RES

NEW YORK CITY

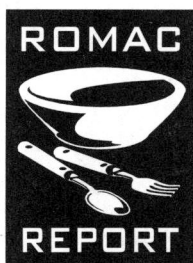

· 1997 ·

PUBLISHED AND DISTRIBUTED BY

ROMAC REPORT
136 Montgomery Ave.
Bala Cynwyd, PA 19004

(610) 668-3636
(610) 668-3603 fax
RomacRpt@AOL.com

ISBN 0-9644383-7-2

PRINTED IN CANADA

Manhattan Neighborhood Map

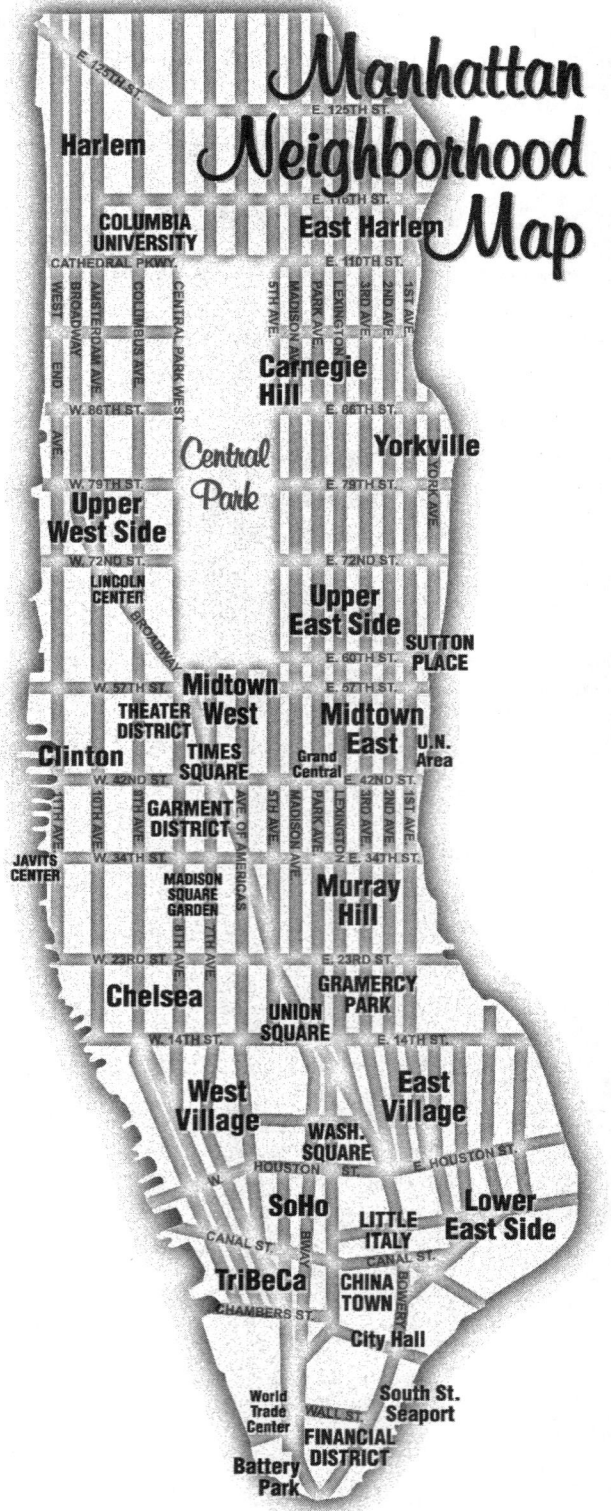

Harlem

E. 125TH ST.

E. 110TH ST.

COLUMBIA UNIVERSITY

East Harlem

CATHEDRAL PKWY.

E. 110TH ST.

5TH AVE.
MADISON AVE.
PARK AVE.
LEXINGTON AVE.
3RD AVE.
2ND AVE.
1ST AVE.

WEST END AVE.
BROADWAY
AMSTERDAM AVE.
COLUMBUS AVE.
CENTRAL PARK WEST

Carnegie Hill

W. 86TH ST.

E. 86TH ST.

Central Park

Yorkville

YORK AVE.

W. 79TH ST.

E. 79TH ST.

Upper West Side

W. 72ND ST.

E. 72ND ST.

LINCOLN CENTER

Upper East Side

BROADWAY

E. 60TH ST.

SUTTON PLACE

W. 57TH ST.

E. 57TH ST.

Midtown West

THEATER DISTRICT

Midtown East

U.N. Area

Clinton

TIMES SQUARE

Grand Central

W. 42ND ST.

E. 42ND ST.

LEXINGTON AVE.
3RD AVE.
1ST AVE.

10TH AVE.
9TH AVE.
AVE. OF THE AMERICAS
5TH AVE.
MADISON AVE.
PARK AVE.

GARMENT DISTRICT

W. 34TH ST.

N. E. 34TH ST.

JAVITS CENTER

MADISON SQUARE GARDEN

Murray Hill

W. 23RD ST.

E. 23RD ST.

Chelsea

GRAMERCY PARK

UNION SQUARE

W. 14TH ST.

E. 14TH ST.

West Village

East Village

WASH. SQUARE ST.

HOUSTON

E. HOUSTON ST.

SoHo

LITTLE ITALY

Lower East Side

BWAY

CANAL ST.

CANAL ST.

BOWERY

TriBeCa

CHINA TOWN

CHAMBERS ST.

City Hall

World Trade Center

WALL ST.

South St. Seaport

FINANCIAL DISTRICT

Battery Park

CONTENTS

PREFACE

The Romac Report is based upon a public opinion poll conducted over the summer of 1996. For restaurants they'd visited in the prior year, poll participants rated the food, room and ambiance, and staff, each on a scale of 0 to 5. Participants also provided commentary, and voted for their favorite spots in dozens of categories, including brunch, dessert, outdoor dining, and many more.

Over 2,000 New Yorkers participated in the poll, yielding over 80,000 individual ratings, tens of thousands of entries in our "Leaders of the Poll" categories, and hundreds of pages of brash, witty, and incisive commentary. We thank our participants heartily!

Each restaurant in this book has its fans, and its critics. While it would be easy to say of each restaurant, as many restaurant guides do, "Some like it, others don't," the Romac poll yields more specific, useful results than that. By carefully examining the votes and commentary for each restaurant, the Romac Report tells you what kind of food and scene you should expect, and passes along our participants' suggestions for when to go, when to stay away, what to order, and so on.

Then, by looking at each restaurant's ranking in context with the other restaurants in the poll, the Romac Report tells you when you are better off simply choosing a different restaurant.

Above all, the Romac staff had as much fun putting this book together as our participants obviously had filling out their questionnaires. We hope you enjoy using this guide as much as we enjoyed writing it.

The Romac editor is Karen Mulligan. The Romac writers are Andrew McElfresh, Joan Lang, Katharine Colton, Russell Carmony, Lea Mazzadra, and Regan Avery. Our copy reader is Sarah McElfresh, and our researcher is Robert Mulligan.

INTRODUCTION

New York City is the restaurant capital of the United States. In no other city will you find the quality and diversity New York offers—from the big-night-out places that have become household names, to the small, chef-owned spots, to the neighborhood joints, pizza places, and so on. Name a cuisine, New York probably has ten or more very fine restaurants that serve it.

The most widely reported news this year concerns closings: Bouley and Le Cirque are the most noteworthy. But don't worry, Sirio Maccioni will reopen next year in a new location, as, we hear, will David Bouley.

Our voters point out to us, again and again, that the big-night-out places have never been hard to find. Even expensive eateries with great locations, big P.R. machines, and only average food, keep drawing diners through their doors.

However, it's the other 95% of restaurants, where New Yorkers do most of their dining out, that our survey participants want to tell us about most. There are scores of very fine establishments, where talented chefs have chucked great jobs, and have opened in just- or way-out of the way locations, to cook the food they've always wanted to cook. And, our participants are just as enthusiastic about their favorite lunch spots, taverns, diners, coffee bars, and assorted dives, as they are about their favorite fine dining restaurants. After all, much of having a rewarding dining experience is about expectations. Lower your expectations, and a great burger at a great dive can be as memorable as any meal.

Our advice: Be adventurous diners. Walk that extra block, to try that place the Romac Report recommends! When next year rolls around, you'll be ready to participate in our 1998 poll. In exchange for your efforts, you will receive a free copy of the 1998 Romac Report.

If you would like to participate, send, fax, or e-mail your name and address to:

Romac Report New York 1998
151 First Ave., Suite 116
New York, NY 10003

(610) 668-3603 fax

RomacRpt@AOL.com e-mail

Charles McElfresh
Lynne Rosen
November, 1996

KEY TO SYMBOLS

Our voters rated restaurants' food, room and ambiance, and staff. The following pictures represent these categories:

= FOOD

= ROOM & AMBIANCE

= STAFF

Voters rated each restaurant's food, room and ambiance, and staff, on a scale of 0 (lowest) to 5 (highest). We averaged the scores, and converted them into the following bar graphs:

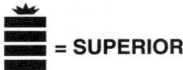

= SUPERIOR

= EXCELLENT

= VERY GOOD

= GOOD

= FAIR

= POOR

Voters also estimated the cost of one meal, with one drink and the tip. The average is printed after the ratings.

Where a restaurant either received too few votes to produce accurate ratings, is new or was written in by our voters, the icons are represented in gray, without ratings:

Bistro Romac

7th St. & Ave. A (212) 358-9759
at Ave. A in the East Village
Boasting the "best new menu in NYC," this brand new spot offers a "fresh look" at a "tired old genre." A "lovely" "fun" staff serves "inspired" "healthy" "creative" fare in a "well-designed" setting. Reservations essential.

HOW TO USE THIS BOOK

The Romac Report is made up of three sections. The first section, **LEADERS OF THE POLL**, details the winners of various categories on the Romac Report poll. The second section, the **RESTAURANT DIRECTORY**, includes ratings and a review of each restaurant, along with its address and phone. The third section is the **INDEX**, which list restaurant names and the page numbers for their directory listings. There are index entries for cuisine types, neighborhoods, and features.

There are three ways to use the Romac Report. First, start with the indexes, where you will find the cuisines and features you enjoy, in the neighborhoods where you plan to dine. Then, look up the reviews of those restaurants in the directory. Or, start with the first section, where you will find the restaurants our participants feel rate highest in several dozen categories; then look up your choices in the directory. Finally, leaf through the directory and start reading-we think you'll enjoy it.

LEADERS of the POLL

NEW YORKERS' TOP 100 FAVORITES

1. Union Square Cafe
2. Gotham Bar & Grill
3. Peter Luger Steak House
4. Gramercy Tavern
5. Carmine's
6. Aureole
7. Nobu
8. Chanterelle
9. Cafe Des Artistes
10. Mesa Grill
11. Four Seasons
12. Zen Palate
13. Sign of the Dove
14. One If By Land Two If By Sea
15. Le Bernardin
16. Tavern on the Green
17. Lespinasse
18. Vong
19. Benny's Burritos
20. Mary Ann's
21. Daniel
22. Cucina
23. Montrachet
24. Angelica Kitchen
25. China Grill
26. America
27. Josie's
28. Dojo
29. Patria
30. Le Madri
31. Yama
32. Hasaki
33. Ollie's Noodle Shop
34. Il Mulino
35. Danal
36. Trattoria dell'Arte
37. Docks
38. Veselka
39. Manhattan Ocean Club
40. Capsouto Freres
41. Pisces
42. Iso
43. Virgil's Real BBQ
44. Tartine
45. Dawat
46. Aquavit
47. Boca Chica
48. La Côte Basque
49. River Cafe
50. Sparks Steak House
51. Smith & Wollensky
52. Odeon
53. Second Avenue Deli
54. Park Avalon
55. Florent
56. John's Pizzeria
57. Cité
58. Yaffa Cafe
59. Ecco-La
60. Rainbow Room
61. Penang
62. Tomoe
63. Periyali
64. Avenue A Sushi
65. Hudson River Club
66. Two Boots
67. Savoy
68. Zoë
69. B. Smith's
70. Barolo
71. An American Place
72. Grand Central Oyster Bar
73. Turkish Kitchen
74. Lemon Grass Grill
75. East
76. Lutece
77. Ruth's Chris Steakhouse
78. Josephina
79. Palm
80. Provence
81. Sevilla
82. Jezebel
83. Blue Ribbon Brasserie
84. El Quijote
85. Cucina Di Pesce
86. Isabella's
87. Ci Vediamo
88. Universal Grill
89. La Reserve
90. Le Chantilly
91. Rain
92. Monsoon
93. Plan Eat Thailand
94. Patsy's Pizza (Brooklyn)
95. Jo Jo
96. Kin Khao
97. Shark Bar
98. Sonia Rose
99. Aja
100. TriBeCa Grill

TOP 100 OVERALL

(2 x FOOD SCORE + ROOM AND AMB. + STAFF)

1.	Lespinasse	51.	Etats-Unis
2.	Les Celebrites	52.	Le Chantilly
3.	Le Bernardin	53.	Sonia Rose
4.	Chanterelle	54.	Solera
5.	Nobu	55.	Halcyon
6.	Terrace	56.	Palio
7.	Daniel	57.	Aquavit
8.	La Grenouille	58.	Taormina
9.	Aureole	59.	Sparks Steak House
10.	Four Seasons	60.	Manhattan Ocean Club
11.	La Côte Basque	61.	Savoy
12.	Il Mulino	62.	Peter Luger Steak House
13.	Lutece	63.	Rao's
14.	Gramercy Tavern	64.	Sushisay
15.	One If By Land Two If By Sea	65.	Stanhope
16.	Petrossian	66.	Carlyle
17.	Union Square Cafe	67.	An American Place
18.	River Cafe	68.	Park Avenue Cafe
19.	La Caravelle	69.	Il Bagatto
20.	Oceana	70.	Le Refuge
21.	Gotham Bar & Grill	71.	Capsouto Freres
22.	La Reserve	72.	Mark's
23.	Hudson River Club	73.	Arcadia
24.	Le Perigord	74.	Water Club
25.	March	75.	Chiam
26.	Montrachet	76.	I. Trulli
27.	Fifty Seven Fifty Seven	77.	Alison on Dominick
28.	Il Nido	78.	Danal
29.	Sea Grill	79.	Aria
30.	Il Monello	80.	Jo Jo
31.	Harry Cipriani's	81.	Il Toscanaccio
32.	Cafe Pierre	82.	Wilkinson's Seafood
33.	Felidia	83.	Patria
34.	Cafe Des Artistes	84.	Dawat
35.	Tse Yang	85.	Da Umberto
36.	Periyali	86.	Windows on the World
37.	Sign of the Dove	87.	Deniz
38.	Vong	88.	Morton's of Chicago
39.	Picholine	89.	Duane Park Cafe
40.	Verbena Restaurant	90.	La Colombe d'Or
41.	Table d'Hote	91.	Jezebel
42.	Rainbow Room	92.	Palm Court
43.	San Domenico	93.	Layla
44.	Cucina	94.	"21" Club
45.	Hangawi	95.	Honmura An
46.	222	96.	Ruth's Chris Steakhouse
47.	Le Regence	97.	Anton's
48.	Water's Edge	98.	Hatsuhana
49.	Post House	99.	Omen
50.	Shun Lee Palace	100.	Remi

TOP 100 FOOD

1. Lespinasse
2. Daniel
3. Le Bernardin
4. Nobu
5. Il Mulino
6. Chanterelle
7. Peter Luger
8. Les Celebrites
9. Aureole
10. Tomoe
11. Terrace
12. La Grenouille
13. La Côte Basque
14. Plan Eat Thailand
15. Totonno Pizzeria Napolitano
16. Lutece
17. Union Square Cafe
18. Four Seasons
19. Elias Corner
20. Montrachet
21. Etats-Unis
22. Gramercy Tavern
23. Picholine
24. Gotham Bar & Grill
25. Patsy's Pizza (Brooklyn)
26. Yama
27. Hasaki
28. Periyali
29. Il Monello
30. Petrossian
31. Oceana
32. Sparks
33. Felidia
34. Il Nido
35. Hatsuhana
36. Sushisay
37. La Caravelle
38. Rao's
39. Table d'Hote
40. Cucina
41. Le Perigord
42. 222
43. Da Umberto
44. La Reserve
45. Manhattan Ocean Club
46. Hudson River Club
47. One If By Land Two If By Sea
48. Park Avenue Cafe
49. Lombardi's
50. March
51. Veniero's
52. Vong
53. Harry Cipriani's
54. Post House
55. Wilkinson's Seafood
56. Sea Grill
57. Shun Lee Palace
58. Jo Jo
59. Fifty Seven Fifty Seven
60. River Cafe
61. Dominick's
62. Taormina
63. Nanni's
64. Mavalli Palace
65. Two Tom's
66. Il Fornaio
67. Tatany 52
68. An American Place
69. Caviarteria
70. Morton's of Chicago
71. Pongsri Thai
72. Verbena Restaurant
73. Dawat
74. Arcadia
75. Sonia Rose
76. Canton
77. Sushiden
78. Aquavit
79. San Domenico
80. Ruth's Chris Steakhouse
81. Chiam
82. Moustache
83. Mesa Grill
84. Luma
85. Sign of the Dove
86. Ess-A-Bagel
87. Lemon Grass Grill
88. Hangawi
89. Tse Yang
90. Patria
91. Cafe Des Artistes
92. La Colombe d'Or
93. Il Bagatto
94. Grand Central Oyster Bar
95. Savoy
96. Aquagrill
97. Palm
98. Le Chantilly
99. Solera
100. Vincent's

TOP 50
ROOM & AMBIANCE

1. Lespinasse
2. Rainbow Room
3. River Cafe
4. Terrace
5. Les Celebrites
6. Windows on the World
7. Nirvana
8. Cafe Pierre
9. Water's Edge
10. One If By Land Two If By Sea
11. Four Seasons
12. Cafe Des Artistes
13. Le Bernardin
14. La Grenouille
15. Chanterelle
16. Palm Court
17. Nobu
18. Petrossian
19. Water Club
20. Sign of the Dove
21. La Côte Basque
22. Temple Bar
23. Le Regence
24. Aureole
25. Gramercy Tavern
26. Boathouse Cafe
27. Daniel
28. Tse Yang
29. Jezebel
30. Palio
31. Hudson River Club
32. La Reserve
33. Stanhope
34. Oak Room & Bar
35. Tavern on the Green
36. Sea Grill
37. Vong
38. Il Buco
39. Barbetta
40. Osteria del Circo
41. Carlyle
42. La Caravelle
43. Lutece
44. World Yacht Cruises
45. Fifty Seven Fifty Seven
46. March
47. 44
48. Verbena Restaurant
49. Hangawi
50. Merlot/Iridium Jazz

TOP 50
STAFF

1. Les Celebrites
2. Lespinasse
3. Chanterelle
4. Le Bernardin
5. La Grenouille
6. Four Seasons
7. La Côte Basque
8. Terrace
9. Aureole
10. Nobu
11. La Caravelle
12. One If By Land Two If By Sea
13. Il Mulino
14. Cafe Pierre
15. Union Square Cafe
16. Lutece
17. Le Perigord
18. Gramercy Tavern
19. Daniel
20. Oceana
21. Fifty Seven Fifty Seven
22. Il Nido
23. Harry Cipriani's
24. Il Monello
25. Petrossian
26. Stanhope
27. March
28. Montrachet
29. La Reserve
30. Gotham Bar & Grill
31. Tse Yang
32. San Domenico
33. Hudson River Club
34. River Cafe
35. Rainbow Room
36. Sea Grill
37. Le Chantilly
38. Periyali
39. Mark's
40. Solera
41. Felidia
42. Le Refuge
43. Carlyle
44. Sonia Rose
45. Rao's
46. Cafe Des Artistes
47. Verbena Restaurant
48. Savoy
49. Hangawi
50. Girafe

TOP VALUES

TOP FOOD ($26-35)

1.	Tomoe	26.	Pisces
2.	Yama	27.	Sala Thai
3.	Hasaki	28.	Malaga
4.	Cucina	29.	Toast
5.	Dominick's	30.	Patrissy's
6.	Tatany 52	31.	Sevilla
7.	Canton	32.	Casani's
8.	Aquagrill	33.	La Luncheonette
9.	Vincent's	34.	Paola's
10.	Iso	35.	Da Tommaso
11.	Danal	36.	L'Ecole
12.	Pietrasanta	37.	Henry's End
13.	Po	38.	Mi Cocina
14.	Tatany	39.	Mary's
15.	Salaam Bombay	40.	Il Buco
16.	Japonica	41.	Jewel of India
17.	Josie's	42.	Becco
18.	La Mediterranee	43.	El Parador Cafe
19.	Jean Claude	44.	13 Barrow
20.	La Bouillabaisse	45.	Arizona 206
21.	Shabu Tatsu	46.	Miracle Grill
22.	El Cid Tapas Bar	47.	Caffe Lure
23.	Baluchi's	48.	Grange Hall
24.	Home	49.	Pamir
25.	Embers	50.	Pesce Pasta

TOP FOOD ($16-25)

1.	Totonno Pizzeria Napolitano	26.	Second Avenue Deli
2.	Elias Corner	27.	New York Noodletown
3.	Patsy's Pizza (Brooklyn)	28.	Gabriela's
4.	Lombardi's	29.	Great Shanghai
5.	Mavalli Palace	30.	Sal Anthony's Caffe Adeline
6.	Il Fornaio	31.	Da Nico
7.	Two Tom's	32.	Word Of Mouth
8.	Pongsri Thai	33.	Agrotikon
9.	Moustache	34.	Zen Palate
10.	Lemon Grass Grill	35.	Sylvia's
11.	Il Bagatto	36.	Regional Thai Taste
12.	Piccolo Angolo	37.	Pastrami King
13.	Candle Cafe	38.	Barney Greengrass
14.	Takahachi	39.	Vinegar Factory
15.	Mitali East	40.	Mingala West
16.	Mandarin Court	41.	Avenue A Sushi
17.	Jai Ya Thai	42.	20 Mott St.
18.	Sweet 'n' Tart Cafe	43.	Carnegie Deli
19.	Patsy's Pizza	44.	Niko's
20.	Thai House Cafe	45.	Haveli
21.	Kang Suh	46.	Negril Island Spice
22.	Tartine	47.	Emily's
23.	Lotfi's Moroccan	48.	John's of 12th Street
24.	Pedro Paramo	49.	Good Enough to Eat
25.	John's Pizzeria	50.	Siam Inn

TOP FOOD (UNDER $15)

1. Plan Eat Thailand
2. Veniero's
3. Ess-A-Bagel
4. Nha Trang
5. Jackson Diner
6. Stick To Your Ribs
7. Cupcake Cafe
8. Soul Fixins'
9. Pintaile's Pizza
10. Wong Kee
11. El Pollo
12. Bo Ky
13. Cafe Lalo
14. Corner Bistro
15. Silk Road Palace
16. Columbus Bakery
17. Two Boots
18. La Caridad
19. Oren's Daily Roast
20. Veselka
21. Katz's Deli
22. La Taza De Oro
23. Sammy's Noodle Shop
24. Big Wong
25. Mee Noodle
26. Benny's Burritos
27. Rose of India
28. Limbo
29. Atomic Wings
30. Eisenberg's Coffee Shop

TOP 40 SLEEPERS*

1. Seryna
2. Joe's Shanghai
3. Sushihatsu
4. Il Menestrello
5. Leopard
6. Savann
7. Kokachin
8. Nino's
9. West 63rd St. Steakhouse
10. Mazzei
11. New City Cafe
12. Da Vittorio
13. Il Tinello
14. Shinbashi
15. Nanni Il Valletto
16. Giambelli Fiftieth
17. Mama's Food Shop
18. Le Boeuf A La Mode
19. Acapella
20. Grifone
21. Pietro's
22. Cinque Terre
23. Royal Siam
24. Meskerem
25. Erizo Latino
26. Wally's and Joseph's
27. What's Cookin'
28. Noodle Pudding
29. Karyatis
30. Uskudar
31. Bruno
32. Habib's Place
33. Le Marais
34. Tang Pavilion
35. O.G. (Oriental Grill)
36. Sahara East
37. Kings' Carriage House
38. Nicola's
39. Adrienne
40. 9th St. Market

*LOW VOTE TOTAL, HIGH FOOD SCORE

TOPS BY CUISINE TYPES

AFGHAN
1. Pamir
2. Khyber Pass
3. Afghan Kebab House

AMERICAN
1. Peter Luger
2. Aureole
3. Union Square Cafe
4. Four Seasons
5. Etats-Unis
6. Gramercy Tavern
7. Gotham Bar & Grill
8. Petrossian
9. Oceana
10. Sparks
11. Table d'Hote
12. Hudson River Club
13. Park Avenue Cafe
14. March
15. Post House
16. Fifty Seven Fifty Seven
17. River Cafe
18. An American Place
19. Morton's of Chicago
20. Verbena Restaurant

ASIAN
1. Aja
2. Kang Suh
3. Zen Palate
4. Cendrillon
5. Bright Food Shop

BAKERY
1. Veniero's
2. Cupcake Cafe
3. Columbus Bakery

BANGLADESHI
1. Nirvana

BBQ
1. Stick To Your Ribs
2. Dok Suni
3. Virgil's Real BBQ

BELGIAN
1. Cafe de Bruxelles

BRAZILIAN
1. Rice 'n Beans
2. Riodizio

BURMESE
1. Mingala

CAJUN
1. Two Boots
2. Mekka
3. Sazerac House

CAL-MEX
1. Burritoville
2. Life Cafe

CALIFORNIAN
1. Michael's
2. California Pizza Kitchen

CARIBBEAN
1. Caribe

CAVIAR
1. Caviarteria

CHINESE
1. Shun Lee Palace
2. Canton
3. Chiam
4. Tse Yang
5. Chin Chin
6. Mr. Chow
7. Wong Kee
8. Mandarin Court
9. Shun Lee/Shun Lee Cafe
10. Sweet 'n' Tart Cafe

CONTINENTAL
1. Gotham Bar & Grill
2. Petrossian
3. 222
4. One If By Land Two If By Sea
5. River Cafe
6. Water's Edge
7. Carlyle
8. Manhattan Cafe
9. Toast
10. Word Of Mouth

CREOLE
1. Great Jones St. Cafe

CUBAN
1. Victor's Cafe 52
2. Cafe Con Leche
3. Tito Puente's

DELI
1. Second Avenue Deli
2. Pastrami King
3. Barney Greengrass
4. Carnegie Deli
5. Ratner's

DOMINICAN
1. Cafe Con Leche

ENGLISH
1. Tea and Sympathy

EUROPEAN
1. Cafe Des Artistes
2. Palm Court
3. Edwardian Room

FRENCH
1. Lespinasse
2. Daniel
3. Le Bernardin
4. Chanterelle
5. Les Celebrites
6. Terrace
7. La Grenouille
8. La Côte Basque
9. Lutece
10. Montrachet
11. Picholine
12. La Caravelle
13. Le Perigord
14. La Reserve
15. Jo Jo
16. Sonia Rose
17. Cafe Des Artistes
18. La Colombe d'Or
19. Le Chantilly
20. Alison on Dominick

GERMAN
1. Heidelberg
2. Roettele A.G.
3. Rolf's

GREEK
1. Elias Corner
2. Periyali
3. Agrotikon
4. Meltemi
5. Gus' Place

HUNGARIAN
1. Red Tulip

INDIAN
1. Mavalli Palace
2. Dawat
3. Darbar
4. Salaam Bombay
5. Mitali East
6. Baluchi's
7. Shaan
8. Jewel of India
9. Haveli
10. Mughlai

INTERNATIONAL
1. China Grill
2. La Metairie
3. Ambassador Grill
4. La Caridad
5. Spring St. Natural

ITALIAN
1. Il Mulino
2. Il Monello
3. Felidia
4. Il Nido
5. Rao's
6. Cucina
7. Da Umberto
8. Veniero's
9. Harry Cipriani's
10. Dominick's
11. Nanni's
12. Taormina
13. Il Fornaio
14. Two Tom's
15. San Domenico
16. Il Bagatto
17. Vincent's
18. Novita
19. Il Toscanaccio
20. Remi

JAMAICAN
1. Negril Island Spice
2. Island Spice

JAPANESE
1. Nobu
2. Tomoe
3. Yama
4. Hasaki
5. Hatsuhana
6. Sushisay
7. Tatany
8. Sushiden
9. Sushizen
10. Omen
11. Iso
12. Honmura An
13. Takahachi
14. Japonica
15. Shabu Tatsu
16. Blue Ribbon Sushi
17. Avenue A Sushi
18. Inagiku
19. La Maison Japonaise
20. Fujiyama Mama

JEWISH

1. Ess-A-Bagel
2. Second Avenue Deli
3. Pastrami King
4. Barney Greengrass
5. Carnegie Deli
6. Ratner's
7. Sammy's Roumanian
8. Katz's Deli
9. Stage Deli
10. Eisenberg's Coffee Shop

KOREAN

1. Hangawi
2. Dok Suni
3. Woo Chon

LATIN

1. Patria

LEBANESE

1. Byblos
2. Cedars of Lebanon
3. Bar Anise

LIGHT FARE

1. Veniero's
2. Ess-A-Bagel
3. Cafe Lalo
4. Vinegar Factory
5. Oren's Daily Roast

MALAYSIAN

1. Penang
2. Rain

MEDITERRANEAN

1. Savoy
2. Cafe Crocodile
3. Zucca
4. Il Buco
5. Gus' Place

MEXICAN

1. Zarela
2. Rosa Mexicano
3. Pedro Paramo
4. Gabriela's
5. Mi Cocina
6. El Parador Cafe
7. Cafe Español
8. Tio Pepe
9. Bright Food Shop
10. Benny's Burritos

MIDDLE EASTERN

1. Moustache
2. Layla
3. Niko's
4. Byblos
5. Cedars of Lebanon

MOROCCAN

1. Lotfi's Moroccan
2. Matthew's
3. Cafe Centro

PAKISTANI

1. Nirvana

PERUVIAN

1. El Pollo

PHILIPPINE

1. Cendrillon

PIZZA

1. Totonno Pizzeria Napolitano
2. Patsy's Pizza (Bklyn)
3. Lombardi's
4. Pintaile's Pizza
5. Patsy's Pizza

POLISH/UKRAINIAN

1. Veselka

PORTUGUESE

1. Il Buco
2. Cabana Carioca

PUERTO RICAN

1. La Taza De Oro
2. Tito Puente's

ROMANIAN

1. Sammy's Roumanian
2. Triplets Roumanian

RUSSIAN

1. Russian Samovar

SCANDINAVIAN

1. Aquavit
2. Christer's

SEAFOOD

1. Le Bernardin
2. Elias Corner
3. Oceana
4. Manhattan Ocean Club
5. Wilkinson's Seafood
6. Sea Grill
7. Aquavit
8. Grand Central Oyster Bar
9. Aquagrill
10. Pisces

SOUL FOOD
1. Soul Fixins'
2. Sylvia's
3. Kwanzaa

SOUTH AMERICAN
1. Boca Chica
2. Riodizio

SOUTHERN
1. Jezebel
2. Sylvia's
3. Emily's
4. Mekka
5. Virgil's Real BBQ

SOUTHWESTERN
1. Mesa Grill
2. Tapika
3. Arizona 206 & Arizona Cafe
4. Miracle Grill
5. Santa Fe

SPANISH
1. Solera
2. El Cid Tapas Bar
3. Bolo
4. Malaga
5. Il Buco
6. Él Rincon de España
7. El Faro
8. Cafe Español On Carmine
9. El Quijote
10. Centro Vasco

STEAKHOUSE
1. Peter Luger
2. Sparks
3. Post House
4. Morton's of Chicago
5. Ruth's Chris
6. Palm
7. Smith & Wollensky
8. Palm Too
9. Smith & Wollensky Grill
10. Embers

SWISS
1. Roettele A.G.

TEX-MEX
1. Santa Fe
2. Canyon Road
3. Tortilla Flats

THAI
1. Plan Eat Thailand
2. Vong
3. Pongsri Thai
4. Jai Ya Thai
5. Thai House Cafe
6. Sala Thai
7. Regional Thai Taste
8. Typhoon Brewery
9. Rain
10. Siam Inn

TIBETAN
1. Angry Monk
2. Tibetan Kitchen

TURKISH
1. Deniz
2. Turkish Kitchen

VEGETARIAN
1. Mavalli Palace
2. Hangawi
3. Candle Cafe
4. Zen Palate
5. Spring St. Natural
6. Apple
7. Caravan of Dreams
8. Burritoville
9. Yaffa Cafe
10. Life Cafe

VIETNAMESE
1. Nha Trang
2. Danal
3. Bo Ky
4. Rain
5. Le Colonial

TOPS BY
NEIGHBORHOODS (Manhattan)

CARNEGIE HILL
E. HARLEM
1. Rao's
2. Table d'Hote
3. Pintaile's Pizza
4. Patsy's Pizza
5. Sala Thai

CENTRAL/W. VILLAGE
WASHINGTON SQ.
1. Il Mulino
2. Tomoe
3. Gotham Bar & Grill
4. One If By Land Two If By Sea
5. Moustache
6. Piccolo Angolo
7. Po
8. Il Cantinori
9. Anton's
10. Cent'Anni
11. Japonica
12. Home
13. Tartine
14. Sevilla
15. Chez Michallet
16. Mi Cocina
17. Mary's
18. 13 Barrow
19. Caffe Lure
20. Grange Hall

CHELSEA/GARMENT DIST.
CONVENTION CTR AREA
1. Da Umberto
2. Luma
3. Gascogne
4. Le Madri
5. Cupcake Cafe
6. Soul Fixins'
7. El Cid Tapas Bar
8. Old Homestead
9. Kang Suh
10. La Luncheonette

CHINATOWN
1. Pongsri Thai
2. Canton
3. Nha Trang
4. Mandarin Court
5. Sweet 'n' Tart Cafe

COLUMBIA U. AREA
HARLEM
1. Terrace
2. Sylvia's

EAST VILLAGE
1. Hasaki
2. Veniero's
3. Il Bagatto
4. Iso
5. Danal
6. Takahachi
7. Mitali East
8. Pisces
9. Pedro Paramo
10. Toast

GRAMERCY/FLATIRON
UNION SQUARE
1. Union Square Cafe
2. Gramercy Tavern
3. Yama
4. Periyali
5. Verbena Restaurant
6. Mesa Grill
7. Patria
8. La Colombe d'Or
9. Novita
10. Follonico

LITTLE ITALY
1. Lombardi's
2. Taormina
3. Il Fornaio
4. Vincent's
5. Wong Kee

MIDTOWN E./SUTTON PL.
UN AREA
1. Lespinasse
2. La Grenouille
3. Lutece
4. Four Seasons
5. Oceana
6. Sparks
7. Il Nido
8. Felidia
9. Hatsuhana
10. Sushisay
11. Le Perigord
12. March
13. Vong
14. Harry Cipriani's
15. Shun Lee Palace
16. Fifty Seven Fifty Seven
17. Nanni's
18. Tatany 52
19. Caviarteria
20. Morton's of Chicago

MIDTOWN WEST
THEATER DIST./CLINTON
1. Le Bernardin
2. Les Celebrites
3. La Côte Basque
4. Petrossian
5. La Caravelle
6. La Reserve
7. Manhattan Ocean Club
8. Sea Grill
9. Aquavit
10. San Domenico
11. Ruth's Chris
12. Halcyon
13. Sushizen
14. Remi
15. Pietrasanta
16. Darbar
17. Tapika
18. Orso
19. Trattoria dell'Arte
20. Palio

MURRAY HILL
1. Mavalli Palace
2. An American Place
3. Sonia Rose
4. Hangawi
5. Jai Ya Thai

SOHO
1. Savoy
2. Aquagrill
3. Alison on Dominick St.
4. Omen
5. Zoe
6. Cascabel
7. Raoul's
8. Honmura An
9. Jean Claude
10. El Pollo

TRIBECA
FINANCIAL DISTRICT
1. Nobu
2. Chanterelle
3. Montrachet
4. Hudson River Club
5. Duane Park Cafe
6. Layla
7. Capsouto Freres
8. Arqua
9. Salaam Bombay
10. Rosemarie's

UPPER EAST SIDE
1. Daniel
2. Aureole
3. Etats-Unis
4. Il Monello
5. Park Avenue Cafe
6. Post House
7. Jo Jo
8. Arcadia
9. Sign of the Dove
10. Le Refuge
11. Le Regence
12. Candle Cafe
13. Elio's
14. Baluchi's
15. Cafe Pierre
16. Carlyle
17. Manhattan Cafe
18. Mark's
19. Lenox Room
20. Matthew's

UPPER WEST SIDE
1. Picholine
2. 222
3. Cafe Des Artistes
4. Gabriel's
5. Josie's
6. Shabu Tatsu
7. Shun Lee
8. John's Pizzeria
9. Gabriela's
10. Docks

YORKVILLE
1. Wilkinson's
2. Quatorze Bis
3. Cafe Crocodile
4. Primavera
5. Malaga

OUTSIDE MANHATTAN

BRONX
1. Dominick's

QUEENS
1. Elias Corner
2. Jackson Diner
3. Stick To Your Ribs
4. Water's Edge
5. Pastrami King

BROOKLYN
1. Peter Luger
2. Plan Eat Thailand
3. Totonno Pizzeria
4. Patsy's Pizza
5. Cucina
6. River Cafe
7. Two Tom's
8. La Bouillabaisse
9. Embers
10. Henry's End

TOPS BY FEATURES

AFTER WORK DRINK

1. Bryant Park Grill
2. Temple Bar
3. 44
4. Monkey Bar
5. Moran's
6. Old Town Bar
7. Heartland Brewery
8. Houlihan's
   (many locations)
9. Rainbow Room
10. Ginger Man

BAGELS

1. H&H
   2239 Broadway (212) 595-8003
   at 80th St. on the Upper W. Side
   639 W. 46th St. (212) 595-8000
   at 12th Ave. in Clinton
   1551 Second Ave. (212) 734-7441
   at 81st St. on the Upper E. Side
2. Ess-A-Bagel
3. Tal Bagels
   977 First Ave. (212) 753-9080
   bet. 53rd & 54th in Midtown E.
4. Pick-a-Bagel
   1083 Lexington Ave. (212) 517-6590
   at 77th St. on the Upper E. Side
   1473 Second Ave. (212) 717-4662
   bet. 76th & 77th on the Upper E. Side
   297 Third Ave. (212) 686-1414
   bet. 22nd & 23rd in Gramercy Park
5. Bagels on the Square
   7 Carmine St. (212) 691-3040
   at 6th Ave. in the Wash. Sq. Area
6. Columbia Hot Bagels
   2836 Broadway (212) 222-3200
   at 110th St./Columbia U. Area
7. Absolute Bagels
   2788 Broadway (212) 932-2052
   bet. 107th & 108th/Col. U. Area
8. Bagelry
   1380 Madison Ave. (212) 423-9590
   at 96th St. in Carnegie Hill
   1324 Lexington Ave. (212) 996-0567
   at 88th St. in Carnegie Hill
9. Daniel's Bagels
   569 Third Ave. (212) 972-9733
   bet. 37th & 38th in Murray Hill
10. Bagel Bob's
    51 University Pl. (212) 533-2627
    bet. 9th & 10th/Central Village

BARTENDERS

1. Splash
   50 W. 17th St. (212) 691-0073
   bet. Fifth & Sixth in Union Sq.
2. Rainbow Room
3. Temple Bar
4. Pete's Tavern
5. Jekyll & Hyde
6. Bear Bar

BARTENDERS (CONT'D)

7. McSorley's Old Ale House
8. dba
   41 First Ave. (212) 475-5097
   bet. 2nd & 3rd Sts. in the E. Village
9. Smith & Wollensky
10. P.J. Clarke's

BATHROOMS

1. 44
2. Bar 89
   89 Mercer St. (212) 274-0989
   bet. Spring & Broome in SoHo
3. Rainbow Room
4. Paramount Hotel
   235 W. 46th St. (212) 764-5500
   bet. Broadway & Eighth Ave.
   in the Theater District
5. Waldorf-Astoria
   301 Park Ave (212) 872-4900
   at 49th St. in Midtown E.
6. Oak Room & Bar
7. Jekyll & Hyde
8. Four Seasons
9. Windows on the World
10. Tavern on the Green

BEER ON TAP

1. Zip City
2. dba
   41 First Ave. (212) 475-5097
   bet. 2nd & 3rd in the E. Village
3. Ginger Man
4. Heartland Brewery
5. McSorley's Old Ale
6. Jekyll & Hyde
7. Chumley's
8. Peculiar Pub
   145 Bleecker St. (212) 353-1327
   bet. LaGuardia Pl. & 6th Ave.
   in the Washington Sq. Area
9. Kinsale Tavern
   1672 Third Ave. (212) 348-4370
   bet. 93rd & 94th in Carnegie Hill
10. Westside Brewing Co.

BREAKFAST

1. Royal Canadian
2. EJ's Luncheonette
3. Sarabeth's Kitchen
4. Veselka
5. Popover Cafe
6. Good Enough to Eat
7. Aggie's
8. Kiev
9. Viand Coffee Shop
10. Ess-A-Bagel

BRUNCH

1. Sarabeth's Kitchen
2. EJ's Luncheonette
3. Popover Cafe
4. Cupping Room Cafe
5. Good Enough to Eat
6. Bubby's
7. Royal Canadian
8. Time Cafe/Fez
9. Friend of a Farmer
10. Capsouto Freres

BURGERS

1. Jackson Hole
2. Corner Bistro
3. Hamburger Harry's
4. Big Nick's
5. Diane's Uptown
6. Old Town Bar
7. "21" Club
8. Cozy Soup & Burger
   739 Broadway (212) 477-5566
   at Astor Pl. in the E. Village
9. Ottomanelli's
   (many locations)
10. McDonald's
    (many locations)

BUSINESS MEALS

1. Four Seasons
2. Union Square Cafe
3. Gotham Bar & Grill
4. Smith & Wollensky
5. "21" Club
6. 44
7. Sparks
8. Hudson River Club
9. Cafe Centro
10. Gramercy Tavern

CELEBRITY SPOTTING

1. Bowery Bar
2. Elaine's
3. Planet Hollywood
4. Nobu
5. TriBeCa Grill
6. Orso
7. Four Seasons
8. Pravda
9. Fashion Cafe
10. Odeon

CHILD-FRIENDLY

1. Two Boots
2. Serendipity 3
3. America
4. McDonald's
   (many locations)

CHILD-FRIENDLY (CONT'D)

5. Jekyll & Hyde
6. EJ's Luncheonette
7. Planet Hollywood
8. Cowgirl Hall Of Fame
9. Carmine's
10. Rumpelmayer's

CIGAR SPOT

1. Beekman Bar & Books
   Lexington Bar & Books
   Hudson Bar & Books
2. Ginger Man
3. Morton's of Chicago
4. Cigar Room at Trumpets
   Grand Hyatt Hotel, 44th & 5th Ave.
   in Midtown E. (212) 850-5999
5. Smith & Wollensky
6. Alva
7. West 63rd St. Steakhouse
8. Club Macanudo
9. Fifty Seven Fifty Seven
10. Keens Steakhouse

COFFEEHOUSE

1. Starbucks
2. Big Cup
3. Limbo
4. Cafe Reggio
5. Timothy's
   (many locations)
6. Cafe Lalo
7. Barnes & Noble Cafe
8. Eureka Joe's
   168 Fifth Ave. (212) 741-7500
   bet. 21st & 22nd Sts. in Flatiron
9. French Roast
10. Cafe Le Figaro

DESSERT

1. Veniero's
2. Cafe Lalo
3. Serendipity 3
4. Aureole
5. Caffe Rafaella
6. Union Square Cafe
7. Cafe Mozart
8. Cafe Des Artistes
9. Sarabeth's Kitchen
10. Park Avenue Cafe

DINER

1. Empire Diner
2. EJ's Luncheonette
3. Brooklyn Diner USA
4. Ellen's Stardust Diner
5. Lucky Dog Diner

DINER (CONT'D)

6. Veselka
7. Moondance Diner
8. Florent
9. Viand Coffee Shop
10. Broadway Diner

DINING ALONE

1. Dojo
2. McDonald's
   (many locations)
3. Zen Palate
4. Union Square Cafe
5. Barnes & Noble Cafe
6. Ollie's Noodle Shop
7. Grand Cent. Oyster Bar
8. Veselka
9. EJ's Luncheonette
10. Kiev

DIVE

1. Corner Bistro
2. Live Bait
3. Ear Inn
4. Dojo
5. Acme Bar & Grill
6. Benny's Burritos
7. Kiev
8. Big Nick's
9. Great Jones St. Cafe
10. Veselka

EAVESDROPPING

1. Elaine's
2. Bowery Bar
3. Barnes & Noble Cafe
4. Four Seasons
5. 44
6. Time Cafe/Fez
7. Dallas BBQ
8. Daniel
9. Carnegie Deli
10. Benny's Burritos

ESCAPE FROM NYC

1. Boathouse Cafe
2. River Cafe
3. Friend of a Farmer
4. Provence
5. Cloister Cafe
6. Cucina
7. Ye Waverly Inn
8. Tavern on the Green
9. Sign of the Dove
10. Peter Luger

ESPRESSO/CAPPUCCINO

1. Starbucks
2. Veniero's
3. Dante's
   1640 York Ave. (212) 717-1180
   bet. 86th & 87th in Yorkville
4. Ferrara's
   195 Grand St. (212) 226-6150
   bet. Mott & Mulberry in Little Italy
   11 Fulton St. (212) 267-4655
   at the South St. Seaport
5. Cafe Le Figaro
6. New World Coffee
   (many locations)
7. Limbo
8. French Roast
9. Cafe Reggio
10. Big Cup

EXOTIC EXPERIENCE

1. Lucky Cheng's
2. Penang
3. Vong
4. Abyssinia
5. Blue Nile
6. Nobu
7. Nirvana
8. Jekyll & Hyde
9. Layla
10. Caribe

FIRST DATE

1. Sign of the Dove
2. One If By Land Two If By Sea
3. Rainbow Room
4. Jekyll & Hyde
5. Ecco-La
6. Isabella's
7. Grange Hall
8. Tavern on the Green
9. Time Cafe/Fez
10. Sonia Rose

GAY SPOT

1. Food Bar
2. Universal Grill
3. Eighteenth & Eighth
4. Big Cup
5. Townhouse
6. Lucky Cheng's
7. Claire
8. Viceroy
9. Manatu's
10. Duplex
    61 Christopher (212) 255-5438
    at 7th Ave. S. in the W. Village

JUKEBOX

1. Corner Bistro
2. John's Pizzeria
3. Great Jones St. Cafe
4. Rudy's Bar
   627 Ninth Ave. (212) 974-9169
   bet. 44th & 45th in Clinton
5. Two Boots
6. Jackson Hole
7. Ellen's Stardust Diner
8. Riverrun Cafe
9. 7B (aka Vazac)
   108 Ave. B (212) 473-8840
   at 7th St. in the E. Village
10. Hard Rock Cafe

KNOWLEDGEABLE STAFF

1. Union Square Cafe
2. Gramercy Tavern
3. Chanterelle
4. Gotham Bar & Grill
5. Four Seasons
6. Montrachet
7. Aureole
8. Lutece
9. Le Bernardin
10. Zoe

LARGE PARTIES

1. Carmine's
2. America
3. Main Street
4. Tavern on the Green
5. Tony di Napoli
6. Gotham Bar & Grill
7. Sal Anthony's S.P.Q.R.
8. Virgil's Real BBQ
9. Ciccio & Tony's
10. Lucky Cheng's

LATE MENU

1. Florent
2. Yaffa Cafe
3. Odeon
4. Around the Clock Cafe
5. Blue Ribbon Brasserie
6. Coffee Shop
7. Kiev
8. Empire Diner
9. French Roast
10. Veselka

LESBIAN SPOT

1. Rubyfruit
2. Henrietta on Hudson
3. Meow Mix
   269 E. Houston St. (212) 254-1434
   at Suffolk in the E. Village
4. Cafe Tabac
   232 E. 9th St. (212) 674-7072
   bet. 2nd & 3rd in the E. Village
5. Cubby Hole
   281 W. 12th St. (212) 243-9041
   at W. 4th St. in the W. Village

LIVE MUSIC

1. Tramps
2. Merlot/Iridium
3. Blue Note
   131 W. 3rd St. (212) 475-8592
   at Sixth Ave. in Wash. Sq. Area
4. Bottom Line
   15 W. 4th St. (212) 228-7880
   at Mercer St. in the Wash. Sq. Area
5. Rainbow Room
6. S.O.B.
7. Manny's Car Wash
   1558 Third Ave. (212) 369-BLUE
   at 87th St. in Carnegie Hill
8. Zinno
9. Time Cafe/Fez
10. Louisiana Comm. B & G

MAITRE D'

1. Union Square Cafe
2. Chanterelle
3. Four Seasons
4. Rainbow Room
5. Lespinasse
6. Daniel
7. Palm
8. Sardi's
9. Le Bernardin
10. La Grenouille

MARTINI

1. Temple Bar
2. Fifty Seven Fifty Seven
3. Marion's Continental
4. Martini's
5. Four Seasons
6. Pravda
7. Rainbow Room
8. Hi-Life
9. Global 33
10. Carmine's

MICROBREWERY

1. Heartland Brewery
2. Zip City
3. Yorkville Brewery
4. Westside Brewing Co.
5. Typhoon Brewery

NOISIEST

1. America
2. Carmine's
3. Hard Rock Cafe
4. China Grill
5. Mangia e Bevi
6. Heartland Brewery
7. Republic
8. Typhoon Brewery
9. Coffee Shop
10. Ernie's

OLDER ADULTS

1. Cafe Des Artistes
2. Rainbow Room
3. Tavern on the Green
4. Gotham Bar & Grill
5. Le Chantilly
6. Four Seasons
7. Oak Room & Bar
8. Lespinasse
9. La Côte Basque
10. La Caravelle

OUTDOOR DINING

1. Barolo
2. Miracle Grill
3. Tavern on the Green
4. Bryant Park Grill
5. Cloister Cafe
6. Grove
7. Boathouse Cafe
8. Yaffa Cafe
9. Verbena
10. Barbetta

OUT-OF-TOWNERS

1. Tavern on the Green
2. Planet Hollywood
3. Hard Rock Cafe
4. Jekyll & Hyde
5. Rainbow Room
6. Carnegie Deli
7. Carmine's
8. Lucky Cheng's
9. America
10. Harley Davidson Cafe

QUIET CHAT

1. Anglers & Writers
2. Tea and Sympathy
3. One If By Land Two If By Sea
4. Cafe Des Artistes
5. Algonquin Hotel
6. Black Sheep
7. Oak Room & Bar
8. Eureka Joe's
   *168 Fifth Ave. (212) 741-7500
   bet. 21st & 22nd Sts. in Flatiron*
9. Terrace
10. Verbena

RAW BAR

1. Grand Cent. Oyster Bar
2. Docks
3. Blue Ribbon Brasserie
4. Oyster Bar at the Plaza
5. City Crab
6. Aquagrill
7. Lundy's
8. Mad Fish
9. Blue Water Grill
10. Fannie's Oyster Bar

ROMANTIC

1. One If By Land Two If By Sea
2. Cafe Des Artistes
3. Rainbow Room
4. Sign of the Dove
5. River Cafe
6. Terrace
7. Sonia Rose
8. Alison on Dominick
9. Tavern on the Green
10. Aureole

STEAK

1. Peter Luger
2. Smith & Wollensky
3. Sparks
4. Ruth's Chris
5. Palm
6. Morton's of Chicago
7. Old Homestead
8. Les Halles
9. Post House
10. Steak Frites

SURLIEST STAFF

1. Carnegie Deli
2. Peter Luger
3. Ratner's
4. Bowery Bar
5. Coffee Shop
6. Smith & Wollensky
7. Katz's Deli

SURLIEST STAFF (CONT'D)

8. Dojo
9. Stingy Lulu's
10. Lucky Cheng's

SUSHI

1. Nobu
2. Yama
3. East
4. Japonica
5. Iso
6. Hatsuhana
7. Tomoe
8. Avenue A Sushi
9. Tatany
10. Hasaki

TABLES CLOSEST

1. Dojo
2. Mary Ann's
3. Les Halles
4. Cucina Di Pesce
5. Carnegie Deli
6. Ecco-La
7. Benny's Burritos
8. La Metairie
9. Antico Caffe
10. Jean Claude

THURSDAY NIGHT OUT

1. Bryant Park Grill
2. El Rio Grande
3. Time Cafe/Fez
4. Moran's
5. Tatou
6. Park Avalon
7. Ñ
8. Lucky Strike
9. Match
10. Merchants

TRENDY SPOT

1. Bowery Bar
2. Pravda
3. Coffee Shop
4. The Lemon
5. Nobu
6. Cub Room
7. Fashion Cafe
8. Match
9. TriBeCa Grill
10. Time Cafe/Fez

VEGETARIAN PLATE

1. Zen Palate
2. Dojo

VEGETARIAN PLATE (CONT'D)

3. Angelica Kitchen
4. Souen
5. Vegetarian Paradise
6. Josie's
7. Candle Cafe
8. Apple
9. Yaffa Cafe
10. Spring St. Natural

VINTAGE NYC

1. Pete's Tavern
2. Old Town Bar
3. Peter Luger
4. McSorley's Old Ale
5. Rainbow Room
6. Katz's Deli
7. Gage & Tollner
8. Second Avenue Deli
9. Palm
10. Carnegie Deli

WATER VIEW

1. River Cafe
2. Water Club
3. Hudson River Club
4. Water's Edge
5. Boathouse Cafe
6. Moran's
7. Windows on the World
8. Harbour Lights
9. World Yacht Cruises
10. Crab House

WEEKEND CROWDING

1. Carmine's
2. EJ's Luncheonette
3. Sarabeth's Kitchen
4. Isabella's
5. Royal Canadian
6. Bowery Bar
7. Time Cafe/Fez
8. Boxer's
9. Mary Ann's
10. Jekyll & Hyde

WINE LIST

1. Soho Kitchen & Bar
2. Sparks
3. Montrachet
4. Union Square Cafe
5. Gramercy Tavern
6. Smith & Wollensky
7. Zoe
8. Four Seasons
9. Cité
10. Lutece

RESTAURANT

DIRECTORY

FOOD ROOM STAFF COST

Abby

$24

254 Fifth Ave. (212) 725-2922
bet. 28th & 29th Sts. in the Garment District
Located in a neighborhood booming with start-up software companies,
the Abby flourishes at lunch. The under-40 techies laud "good burgers"
but are less enthusiastic about the rest of the American Bistro standards.
The room is "nice with raised wooden booths," voters say this place
"could be better" and suggest "less attitude, more food."

Abruzzi

$38

37 W. 56th St. (212) 489-8110
bet. Fifth & Sixth Aves. in Midtown W.
While this Upper Midtown Italian has "good" food (it's an area
business-luncher fave), the room and staff don't live up to the
location—the "atmosphere is strange" with a "nervous staff."
However, some find it "cozy," with "great hors d'oeuvres.

Abyssinia

35 Grand St. (212) 226-5959
at Thompson St. in SoHo
Eat with your fingers at this SoHo Ethiopian. "Great prices," "great
decor" and "great food" in an "authentic atmosphere" equal a
"spicy and delicious" evening for the more exotic and adventurous
diner. So the service is "crummy": You can't have everything.
Herbivores and carnivores are welcome.

Acapella

$42

1 Hudson St. (212) 240-0163
bet. Chambers St. & W. Broadway in TriBeCa
This Northern Italian sleeper offers "great complimentary
appetizers" and "good fish" to the Wall Street crowd. Don't worry
about parking: they have valet service.

Acme Bar & Grill

$19

9 Great Jones St. (212) 420-1934
bet. Lafayette St. & Broadway in the E. Village
Amazingly popular despite itself, Acme is "not the best of
anything" except perhaps in the "loud" "dive" with "huge portions"
category. Of the "down-home" Southern/Cajun fare, voters "kill
for" the "dirty mashed potatoes," "corn fritters," and a "huge
variety of hot sauces." Live "yee hah!" music downstairs gives this
place a "real roadhouse feel."

Adrienne

$53

Peninsula Hotel, 700 Fifth Ave. (212) 903-3918
at 55th St. in Midtown W.
Contemporary American food in a European setting, accompanied
by live piano music, overlooking Fifth Avenue: Are you relaxed
yet? "Simply wonderful" and "beautifully prepared and presented"
gush admirers. It's "soothing for the older, slower crowd" who
want to eat in style without the trendy pace. Dress up.

= SUPERIOR = EXCELLENT = V. GOOD = GOOD

Aesop's Tables

1233 Bay St., (at Maryland St.) Staten Island (718) 720-2005
Let's put the cards on the table: Three years of operating in Staten Island and only 35 seats are the reasons behind this Contemporary American's low number of votes. But the warm, country setting (hardwood floors, antique brushed-tin walls, rattan chairs, and outdoor garden) has fended off any detractors. The "delicious vegetable spread" and "well-prepared" fare with an Italian/Mediterranean flair wins praise. This "lovely spot" is "worth the trip to SI."

Afghan Kebab House

 $17

155 W. 46th St. (212) 768-3875 (bet. Sixth & Seventh/Midtown W.)
764 Ninth Ave. (212) 307-1612 (bet. 51st & 52nd Sts. in Clinton)
1345 Second Ave. bet. 70th & 71st Sts./U.E. Side (212) 517-2776
These "tiny," "no-frills" Afghans provide "decent" kebabs in Midtown and on the Upper East Side. Reviewers skewer "no-nonsense" service with "going-on-jihad" attitude but "bargain" prices and convenient locations keep them coming back.

Aggie's

146 W. Houston St. (212) 673-8994
at MacDougal St. in the W. Village
Breakfast in the West Village. "Great pancakes, pancakes, pancakes" in a crowded local hangout and dig those "free refills" on the java. Aggie's has lunch and dinner as well, but inaugurate yourself to this one with "home cooking" at daybreak.

Agrotikon

 $25

322 E. 14th St. (212) 473-2602
bet. First & Second Aves. in the E. Village
"Here comes the neighborhood!" say thankful fans of the "fresh and delicious" fare at this "gourmet Greek." "Imaginatively prepared" regional dishes are served by a "happy staff" in an "elegant" and "very European" setting: ambrosia in the East Village.

Aja

 $41

937 Broadway (212) 473-8388
at 22nd St. in the Flatiron District
"It's no hype": Aja "survives in-spot status" by serving "fusion at its finest." Gary Robins, whom fans vote "best Eclectic/Asian chef in the city," constructs "creative skyscraper dishes"—occasionally "taller than they are tasty," but more often "sumptuous" and invariably "innovative." The atmosphere: "a perfect balance of intimate and lively." And in-spot addicts, rest easy: It still has "a great people-watching bar."

Akbar

 $30

475 Park Ave. (212) 838-1717
bet. 57th & 58th Sts. in Midtown E.
Midtown/Upper East Side Indian food distinguishes itself from East Village Indian food with higher prices, "small portions," and a business-friendly ambiance ("quiet in the evening"). The food is "good," but nothing to levitate over.

■ = FAIR   [blank] = POOR   ▦ = NOT RATED   **29**

FOOD ROOM STAFF COST

Al Bustan

$31

827 Third Ave. (212) 759-5933
bet. 50th & 51st Sts. in Midtown E.

Among the fancier ethnics (a bit north of others in the UN area), the
food at this East Side Middle Eastern is "fair." Voters find it "dull,
dull, dull," and say the "kitchen and staff do not match the decor."

Alejandra's Adopt

190 Ave. B (212) 353-2291
at 12th St. in the E. Village

This new Richard (Shark Bar, Mekka) Wright offering serves
"comida de bodega," food made from everyday Brazilian peasant
ingredients, in a comfortable setting.

Algonquin Hotel

$38

59 W. 44th St. (212) 840-6800
bet. Fifth & Sixth Aves. in Midtown W.

"The history is appetizing enough" to make up for the lackluster
American food at this "civilized and cosmopolitan" "flashback to
old New York." Kids will cotton to the resident cat; Grown-ups will
go for the "great lobby bar," the ideal after-work or after-theater
drink spot. The prix fixe pre-theater lunch and dinner are at best
convenient, at worst "appalling."

Alison on Dominick

$47

38 Dominick St. (212) 727-1188
bet. Varick & Hudson Sts. in SoHo

Better even than the "wonderful" food at this TriBeCa Country
French is the "very cozy and romantic" atmosphere voters call
"unpretentious," "understated elegance." Among the top romantic
spots in town, the "staff pampers you" to the point that, in less than
ten years, Alison is "an institution—but still fresh!"

Alley's End

$28

311 W. 17th St. (212) 627-8899
bet. Eighth & Ninth Aves. in Chelsea

Since "most people can't find it," this "quiet, relaxed" Chelsea
American remains a "well-kept secret" and "ideal for illicit trysts."
Those in the know appreciate the "hidden garden" and
"thought-provoking atmosphere" that make them feel far from
NYC. Though the food is "not always consistent," it remains a local
favorite. Look for the neon knife and fork.

Allora

$29

1321 First Ave. (212) 570-0384
at 71st St. on the Upper East Side

While "a pleasant neighborhood spot," with sidewalk dining and
delivery, this Northern Italian seafooder "doesn't stand out from the
rest of the other East Side Italians." Just as well: It's laid back and
comfortable for families.

= SUPERIOR ⬛ = EXCELLENT ⬛ = V. GOOD ▬ = GOOD

Alt.Coffee

$11

139 Ave. A (212) 529-2233
bet. St. Mark's Pl. & 9th St. in the E. Village
High-speed Internet access and "good music" make this "friendly
cafe" with "East Village grunge appeal" a "fun place to sit" and
schmooze. Don't go for the food, you'll be disappointed by the quality
and the "small selection, small servings." Our Gen X reporters warn
"the tables are so close" that the room is "not for claustrophobics."

Alva

$37

36 E. 22nd St. (212) 228-4399, (212) 228-4584
bet. Broadway & Park Ave. S. in the Flatiron District
"Good bistro food" but "cramped quarters" sums up the sentiment
on Fernando Saralegui and Charles (Aureole) Palmer's
Gramercy/Flatiron "trendy"-teria. The "amazing" au courant
Continental/American menu, "charming staff" (ponytails much
apparent), and "crowded" bar scene make this one "fun," but
despite the electric atmosphere that would do its namesake Edison
proud, you had better like your dining room "dark."

Ambassador Grill

$39

Hyatt UN Park Plaza Hotel, I U.N. Plaza (212) 702-5014
at 44th St. in the UN Area
"Very good" Sunday buffet brunch and valet parking draw a
worldly over-30 crowd to this International/Eclectic. Proximity to
the UN makes it popular with diplomats, but dinner options from
the "limited menu" are "nothing to write home about." The staff can
get "confused," and expect to pay high prices for the mirrored,
"polished atmosphere."

America

$23

9 E. 18th St. (212) 505-2110
bet. Broadway & Fifth Ave. in the Flatiron District
Whether America is "crazier than Times Square on New Year's
Eve," or "everything that sucked about the '80s," this Flatiron
American excels at excess. From the "overwhelming" regional
menu to the "diverse" crowds of kids, tourists, and big groups, you
will feel "like you're eating at the Gap" or in a "cheery" "airplane
hangar." Head here if you have to feed "different types of eaters"
and they aren't too fussy about "big portions" of "uneven" eats and
a staff that "tries to do everything but rarely gets it right."

American Festival Cafe

$34

Rockefeller Center, 20 W. 50th St. (212) 332-7620
bet. Fifth & Sixth Aves. in Midtown W.
You've got a great idea: nab "a window seat at Christmas" for
"great views of the skating rink." But you're not the only one
checking out the Rockefeller Center tree and all the aspiring Tonya
Hardings as you chow down on "overpriced" "average" American
fare. Read: It's "noisy" and tourist central, but "fun" nonetheless.
The best bet is weekend brunch. Reserve to avoid "long lines."

FOOD ROOM STAFF COST

Amici Miei

$30

475 W. Broadway (212) 533-1933
at Houston St. in SoHo

With friends like this, who needs enemies? Sure the SoHo crowd is "good-looking" and the location "trendy," but "that's about all it has going for it." If you want to people-watch, it's "nice outdoors," so "enjoy snacks and wine" in the "sidewalk garden" but don't rely on the "lame service" or sometimes "greasy" Italian food.

Amir's Falafel

$9

2911 Broadway (212) 749-7500
at 114th St. in Harlem

Pass the "paper plates" and go for a good, "cheap," "Middle Eastern fix." You'll make your two o'clock class with this "dependable," "fast-food -type" meal, as long as the waitstaff can get its falafel in gear.

An American Place

$44

2 Park Ave. (212) 684-2122
at 32nd St. in Murray Hill

Chef/owner Larry Forgione creates "imaginative regional specialties" at this Murray Hill American, to the delight of our voters. Food and staff are both in the top 100 on our poll, and Romac Reporters say "you couldn't ask for more flavors" or more "generous portions," served up with "great service."

Andalousia

$26

28 Cornelia St. (212) 929-3693
bet. W. 4th & Bleeker Sts. in the Washington Sq. Area

Hey, there's a tassel in my soup! The belly dancer entertains as you feast on exotic Moroccan dishes in the West Village. The staff gets a "B+" and the food is "delicious." And you can't beat the three-course prix fixe for $19.95. It's "a wee bit noisy" so bring your tambourine: If you can't beat 'em, join 'em.

Andrusha

1370 Lexington Ave. (212) 369-9374
bet. 90th & 91st Sts. in Carnegie Hill

You can expect traditional fare at this favorite Russian/Czech spot in its new location: potato pancakes, borscht, goulash and Russian tea. Czech it out.

Angelica Kitchen

300 E. 12th St. (212) 228-2909
bet. First & Second Aves. in the E. Village

Go ahead "laugh at its hard-core veggie-ness, but the food is great." Whatever kind of naturalist you are, vegan, macrobiotic or lettuce cult member, this East Village spot is "inexpensive" and "cool" with a "hip and diverse crowd." "If there were more places like this, everyone would give up meat."

▮ = SUPERIOR ▮ = EXCELLENT ▮ = V. GOOD ▬ = GOOD

Angelo's of Mulberry St.

$31

146 Mulberry St. (212) 966-1277
bet. Grand & Hester Sts. in Little Italy
One of Little Italy's oldest (circa 1902), this sometimes-crowded trattoria is "worth the wait" for "fresh" Italian fare. It can be "touristy" and some say "overpriced" but voters praise the authentic "tasty sauce" and old-world, "Godfather" atmosphere.

Angels

$20

1135 First Ave. (212) 980-3131
bet. 62nd & 63rd Sts. on the Upper East Side
Italian cherubs smile down on diners, who smile down on "giant portions" of "cheap" Italian pastas, seafood and chicken. Not fine dining by any stretch, though the "lots of choices" on the menu, including many heart-healthy options, has made it an "Upper East Side fixture with Lower East Side prices."

Anglers & Writers

$22

420 Hudson St. (212) 675-0810
at St. Lukes Pl. in the W. Village
"Picturesque" decor lures a steady stream of voters to this "quaint, quiet and charming" Country American, particularly for its traditional brunches of chicken pot pie, stew or roast turkey with all the trimmings. While the consistency of the food may have suffered of late, all agree it's the right place to warm up "on a cold winter Sunday," with "hearty food or a simple tea break." "Pretty" decor to some is "tres fey" to others, but all agree "those Wisconsinites know how to make a pie!"

Angry Monk

$18

96 Second Ave. (212) 979-9202
bet. 5th & 6th Sts. in the E. Village
"Exotic" Tibetan food in the "delightful garden" will lift the angry out of any monk or anyone else for that matter. "Wonderful veggie" dishes and "incredible dumplings" earn praise, but half the menu slips into "blandness"—nothing a little of that Himalayan chili sauce won't cure.

Annie's

1381 Third Ave. (212) 327-4853
at 77th St. on the Upper East Side
Jim McMullen's new family-style restaurant serves American fare with International hints: Mexico, Italy and Asia. It also has a big breakfast menu. Bring the babies.

Ansonia

329 Columbus Ave. (212) 579-0505
bet. 75th & 76th Sts. on the Upper West Side
This new, renovated upscale Upper West Side spot features chef Bill Telepan, whose resume includes four years as sous chef at Gotham Bar and Grill: See what he's cooking up here.

FOOD ROOM STAFF COST

Antico Caffe $20

1477 Second Ave. at 77th St. on the U.E. Side (212) 879-4824
For "inexpensive pasta, unbeatable bread and funky painted tables,"
this "local hangout" can't be beat. Dine outside, try the takeout, or
rub elbows with your neighbor—the "tight" tables make for "very
cramped quarters." And "it's a shame the staff is so terrible," but as
a "good value neighborhood place when money is an issue," this
place is "a student's dream."

Anton's $38

259 W. 4th St. at Perry St. in the W. Village (212) 675-5059
Still a sleeper, this "chef-run jewel" boasts "friendly" service and a
daily-changing Eclectic menu. A "quaint" and calming atmosphere
with music at a "perfect volume" makes it "a nice neighborhood
place" for regulars who know a "gem" when they see one.

Apple $20

17 Waverly Pl. (212) 473-8888
bet. Greene & Mercer Sts. in the Washington Sq. Area
"Calm, serene, and very granola" say our reviewers of this rather
large, NYU-area Vietnamese/Vegetarian. That's right, veggies and
carnies alike appreciate the good food, since this spot scrupulously
maintains two separate kitchens. Most voters give a thumbs up to
the "tasty and healthy" offerings but others think the Pacific
Rim/Fusion influences are "weird." Service is "inattentive": So
what—this place is kid-and karaoke-friendly.

Aquagrill $35

210 Spring St. at Sixth Ave. in SoHo (212) 274-0505
How, in less than six months, has this SoHo American seafooder
managed to squeak into the Top 100 for food? The "scrumptious" fish
fare is "inspired." "Fresh," "imaginative," and a "bit pretentious (but so
what?)," Aquagrill has the "best raw bar" that, unusually, is included in
the prix fixe lunch (1/2 dozen oysters, soup and salad). It's the "best new
seafooder this year," but voters hope "the service will match it some day."

Aquamarine

Pier 64, 26th St. at the Hudson River in Chelsea (212) 243-9500
Situated on Pier 64, this new seafooder overlooks the Hudson. It
serves progressive American cuisine featuring pastas and seafood.
Tell us what you think on next year's poll.

Aquavit $51

13 W. 54th St. bet. Fifth & Sixth/Midtown W. (212) 307-7311
You get "austere Modern Scandinavian everything" at this "lovely, serene,
pricey " upscale Midtowner. Aquavit has a split personality: While the
upstairs cafe-cum-bar is "fun for light food, downstairs is for a serious
meal out." Sure this place offers traditional dishes like Swedish meatballs
and gravlax, but adventurous types might try the sundried-cherry-crusted
rack of lamb. The Rockefeller Townhouse boasts a glass atrium and
two-story waterfall that attracts a predominantly boomer crowd (the
"restaurant of the '80s"). Voters rate Aquavit one of their top 50 favorites,
and advise that for "such a soothing experience," reservations are essential.

Arcadia  $55

21 E. 62nd St. (212) 223-2900
bet. Fifth & Madison Aves. on the Upper East Side
The "tables are tiny" but the cuisine "heavenly" and "inventive" at
chef/owner Anne Rosenzweig's "intimate" Contemporary
American Upper East Sider. An over-30 "see-and-be-seen" crowd
fits snugly (is "crammed") into the "elegant, tasteful room" and
advises that it's "cramped" if you aren't "in a booth." So "bring
your corporate card" or try the prix fixe "lunch for a better bargain."

Aria  $42

253 E. 52nd St. at Second Ave. in Midtown E. (212) 888-1410
This Italian sleeper is about to wake up. Located on the East Side
where there's not too much sidewalk traffic after rush hour, it quietly
shows up on the tops list in both food and service. "Why is it always
so empty? Food, service, and ambiance really are above average."

Arizona 206 &  $34
Arizona Cafe
206 E. 60th St. (212) 838-0440
bet. Second & Third Aves. on the Upper East Side
Chef Walzog's departure and frequent chef changes have put a
damper on the food ratings at this Upper East Side Southwestern
(though still "very good"), but new-chef Miles Angelo is "upholding
its innovative reputation" and may just blast the scores into the
stratosphere. "Supreme food both in taste and preparation" say recent
visitors, who also appreciate the "better deal" Tex-Mex (simpler) cafe
next door. P.S. The pueblo-style room often hosts a "noisy bar scene."

Arlo's  $33

1394 York Ave. at 74th St. in Yorkville (212) 327-0870
Expect "generous portions" of "very tasty" American fare at this
little-known Yorkville yearling. Sidewalk seats, Thursday night live
jazz and reasonable prices make it an inviting local option. Voters
praise the "great brunch deal" and "efficient, courteous" service but
warn: The "walls are an alarming shade of red."

Around the Clock Cafe

8 Stuyvesant St. at Third Ave. in the E. Village (212) 598-0402
Only in New York City can you satisfy the munchies with "great"
American/Continental food in "always lively" surroundings, 24
hours a day. This is the "quintessential East Village"/"NYU hang."
"Don't miss it for pancakes or a light dinner before a movie."
"Thank God it's open around the clock."

Arqua  $44

281 Church St. (212) 334-1888
at White St. in TriBeCa
Food is the focus—what a novelty!—at this "minimalist" TriBeCan
Northern Italian, where the "inherent, incredible beauty" of the room
vies with that of the crowd (well, they're incredibly beautiful, anyway;
the inherent part is open to discussion). The food's "authentic,"
"atypical," and "good, good, good," especially the "truly wonderful"
homemade pastas. Lunchtime's the right time to hear yourself talk.

	FOOD	ROOM	STAFF	COST

Arriba Arriba

1463 Third Ave. (212) 249-1423
bet. 82nd & 83rd Sts. on the Upper East Side

Thank heaven there's a place you can grab "great tacos" (read: "standard Mexican fare") after midnight. This Upper East Sider also has a "great bar" so if the drinking causes a munchies invasion, you won't have to go too far to fight them off. Smoke in the bar, yes on the credit cards.

Arte $29

21 E. 9th St. (212) 473-0077
bet. University Pl. & Fifth Ave. in the Central Village

This Central Village Italian lacks food 'Arte'stry but it has "good pastas and risotto" with "warm, friendly, responsive service." See if you mind relaxing in the garden or in front of a fire with a fairly priced pre-theater meal at hand. Five dollar validated parking across the street.

Artepasta $20

81 Greenwich Ave. (212) 229-0234
at Bank St. in the W. Village
106 W. 73rd St. (212) 501-7014
bet. Columbus & Amsterdam Aves. on the Upper West Side

There's "nothing fancy" about "one of New York's best bargains": "Boy do you get your money's worth" for the West Village. The ridiculously inexpensive Northern Italian prix fixe lunch and dinner menu (both under 10 bucks) is a steal. Probably a good thing too, the food is "okay but nothing to write home about" and the service can be "lousy" at times. "Colorful and conversational" murals make it pleasant. No smokes, no cards, and the kitchen is open until midnight.

Artos $42

Historic Timekeeper's Bldg., 307 E. 53rd St. (212) 838-0007
bet. First & Second Aves. in Midtown E.

It is still too soon to get an accurate bead on this new East Midtown Greek. Early reports are very good, with raves about the "terrific" dishes, the "bartender of the year," and "wonderful breads, warm from the oven." "Cool and dark," it's still an unknown.

Arturos $18

106 W. Houston St. (212) 677-3820
at Thompson St. in the Washington Sq. Area

"Stick with the pizza" and "great" live jazz at this Washington Square "old hand." With "dim," "no-frills" service and atmosphere, there's no "scene" but convenience,"reasonable" prices and "tasty" pies make it a neighborhood "tradition."

Artusi

36 W. 52nd St. (212) 582-6900
bet. Fifth & Sixth Aves. in Midtown W.

The owners of Villa d'Este on Lake Como in Northern Italy recently changed the name of their New York restaurant, Cesarina, to honor the author of Italy's most famous cookbook: Pellegrino Artusi. The new chef, Artusi admirer Mauro Mafrici, cooked at Felidia and at San Domenico in Imola, Italy, and now runs the kitchen at this comfortable spot.

▤ = SUPERIOR ▤ = EXCELLENT ▤ = V. GOOD ▬ = GOOD

Asti

⑂ 🌹 ⛲ $34

13 E. 12th St. (212) 741-9105
at Fifth Ave. in the Central Village
"Oh what fun we all had" chime voters about this "entertaining" Central Village Italian where you should "open your mouth to sing, not eat." Kudos for the "very attentive" "singing waiters" who rank in the top 100. The "cool opera memorabilia" sets the "jovial" musical scene. Unfortunately, "even an average cook could do better at home." Half-priced parking next door.

@Cafe

⑂ 🌹 ⛲ $15

12 St. Mark's Pl. (212) 979-5439
bet. Second & Third Aves. in the E. Village
Surf's up in the East Village! But don't get caught in The Net, you could be here all night. If you're not a "computer geek" this is not your place: "Go for the @, not the cafe." Download "nice" drinks @ the bar; the eats draw unanimous thumbs down. At best it is a "good place for studying and researching if you don't mind the music."

Atomic Wings

⑂ 🌹 ⛲ $13

175 W. 4th St. (212) 627-9500
bet. Sixth Ave. & Seventh Ave. S. in the W. Village
2nd Ave. & 92nd St. (212) 410-3800
in Carnegie Hill
2180 Broadway (212) 877-1010
at 77th St. on the Upper West Side
1446 First Ave. (212) 772-8400
bet. 75th & 76th Sts. in Yorkville
These Buffalo-style wings joints are more a commodity than a chain: Originally offered as a service to bar owners who wanted to serve better food, in some cases the wings have eclipsed the bars they meant to help. Whatever. They're "spicy and cheap," and by most accounts "the best wings in NYC."

Au Bon Coin

⑂ 🌹 ⛲ $28

85 MacDougal St. (212) 673-8184
bet. Bleecker & Houston Sts. in the Washington Sq. Area
While this "nice little French" bistro in the Washington Square area is "intimate," and tries to "capture the feel of a Paris restaurant, it is off in one detail: The staff is "friendly" and "sweet." The food is a bit unsophisticated and draws mixed reviews.

Au Mandarin

⑂ 🌹 ⛲ $26

200 Vesey St. (212) 385-0313
at West St. in the Financial District
In trying to be upscale, this restaurant's "fresh," "tasty" Chinese food is simply "overpriced" to many. The service is competent enough to handle the Financial District power crowd, so stop in after a tough morning at the office for a change-of-pace business lunch. The "imitation imperial court setting" in an indoor atrium only about half works. There's a weekend brunch if you're doing downtown, out-of-towner, top-of-the-Trade-Center stuff.

▬ = FAIR   [blank] = POOR   ▦ = NOT RATED

FOOD ROOM STAFF COST

Aunt Suzie's

126 E. 28th St. *bet. Park & Lex./Gramercy (212) 689-1992*
247 Fifth Ave., *Carroll & Garfield Sts., Brooklyn (718) 788-3377*
If you come to these Italian siblings, be prepared for "huge portions
you must share." The pulls are the "modest prices," the "cozy
atmosphere," and the "fast service."

Aureole
$67

34 E. 61st St. (212) 319-1660
bet. Park & Madison Aves. on the Upper East Side
Chef/owner Charlie Palmer "is a wizard: He works magic with the
food" at this very Upper East Side progressive American fixture,
one of New York's 10 best restaurants. The kitchen serves
"transcendent," "heavenly" fare in a "soothing," "elegant" and
"relaxed atmosphere." Some bits of good advice: "Save yourself for
dessert" ("almost too pretty to eat"), the $32 "prix fixe lunch is an
excellent value," and there's a pretty garden open May-October.

Au Troquet
$35

328 W. 12th St. at Greenwich Ave./W. Village (212) 924-3413
An "attentive" staff and amiable chef who "likes to meet
customers" make this "true bistro" a "solid" choice. Expect reliable
French fare in a "cute," "country" atmosphere that's "especially
nice in the summer." If you're looking for low-key dining, this
"romantic hideaway" in the West Village has a "real French feel."

Avanti
$31

700 Ninth Ave. at 48th St. in Clinton (212) 586-7410
"Consistently good" for a leisurely lunch or pre-theater dinner,
this Clinton Italian charms voters with its "warm and cozy
fireplace"and "country" atmosphere. Get comfortable and "plan
time" to enjoy "inventive," "made-to-order" fare that takes longer
to prepare. Though "knowledgeable," the staff can be "slow," so
"don't go if you're in a rush."

Avenue A Sushi
$23

105 Ave. A bet. 6th & 7th Sts. in the E. Village (212) 982-8109
"Funky" East Village "hipsters" crowd this "dark" Japanese for
"unusual," "surprisingly good" eats at "fairly cheap" prices. If
you're into the "eclectic" art, black lights and "psychedelic neon"
decor, "the ambiance is fabulous" but "forget about conversing,"
the "hip" DJ keeps the music loud. "Perfect for out-of-towners"
looking for something "different," it's "unforgettable" for late-night
"people-watching" and "disco sushi."

Azusa of Japan
$25

3 E. 44th St. (212) 681-0001
bet. Fifth & Madison Aves. in Midtown E.
Manhattan's only a la carte skewer counter is the centerpiece to
this Midtown Japanese yearling, serving authentic, lighter cuisine
to a less-than enthusiastic crowd. Sure, they do serve fugu (blow
fish) in season, but with only so-so food and "service" that is "not
good," is it worth the risk?

Baby Jake's $17

14 First Ave. (212) 254-2229
bet. 1st & 2nd Sts. in the E. Village
"Bring your sense of humor" to this cheap, "laid back" East Village
Cajun. It is "down-to-earth" with a "funky" space and "free jukebox,"
but the "bland" food and "worst" service make most diners cranky.
It's open late on weekends and after you've had a few cocktails you
might not mind the "grease, grease and more grease."

Bachue

36 W. 21st St. (212) 229-0870
bet. Fifth & Sixth Aves. in the Flatiron District
If you are interested in pasta sans the chicken, fish, or veal, and are
looking for more vegetarian places to dine out, this Flatiron Italian
will do fine. "Healthy food" in "huge portions" "make it worth
while," so who cares if there's "no atmosphere?"

Bali Nusa Indah $19

651 Ninth Ave. (212) 974-1875
bet. 45th & 46th Sts. in Clinton
There aren't many Indonesian eateries in NYC, and word is, this
Clinton outpost serves "spicy, fresh" fare at bargain prices. Solid
scores for "friendly" service and "wonderful ambiance"—complete
with "unusual batik tablecloths"—make it an "interesting" option,
especially pre-theater.

Ballato's $26

55 E. Houston St. (212) 274-8881
bet. Mott & Mulberry Sts. in SoHo
You can bring your own beer and wine to this SoHo: Too bad you
can't bring your own service and atmosphere. For "bargain" prix fixe
specials at lunch and pre-theater it's a decent "value." However, dull
service and worn, "homey" decor make voters lament that this
Neapolitan was "once good," but now that's "just a memory."

Baluchi's $27

1565 Second Ave. bet. 81st & 82nd/U.E. Side(212) 288-4810
193 Spring St. bet. Thompson & Sullivan in SoHo (212) 226-2828
361 W. 4th St. at 6th Ave./Washington Sq. Area (212) 929-2441
"A step above the usual Indian" these "elegant" siblings impress
voters with "consistent," "delicious" fare at "moderate prices." Tables
are "tight," but the "beautiful," "authentic" decor and "courteous staff"
make these restaurants very popular.

Bambou

243 E. 14th St. (212) 358-0012
bet. Second & Third Aves. in the E. Village
This comfortable new spot features contemporary Caribbean
cooking complete with elements like callaloo, cassava and coconut.
Visit this place to be transported.

FOOD ROOM STAFF COST

Bandito's

153 Second Ave. (212) 777-4505
at 9th St. in the E. Village
For "great margaritas" and "adequate" Mexican fare, steal on over to this "casual, fun" East Village write-in. Late-night dining and sidewalk seating make it a local "standard."

Bangkok Cafe — $25

27 E. 20th St. (212) 228-7681
bet. Broadway & Park Ave. S. in the Flatiron District
This little Thai, after slightly more than a year in service, is managing to find a following (of mostly twentysomething diners) in the bursting Flatiron dining scene. While rarely described in superlatives, the "pretty space, very nicely done," the "very pleasant staff," and the "solid," "straightforward" and "low-key food" follows an appropriately Eastern sense of balance and restraint. It's not the cheapest Thai in the book, but you get what you pay for here.

Bangkok Cuisine — $24

885 Eighth Ave. (212) 581-6370
bet. 52nd & 53rd Sts. in the Theater District
Prices are low and the food is "hot" at this Theater District Thai. "Authentic," "consistent" fare lures lunchtime and pre-theater crowds who tolerate the generic decor and lackluster service.

Bar Anise — $29

1002 Third Ave. (212) 355-1112
bet. 60th & 61st Sts. on the Upper East Side
Can't make it to Club Med? This North African restaurant has a "relaxing," "transporting atmosphere" and "excellent Mediterranean salads and chick-pea pasta." You must do the dance of seven veils to get some service, but hey, nobody's perfect. Ride your camel over for brunch on Saturday and Sunday.

Baraonda — $33

1439 Second Ave. (212) 288-8555
at 75th St. on the Upper East Side
"Expect to be ignored" by the "Euro-chic" staff at this Upper East Side Northern Italian. The "pasta with personality" is "good," but not as compelling as the "lively," "attractive" clientele and suave setting that make the atmosphere "addictive" for some diners. It can get "loud on the weekends" so try the sidewalk tables, and bring cash—no plastic.

Barbetta — $46

321 W. 46th St. (212) 246-9171
bet. Eighth & Ninth Aves. in Clinton
Family-owned for 90 years, this Clinton Piedmontese Italian boasts one of the prettiest rooms in the city. An "elegant special-occasion place" to some, others go more frequently for the "best garden for summer dining" and the "great prix fixe dinner." While the staff has its ups and downs, owner Laura Maioglio is "among the most gracious hosts in the city." The food, however much "like Mom's," just can't live up to the setting.

≡ = SUPERIOR ≣ = EXCELLENT ≡ = V. GOOD ━ = GOOD

Barking Dog Luncheonette

$17

1678 Third Ave. at 94th St. in Carnegie Hill (212) 831-1800
"A comprehensive canine collection of tchatchkas" adorns every nook and cranny of this "southern homey" American diner in Carnegie Hill. Neighborhood regulars claim the "home cooking" tastes "steps above NY diner food" and rarely go anywhere else for "great salads," "big sandwiches," and "brunch—yum yum, the best French toast." Non-dog owners who call it a "yuppie-puppy hangout" are mad because they can't eat on the sidewalk while their dogs drink from the special outside trough. No plastic.

Barnes & Noble Cafe

$10

Citicorp Bldg., 160 E. 54th at Third//Midtown E. (212) 750-8033
675 Sixth Ave. bet. 21st & 22nd Sts. in Chelsea (212) 727-1227
4 Astor Pl. bet. Broadway & Lafayette/E. Village (212) 420-1322
1960 Broadway at 66th St. on the U.W. Side (212) 595-6859
Starbucks coffee, many teas and the freedom to read books from the bookstore make these little in-store coffeehouses (complete with live fiction and poetry readings) very popular hangouts (and "meet" markets, by God). Sandwiches and light fare are uneven at best, leaving your mouth free for a quiet chat.

Barney Greengrass

$19

541 Amsterdam Ave. (212) 724-4707
bet. 86th & 87th Sts. on the Upper West Side
Celebrating its 88th birthday, Barney's is still the Sturgeon King, though more by divine right than by democratic process. Its many fans tout it one of the top brunches in the city, calling the predominantly smoked-fish menu "Jewish soul food" (especially the "chopped liver like Grandma's" and the "best lox in NYC — hands down"). However, it can be "disappointing during the week," and such a long-lived place is bound to have voters saying it has become "overpriced." All agree, the "tacky," "'50s decor," while providing "character galore," has seen better days: This emperor is due for some new clothes.

Barocco

$35

301 Church St. (212) 431-1445
at Walker St. in TriBeCa
"Still reliable" and always a scene with a crowd of "very hip," "eccentric," even "crazy" clientele, say voters of this Tuscan TriBeCan. They come for the "bossa nova atmosphere" and great drinks, and find the food trade-off acceptable: "medium priced, medium good."

Barolo

$40

398 W. Broadway (212) 226-1102
bet. Spring & Broome Sts. in SoHo
"How much more romantic can you get?" Not much, unless you're at a favorite vacation hideaway, because this Northern Italian is "like being in Europe." The best outdoor dining in New York, bar none, say participants. It's "beautiful in the Spring" and the gargantuan wine list has something for everyone. "It's a shame the service is so abysmal" at one of voters' favorite places in town. Free parking on the street after 6 p.m.

FOOD ROOM STAFF COST

Bar Pitti
$27

268 Ave. of the Americas (212) 982-3300
bet. Bleecker & Houston Sts. in the W. Village
There's nothing like a good "neighborhood favorite." Too bad if this Tuscan's not in yours: West Village people think it's "an amazing bargain." It can "be too noisy when crowded" but it's "a great date place" and the "genuine, homemade" fare "makes you feel as if you're in Florence." "The staff is getting too big for its britches"; deal with it.

Bar 6

502 Sixth Ave. bet. W. 12th & W. 13th/W. Village (212) 645-2439
If you're near the West Village and your three favorite things are "cigars," "lively, decadent" French/Moroccan food, and "beautiful barmaids"—in that order—you've come to the right place. This is a place of worship for The Cigar, so don't leave home without 'em. There's a DJ after 11 p.m., and the kitchen stays open until 2 or 3 a.m. every night.

Bayamo

704 Broadway (212) 475-5151
bet. 4th St. & Washington Pl. in the Washington Sq. Area
If you ever find yourself with the same cravings as people of Cuban/Chinese descent, this "exotic" spot in the Village will cure you. There's a "huge bar," "nice staff," and a "colorful," "surreal setting," where you can slurp "great frozen drinks." You won't find many Cuban-Chinese kitchens around and the good news is this one is open until 2 a.m.

Bay Leaf Indian Brasserie
$27

49 W. 56th St. bet. Fifth & Sixth Aves./Midtown W.(212) 957-1818
Ask some five-year-olds to point to India on an atlas, and you'll get the same results voters give this Midtown mediocrity: all over the map. It gets points for its garden and for striving to transcend the typical, but while some consider the "small servings" of "New-Age Indian" worth a return visit (especially if you're struck by a pre-/post-theater curry craving), most find the fare "more expensive" than other Indians, but "not better."

Bear Bar
$15

2156 Broadway at 76th St. on the Upper West Side (212) 362-2145
Though most twentysomething respondents "can't remember the food" at this Upper West Side bar, they wisely suggest: "don't go if you're claustrophobic or your date is sober." It's "crowded" and rowdy and the "staff sucks." If you can bear the acoustics, it can be "good for drinks" but not much else.

Becco
$31

355 W. 46th St. bet. Eighth & Ninth Aves./Clinton (212) 397-7597
Owned by the Bastianich (Felidia, Frico Bar) family, the Clinton/Theater District's "best buy" is "warm and festive," and "always crowded." The "endless" "pasta special" is an "excellent value," and our reporters also like the "great" pay-one-price ($15) "wine policy, "bountiful" antipasto, and "gracious service." "Mangia," for "heaven is definitely Italian."

≣ = SUPERIOR ≣ = EXCELLENT ≣ = V. GOOD ▬ = GOOD

Beekman Bar And Books

$29

889 First Ave. at 50th St. in Midtown E. (212) 980-9314

"The closest most cigar smokers get to heaven," (presumably while they're still alive) say voters of this hors d'oeuvres and light menu bar just north of the UN, where neoconservatives "debate their favorite brand of Republicanism while smoking Cuban cigars." It's the No. 1 cigar spot on the poll, and while the food is low fidelity, the mood is high Fidel. Jacket required.

Bella Donna

307 E. 77th St. bet. First & Second Aves./Yorkville (212) 535-2866
1663 First Ave. bet. 86th & 87th Sts./Yorkville (212) 534-3261

"Prepare to wait on long lines": Bella Donna is "small" and "always packed" because the Italian food is "delicious," the prices reasonable, and the Yorkville atmosphere "homey." "Great for lunch," no plastic.

Bella Luna

584 Columbus Ave. (212) 877-2267
bet. 88th & 89th Sts. on the Upper West Side

Brunch is never a four letter word, but it's especially nice before a Saturday or Sunday afternoon at the Natural History Museum. This "good neighborhood" Italian on the Upper West Side beckons diners to try "good pasta" "at fair prices" in a "classy space."

Bell Caffe

$16

310 Spring St. (212) 334-2355
bet. Hudson & Greenwich Sts. in SoHo

The "comfy couches" and mismatched "bohemian"setting make this West Villager good for "long conversations and drinks." "Great" live music "is a plus," but "order your food from another place" because the Ethno-healthy cuisine doesn't ring true and "tastes like microwave dinners." "Trendy" Gen-X regulars tolerate the often "rude" and "grungy" staff and tout the backyard garden as "wonderfully bizarre."

Bellissima

$24

1179 Second Ave. (212) 751-1536
bet. 62nd & 63rd Sts. on the Upper East Side

In its second year, this little Upper East Side Italian isn't winning any awards for its room or staff, but steadily gaining on its competition for the "nice neighborhood spot"-good-eats-at-low-prices crowd. Plus, it travels well: "the best home delivery I ever had; hot and plenty."

Bello

$31

863 Ninth Ave. (212) 246-6773
at 56th St. in Clinton

The name of this restaurant means 'beautiful' so, if you plan on eating at this Northern Italian, check the mirror, grab your jacket and tie and make reservations. We hear there's a "phenomenal veal-chop special," and "good food and ambiance." Late-night menu, free indoor parking.

FOOD · ROOM · STAFF · COST

Ben Benson's

$45

123 W. 52nd St. (212) 581-8888
bet. Sixth & Seventh Aves. in Midtown W.

You'll have a "loud," "high-testosterone experience" at this suit-and-tie West Midtowner that serves up "huge meat" and "out-of-this-world" hash browns. Though some find the atmosphere "sterile," it's popular for "business lunch" and "group heaven" at dinnertime. Expect a "mature crowd" that appreciates cigars and "great steaks" and doesn't mind "expense-account" prices. Compared to the beef, the service is "solid" but "unspectacular."

Bendix Diner

219 Eighth Ave. (212) 366-0560
at 21st St. in Chelsea

Head for Chelsea, if your party wants a choice of "get fat diner" fare or Thai food, at the same restaurant. BYO to a "good, inexpensive" local pit stop with "good food, good prices." Satisfy the brunchies on the weekends. Bring the kids.

Benihana

47 W. 56th St. (212) 581-0930
bet. 5th & 6th Aves. in Midtown W.
120 E. 56th St. (212) 593-1627
bet. Lexington & Park Aves. in Midtown E.

These one-of-a-kind "classic" Japanese steakhouses with "suprisingly good food" and "entertainment" are tourists havens. They're quiet stops after a long day on your feet and you can watch the knife-twirling chefs prepare steak and vegetables right before your eyes. Duck! Bring the little samurais.

Benito's I & II

$26

174 Mulberry St. (212) 226-9171
163 Mulberry St. (212) 226-9012
bet. Grand & Broome Sts. in Little Italy

Folks like the food better at one, that is Benito's I, and the ambiance a little better at Little Italy "home-style" Italian's newest incarnation, creatively named Benitos II. Those are Roman numerals, get it? Both are "fun in the old style," casual places, where you "let the waiter order for you," and while I is "quiet," II is the kind of place where you don't have to cringe when the kids act up.

Benny's Burritos

$14

113 Greenwich Ave. (212) 727-0584
bet. Jane & W. 12th Sts. in the W. Village
93 Ave. A (212) 254-2054
at 6th St. in the E. Village

Cal-Mex is too mild for some of our more serious spice hounds, who have to satisfy themselves with a shot of old Mexico at the bar of these Burrito joints. Kitschy-'50s decor and tiny tables set the scene for "some of the biggest burritos around." "Good food" at these prices means "one of the best deals in town." Outside dining in nice weather makes for great Village people-watching.

☰ = SUPERIOR ☰ = EXCELLENT ☰ = V. GOOD ▬ = GOOD

Bereket

187 E. Houston St. (212) 475-7700
at Orchard St. on the Lower East Side
"Don't expect service, it's self serve," do expect an "authentic" Turkish spot that serves "cheap" "fine food," "good for after hours": the more adventurous "take out and spread a tablecloth in Tompkins Square Park." "The best place for a quick bite on the Lower East Side."

Between The Bread

$16

141 E. 56th St. (212) 888-0449
bet. Lexington & Third Aves. in Midtown E.
145 W. 55th St. (212) 581-1189
bet. 6th & 7th Aves. in Midtown W.
If the Earl of Sandwich ever collected royalties on his invention, These places would owe him a fortune. Focusing mainly on corporate catering, these Midtowners also serve a "pleasant" breakfast ("great muffins") and other light fare on the healthy side.

Bice

$45

7 E. 54th St. (212) 688-1999
bet. Fifth & Madison Aves. in Midtown E.
A "too-trendy" "scene" keeps this pricey Midtowner "crowded" with "stars" and other "beautiful people." Most enjoy the "great" Italian fare, especially for business lunch, though some cry: "overrated and overpriced." Outdoor dining and fresh flowers add to the lively atmosphere, but service doesn't measure up.

Big Cup

228 Eighth Ave. (212) 206-0059
bet. 21st & 22nd Sts. in Chelsea
What's a coffeehouse without eavesdropping? Not much fun, that's what. There's also a lot of "cruising and flirting" going on in this one which rolls in to top spots for java, espresso, and gay hangout. Bagels, desserts and sandwiches complement the joe but be prepared for "rude" service and something called "gen-x attitude."

Big Nick's

2175 Broadway (212) 362-9238
at 77th St. on the Upper West Side
This Upper West Sider is such a "quintessential New York dive" that participants couldn't help but comment about it. "Great huge burgers," pizza, and hot dogs for the kids says it all. It's "fun," "tasty," "inexpensive," open 24 hours.

Big Sur

$25

1406 Third Ave. (212) 472-5009
at 80th St. on the Upper East Side
The staff of "models" might be "waiting to be discovered" but they sure aren't waiting tables at this "trendy" Upper Eastsider. Go late for the "good bar action" if you want a "bit of the Village Uptown," but say "no sir" to the inadequate Southwestern fare.

▬ = FAIR   [blank] = POOR   ▤ = NOT RATED   **45**

FOOD ROOM STAFF COST

Big Wong

$12

67 Mott St. (212) 964-0540
at Canal St. in Chinatown
This Chinatown "dive" "has been around forever, and looks it" with "no-frills ambiance" and "poor" service. If you can get beyond the lackluster conditions, head here for "large" portions of "good," "authentic Cantonese" at prices so "cheap," "a sumo" could chow down "for under $15." Regulars know it's cash only and claim it has the "best roast pork in New York."

Bill Hong's

$36

227 E. 56th St. (212) 355-2031
bet. Second & Third Aves. in Midtown E.
Nowhere near Chinatown? The food here is "really great but I wish it were a little less costly." It "has not aged well," but who has? The late menu doesn't run out of steam until midnight on Friday and Saturday.

Billy's

948 First Ave. (212) 753-1870
bet. 52nd & 53rd Sts. in Midtown E.
"New York's oldest and best pub" and "landmark" steakhouse opened in 1870 on the border of Midtown East and Sutton Place. And it's still alive and kicking. The "huge portions of great steaks" served by "nice waiters" give the "older crowd" a quiet "staple" to return to again and again.

Birdland

2745 Broadway at 105th St./Columbia U. Area (212) 749-2228
315 W. 44th St. at 8th Ave./Theater District (212) 581-3080
Jazz, jazz, and more jazz for Bird lovers everywhere. "Cool Manhattanites flock" to these Times Square and Upper West spots on the weekends to pay no cover for all that music.

Biricchino

$38

260 W. 29th St. (212) 695-6690
bet. Seventh & Eighth Aves. in Chelsea
In its ten years of existence, this Chelsea Northern Italian has been popular with the over-30, B&T Madison Square Garden crowd, though less so with the area residents. Best known for homemade sausages and charcuterie, the relatively high price tag is worth it to some for the easygoing, casual atmosphere.

Bistro Du Nord

$36

1312 Madison Ave. (212) 289-0997
at 93rd St. in Carnegie Hill
There's pretty much zilch in the way of restaurants on Madison Avenue, so if you're starving, and you find yourself North, this one's as good as any. It's "somewhat overpriced" for average French food but the "good deal" prix fixe slices the cost in half. The "tight tables" can make for "uncomfortable" seating when it's crowded, but become "jewelry box" "cozy" on snowy winter nights when it's less packed.

≡ = SUPERIOR ≣ = EXCELLENT ≡ = V. GOOD ▬ = GOOD

Bistrot Margot

26 Prince St. (212) 274-1027
bet. Mott & Elizabeth Sts. in SoHo
This tiny, newish "delightful hole in the wall" with "good," even "excellent" French bistro fare has a small, loyal neighborhood following. An "impressive small kitchen" that serves "good cheap French" is a rarity in SoHo.

Black Finn

 $20

994 Second Ave. (212) 355-6993
bet. 52nd & 53rd Sts. in Midtown E.
No one rages 'bout the Cajun served at this East Midtowner. "It's great for an after-work drink and that's about it," although sometimes you simply need to kick back by a fireplace, smoke a cigar and watch a game. The good news is it has satellite TV so you can channel surf right past the Jets.

Black Sheep

 $38

344 W. 11th St. (212) 242-1010
at Washington St. in the W. Village
An "off-the-beaten-path" location and "cozy, rustic" ambiance make this West Villager a refuge for romantics. With a working fireplace and "good" homestyle French/Italian fare, it's "great" for dates and quiet conversation. Though service is somewhat sheepish, this "bit of the country" satisfies flocks who like the "far-from-NYC" feel.

Blockhead's Burritos

499 Third Ave. (212) 213-3332
bet. 33rd & 34th Sts. in Murray Hill
"Burritos!!" They believe in "great big food!" here so bring your ruler—the "burritos are humongous." "Huge portions" of "cheap" "healthy, ample Mexican" in a "clean, friendly" environment with "great living room furniture," "salads and Margaritas"...gee, that's too bad. Console yourselves in the "nice lounge area" and "sit back and dip the chips."

Blue Moon East

1444 First Ave. (212) 288-9811
at 75th St. in Yorkville
"Eat outside" at this "quaint" Yorkville Mexican—a popular write-in for solid eats and "great brunch." It's "fast" and "clean" and portions are "generous."

Blue Nile

103 W. 77th St. (212) 580-3232
at Columbus Ave. on the Upper West Side
A Top 5 New York exotic experience (appropriately located across from the Natural History Museum), this is real "traditional Ethiopian—you eat with your fingers." You also order mead (honey wine) and "tasty marinated food" that's "hotter than Abyssinia" (the restaurant, not the location). It's a "fun place," and you may want to limber up and wash your hands ahead of time.

FOOD *ROOM* *STAFF* *COST*

Blue Ribbon Brasserie

$36

97 Sullivan St. bet. Prince & Spring Sts. in SoHo (212) 274-0404
"The scene can be a bit tiresome" at this SoHo Eclectic but "the food never disappoints." An "outstanding raw bar" and "top late-night" menu keep it "alive and kicking till 4 a.m." Though the no-reserving policy means it's packed after dark, the faithful are willing to wait for "a cool place that hasn't been invaded by B &Ters."

Blue Ribbon Sushi

$38

119 Sullivan St. bet. Prince & Spring Sts. in SoHo (212) 343-0404
Not yet a year old, this Soho Japanese (sibling of the popular Blue Ribbon Brasserie next door) has zoomed into the Top 20 sushi spots in New York, receiving a blue ribbon for its "very good" "fresh" food and "staff that really seems to like you." It's a "nice place" "mostly due to the location" and the hip under-30 crowd makes for "great people-watching," especially after hours. Hey, this is SoHo: You can smoke, and it's open until 2 a.m. No reserving.

Blue Water Grill

31 Union Sq. W. at 16th St. (212) 675-9500
Get your seafood fix "right off the boat" on Union Square where you can pick from the "creative," "ultra fresh," "well-prepared" "eclectic fish menu with tastes from all over" "in a cool, relaxed yet hip atmosphere" at "reasonable prices." This "cheery neighborhood place" houses a world class raw bar, so get your hat. Jazz downstairs Monday thru Saturday.

Boathouse Cafe

$32

Central Park Lake (212) 517-2233
72nd St. & E. Park Dr. in Central Park
The "pastoral view" over the Central Park pond really does take you light years away from the bustle of the city. Try this restaurant on a special occasion: an anniversary or before that carriage ride proposal. It's "great to take visitors for a drink," and for a "beautiful view at sunset" there's "no better place in the summer," though the food ("very average") doesn't live up to the setting, and the staff doesn't score any higher.

Bobby O's City Bites

560 Third Ave. at 57th St. in Midtown E. (212) 681-0400
It's "yuppie yet yummy" at this Midtown American with Italian accents. Since you'll be spending most of your money at the hot bar scene on the weekends ("always busy"), they know your pockets will be lighter come morning, so the brunch is accordingly cheap.

Bobby Van's Steakhouse

$41

Helmsley Bldg., 230 Park Ave. at 46th/Midtown E. (212) 867-5490
Tight-lipped voters have few words for this newcomer, solid scores show they appreciate the tasty steaks and capable service. Housed in a circa-1927 landmark building, it's a promising Midtown outpost of the Bridgehampton original. Check out the private cigar room.

▦ = SUPERIOR ▦ = EXCELLENT ▦ = V. GOOD ▬ = GOOD

Boca Chica $22

13 First Ave. (212) 473-0108
at 1st St. in the E. Village
Hordes of "attractive" twentysomethings hit this "festive" South American for "killer drinks" (especially the "kicky caipirinhas") and "tasty," "spicy" food. Be warned: This chica is packed—it's "hard to get a table" and "very loud," so "keep pouring the sangria" and beware the "vacant" staff that "just doesn't care."

Bodega

136 W. Broadway (212) 285-1155
at Thomas St. in TriBeCa
The owner, manager and chef (Lynn Wagenknecht, Edward Youkilis and Stephen Lyle) of Odeon have opened a family-friendly restaurant across the way, serving sandwiches, Mexican-styled dishes and standard dinner fare. Bring the kids.

Bo Ky $10

80 Bayard St. (212) 406-2292
at Mott St. in Chinatown
"The world's best meal in a soup bowl" is "the best thing on a cold winter's day," and this Chinatown noodle shop is the paragon of bargains. There's "no decor" and they bring your food as fast as they can, so don't be insulted if they set it down without a word and scurry off to help the next hundred customers. No reservations, no plastic.

Bolo $44

23 E. 22nd St. (212) 228-2200
bet. Broadway & Park Ave. S. in the Flatiron District
"Bobby Flay has done it again" with this "fantasy trip to España," via "exciting tastes," an "airy" "great space," and a "lively" local scene. Though the service can be "rushed" and traditionalists grumble that "the chef is trying to be too inventive," fans suggest "you'll be boloed over by the food." "Suckling pig," "great octopus salad," and sangria that's "tops" come in for extra points.

Bombay Palace $27

30 W. 52nd St. bet. Fifth & Sixth/Midtown W. (212) 541-7777
This West Midtown restaurant is a little on the "pricy" side for Indian, but if you aren't near little India—which you aren't if you're here—then this will do. The "food is prepared with care" and you'll feel "pampered and welcome."

Bondini $33

62 W. 9th St. (212) 777-0670
bet. Fifth & Sixth Aves. in the Central Village
You've shopped till you've dropped at Balducci's, and now you're too tired to cook dinner: Why not head around the corner to Bondini where there's a little of everything, and it's all "good?" You'll also find "charming, elegant" decor and "friendly service" at this Central Village Northern Italian.

| | FOOD | ROOM | STAFF | COST |

Boonthai

$22

1393 Second Ave. (212) 249-8484
bet. 72nd & 73rd Sts. on the Upper East Side
With a nondescript, "quiet" atmosphere and "good" fare, this Upper East Sider serves locals who seek the "usual" Thai options. Though service falters, prices are "reasonable" for this part of town.

Borgo Antico

$29

22 E. 13th St. (212) 807-1313
bet. University Pl. & Fifth Ave. in the Central Village
This year-old Tuscan Italian is one of the "best newcomers of the year." It's "worth the walk up a flight of stairs" to the "lovely" dining room, with its "warm," country-house ambiance and "welcoming service." The food may not be "as consistent" as the "great staff," but it comes in for its share of kudos.

Borsalino

$27

255 W. 55th St. (212) 246-0710
bet. Broadway & Eighth Ave. in Midtown W.
Another "nice, quiet Italian" in West Midtown can never hurt. Everything about this place is adequate, even good. The menu stays active until 11:30 p.m. Friday and Saturday and there's a $20 pre-theater. It serves "the smallest portions ever" though, so order twice.

Bouterin

420 E. 59th St. (212) 758-0323
bet. First Ave. & Sutton Pl. at Sutton Pl.
Chef/proprietor Antoine Bouterin brings to his still-new restaurant 14 years experience at Le Perigord, along with the cuisine of his home region: southern France. Big recent press makes this one a tough res.

Bowery Bar

$31

358 Bowery at E. 4th St. in the E. Village (212) 475-2220
"Bum food," "lousy service," "crummy location" and "the velvet rope entry is a joke" about sums it up. So no one goes there, right? Umm, not exactly. Look up "trendy" in the dictionary and there's a picture of this joint. Models, celebs, "beautiful people" and all "those under 28 who wish to be seen" jam the place. It can be fun to drink here but it's also "fun to watch middle-aged record execs play with anorexic high school girls." If you do order from the menu, be in it for the long haul, the "wanna-be models serving the food with super attitude" are "so slow you'll be eating dinner around midnight"—but "are you really going here for the food?"

Boxer's

190 W. 4th St. bet. 6th & 7th Aves./Wash. Sq. (212) 633-BARK
This Washington Square American and European has "great food, but is often overcrowded," especially on weekends. Otherwise, it's "a casual place to relax," a "good place for a date" or an after work drink at the large, central bar.

▆ = SUPERIOR ▆ = EXCELLENT ▆ = V. GOOD ▆ = GOOD

Box Tree  $60

Box Tree Hotel, 250 E. 49th St. (212) 758-8320
bet. Second & Third Aves. in Midtown E.
This dressy Turtle Bay French was once the epitome of romantic.
Today it doesn't even make the Romac Top 20 romantic spots, though
the room is still among the Top 75 in town. What happened? Some
say it has become "inconsistent," and that (like its core clientele) it is
still "good looking, but has gone downhill." Let's hope it's not "past
its prime," and that it will soon return to its former glory.

Bravo Gianni  $51

230 E. 63rd St. (212) 752-7272
bet. Second & Third Aves. on the Upper East Side
"Very good" food brings in high ratings, but makes voters a bit
"crazy": This upscale Upper East Side Italian keeps out the riffraff
with high prices and a "made man" attitude.

Brawta Caribbean Cafe  $18

347 Atlantic Ave., at Hoyt St. in Brooklyn (718) 855-5515
This Caribbean has wowed 'em in Brooklyn in its first two years,
serving "excellent food in an appropriately informal setting."
"Reasonably priced, and the people are always nice," at this "great
neighborhood joint," voters "hope they move to Manhattan!"

Bridge Cafe  $34

279 Water St. at Dover St./South St. Seaport (212) 227-3344
Charm and history drip from the tin ceilings of this slice of old New
York located under the Brooklyn Bridge. It "feels off the beaten
track," and indeed it is, though that doesn't stop the crowds from
stampeding into this small, "friendly" spot in search of "great
buffalo" and other "great"-raters, including the single-malts (with
sample tastings) and the Sunday brunch. Variety, however, does not
rate a "great," and the "nice and cozy" atmosphere in this
202-year-old building is at least as big a draw as the food.

Bright Food Shop  $19

216 Eighth Ave. (212) 243-4433
at 21st St. in Chelsea
"Bright" means a "stark luncheonette setting" at this"eclectic"
Chelsea eatery. "The Asian/Mexican menu is often baffling, but
when it works, it's great," though "they could stand a few items on
the menu for the jalapeño impaired," whatever that means. The
"inventive," "tangy, nouvelle Southwestern fare" is "dirt cheap,"
and we hear that "not eating here isn't a bright thing to do." Voters
call it "a well-kept secret" and urge you not to "let everyone in on
it." Well, we can't make any promises.

Brio  $36

786 Lexington Ave. at 61st St. on the U.E. Side (212) 980-2300
The fact that it's a "little crowded" may mean you have to "be
prepared to wait," but the homemade pastas and "super" desserts
add up to "fine Italian" in Midtown.

FOOD   ROOM   STAFF   COST

Broadway Diner

$17

1726 Broadway at 55th St. in Midtown W. (212) 765-0909

Like the talk show that is filmed across the street from the Broadway location, these American diners have slipped over the past few years—check out those ratings!—and prices are on the wrong side of cheap. An "okay" stop "before theater time," their "good French toast," "great greasy burgers," and "convenient locations" put them on our top 10 list for NYC Diners.

Broadway Joe Steakhouse

$36

315 W. 46th St. (212) 246-6513
bet. Eighth & Ninth Aves. in Clinton

When I was a kid, "Broadway Joe" was Joe Namath. Now the Jets stink and this Clinton joint's not much better, according to voters, who say it's at best "average," with service that wants to "rush you out." This "tourist trap" is baited, however, with steaks that are at least in "generous portions," if only "okay."

Brooklyn Diner USA

$23

212 W. 57th St. (212) 977-1957
bet. Seventh Ave. & Broadway in Midtown W.

Here's a question for our voters that call this place "overpriced": Didn't it occur to you, as you walked along 57th Street, that this year-old diner might just be the tiniest bit touristy? With only slightly "better than diner food," a dressy staff and Brooklyn Dodger decor actually make this place worthwhile to most, especially those with kids. P.S. "USA" in the name means "touristy." Jeez!

Brother Jimmy's Bar B Que

$19

1461 First Ave. at 76th St. in Yorkville (212) 545-7427

A "casual, noisy" bar with borderline scores for food, decor and service must be doing something right if it's packing 'em in. It's top twenty both for child-friendliness and Thursday night out. This is "down-and-dirty homestyle BBQ" with "heavy Southern soul," "it's like going to an outdoor picnic all year round." Try the "Brunswick stew," and stick some ribs in your ears to drown out the "too loud" music.

Brother's BBQ

225 Varick St. at Clarkson St. in the W. Village (212) 727-2775

If the "good Southern roadside food" doesn't grab ya the "funky and friendly" bar probably will. It's "noisy but fun" which makes it a lot like Bigtown.

Brunettas

$19

190 First Ave. bet. 11th & 12th/E. Village (212) 228-4030

"The garden is unbeatable" at this East Village "hideaway," but Downtowners know they can frequent this unassuming place for "affordable" Italian all year long. The food rates in the middle of the pack but the "brunch menu is the best" and prix fixe dinner is only $9.95. "Service depends on the student of the moment." In the winter, the chair count shrinks to half, but walk on over when the snow melts, and order "the Monday night special and sit in the garden."

▇ = SUPERIOR ▇ = EXCELLENT ▇ = V. GOOD ▬ = GOOD

Bruno

⟨icons⟩ $42

240 E. 58th St. (212) 688-4190
bet. Second & Third Aves. in Midtown E.

Get your Italian fix in Midtown at a restaurant that receives consistent kudos across the board. Bite into "excellent food, service and atmosphere," the check may bite back, but we hear it's worth it. This place is also "excellent for special times with a date or friends." Enjoy live piano music, sitting by the fire, or relaxing on the terrace with the late-night menu. Reservations are essential; dress up.

Bryant Park Grill

⟨icons⟩ $34

Bryant Park, 40th St. bet. 5th & 6th/Garment Dist. (212) 840-6500

"Location, location, location" in the "now-beautiful" renovated Bryant Park douses any complains about "slow service," "stiff prices" and a kitchen that may need a little more time to hit its stride. Sure, the "crowds" can be "irritating" and the Contemporary Continental menu is "nothing special," but this "totally NY experience" brings a "touch of class to the neighborhood," and it's "the best outside dining" in the city. In short, "If I were in Europe in this atmosphere, I'd go through a roll of film."

B. Smith's

⟨icons⟩ $34

771 Eighth Ave. at 47th St. in the Theater District (212) 247-2222

Once supermodel, now superhost Barbara Smith, together with chef Henry Chung, has been packing in a diverse, good-looking and mostly boomer crowd for—can it be?—over ten years now. With solid ratings all around by a high volume of voters, the "beautiful people" come pre-/post-theater for the great staff ("the best management in town") serving up "very good Soul Food": Potato-leek pancakes topped with smoked salmon wins special mention. Be aware that a jumping bar scene and jazz upstairs can make it a "bit noisy."

Bubby's

⟨icons⟩ $20

120 Hudson St. (212) 219-0666
at N. Moore St. in TriBeCa

If you miss "wonderful, healthy, homemade food" you might try this TriBeCa winner. Everything is consistently "fresh" and "delicious," served in "generous portions" with a "friendly neighborhood feel." "Don't miss the mashed potatoes," the "great homemade desserts," "the quintessential breakfast," (top 20) or the Saturday and Sunday top 20 brunch. Kids are welcome here.

Bull & Bear

⟨icons⟩ $37

Waldorf-Astoria, 301 Park(212) 872-4900
at 49th St. in Midtown E.

Harumph! With so many Midtown spots competing for the business lunch crowd, the B&B has been setting the standard since the days when three martinis were de rigeur for the man in the grey flannel suit. Steaks, chops and seafood, including dry-aged Black Angus are the order of the day. Sure, there are better steakhouses around, but none stodgier, and "phenomenal service for business lunch" for some is "too stuffy" for others. It even has its own humidor at the bar—double harumph!

	FOOD	ROOM	STAFF	COST

Burritoville

$10

141 Second Ave. bet. 8th & 9th Sts./E. Village (212) 260-3300
36 Water St. at Broad St. in the Financial District (212) 747-1100
451 Amsterdam bet. 81st & 82nd Sts./U.W. Side (212) 787-8181
1489 First Ave. bet. 77th & 78th Sts. in Yorkville (212) 472-8800
1606 Third Ave. bet. 90th & 91st in Carnegie Hill (212) 410-2255

Impressions of this Cal-Mex chain are as mixed as you can get: It seems the "Cal" influences get in the way of the "Mex" that many eaters (mostly for takeout) expect ("can't they just make a plain burrito?"). Still, if you have special dietary needs (like lactose-intolerance, vegan), and you are on a budget, try it. P.S. The "giant portions" of beans and brown rice are "about as much as your digestive tract can take."

Bus Stop Cafe

$15

597 Hudson St. at Bethune St. in the W. Village (212) 206-1100

There's nothing like hanging out in a West Village cafe where the food is "inexpensive" enough to make a "home for actors." "Breakfast always includes newspapers" and classical music. The American food isn't the best in town, but at least it isn't trying to be something it's not.

BUtterfield 81

168 E. 81st St. bet. Third & Lex. on the U.E. Side (212) 288-2700

Veteran restaurateur Ken Aretsky (Arcadia, "21" Club) brings daughter Beth as co-chef and son Jon as bartender in this new American neighborhood spot. This is one to check out.

Byblos

$21

200 E. 39th St. at Third Ave. in Murray Hill (212) 687-0808

If you're in Murray Hill and you're hankering for Lebanese/Middle Eastern, here's a solid, "inexpensive" place with "helpful service and great appetizers." There is a prix fixe lunch and dinner deal, but strangely, the regular menu may be a better bargain. Friday and Saturday night a keyboard player stops in to tickle your fancy, not to mention the ivories.

Cabana Carioca

$22

123 W. 45th St. bet. Sixth & Seventh/Midtown W. (212) 581-8088

"Stuff yourself silly" at this "yummy" Midtown South American that some say is "like being back in Sao Paolo." The lunchtime crowds know to go to the "top floor" and expect "semi-hostile service" and "super-cramped," wildly decorated quarters. The $6 all-you-can-eat buffet lunch may be the "best bargain in town."

Cafe Beulah

$33

39 E. 19th St. bet. Bdwy & Park Ave. S./Flatiron (212) 777-9700

Just 'cus its "upscale" honey sure don't mean it ain't down-home. The South Carolina Soul cooking at this Flatiron cafe earns consistent kudos from students to seniors. The "great ambiance" takes you back to the coastal Carolina lowlands and the service is equally good. Rest assured that the "great fried chicken" is the real southern deal and not a borrowed recipe. Yes, it's a bit pricey for some wallets but surprised first-timers call it "a sleeper."

▤ = SUPERIOR ▤ = EXCELLENT ▤ = V. GOOD ▬ = GOOD

Cafe Botanica $38

Essex House, 160 Central Park S. (212) 484-5120
59th St. bet. Sixth & Seventh Aves. in Midtown W.
The Sunday brunch and the prix fixe dinner make Cafe Botanica's
Contemporary American fare a "great value," but it's the relaxing
ambiance, the "good" service and the "beautiful floral setting
overlooking the park" that make it a class act. It may be a bit too
fancy for some, but it's "bound to impress." Make sure you dress
up, lest the decor put you to shame.

Cafe Centosette $17

107 Third Ave. at 13th St. in the E. Village (212) 420-5933
Though the menu and service are "limited," this East Village
Italian provides a "romantic," "relaxing" atmosphere that satisfies
some who go for "dessert and coffee." Others bemoan the
"garlicky reek" and unmemorable eats, but low prices mean
"there's always plenty of people."

Cafe Centro $37

MetLife Bldg., 200 Park Ave. at 45th/Midtown E. (212) 818-1222
To embrace the sheer Midtownness of Midtown, head for this
French/American brasserie, where expense-accounting suits don't
mind spending "grand centos" for "tasty food"— including
Moroccan and rotisserie specialties—and "an even better beer
menu," plus 15 wines by the glass. Believe it or not, "business and
fun" do mix, especially at lunchtime; the art-deco decor and "noisy,
crowded, and exciting" atmosphere overcome sometimes "uneven"
food" and offer all sorts of distractions from tedious shoptalk.

Cafe Colonial $28

73 E. Houston St. at Elizabeth St. in SoHo (212) 274-0044
"In Style," this Lower East Side New American with Brazilian
accents "lives up to its name." In general the "overhyped, standard
fare" and "fair" service could use some work. The breakfast and late
night menus through the week do make it convenient, as does the
Brunch on Saturdays and Sundays. Sidewalk dining, smoking
permitted in the evening.

Cafe Con Leche $17

424 Amsterdam Ave. bet. 80th & 81st/U.W. Side (212) 595-7000
"Standout" Cuban/Dominican food is the stock-in-trade of this "fun,"
"authentic" dive on the Upper East Side. Sure, it's "dark" and
"cramped," but for "fair prices," "friendly staff," and a "delightful"
"neighborhood" experience, this is the "real" thing. "Take home some
garlic sauce and hot sauce; it's good on anything."

Cafe Crocodile $40

354 E. 74th St. bet. First & Second/Yorkville (212) 249-6619
Some folks find it hard to believe that this Upper East Side
French/Mediterranean is coming up on a twenty year anniversary. It's
still so "cute," "small and intimate," with a "charming staff" and what
some think is "the most underrated food in town." Sometimes the
"crush can" make it "unappetizing, though the food still rates."

FOOD ROOM STAFF COST

Cafe de Bruxelles

$35

118 Greenwich Ave. at W. 13th St./W. Village (212) 206-1830
Let's get one thing straight: it's "frites" not "French fries" (try the
yam variety) at this West Village Belgian cafe. "An authentic
charmer" say the fans, and "without being Euro-trash" say the
grateful. Try the Liegeoise salad, waterzooi chicken or dark Belgian
beer beet stew. The "amazing European bar selection," the special
mayonnaise sauce and "friendly service" also receive lots of
mentions. Prices can creep up just a tad but the prix fixe lunches
and dinners (both under $20) are reasonable. Smoking is allowed.

Cafe De Paris

$33

924 Second Ave. at 49th St. in Midtown E. (212) 486-1411
Though few of our Romacateers know it, this "romantic" little
French bistro in Murray Hill offers a beautiful terrace and a couple
of good-value prix fixe menus that court a small but loyal local
following. So the food's "nothing special?" It's so romantic you can
"turn and kiss the cute stranger" at the next table.

Cafe Des Artistes

$50

1 W. 67th St. (212) 877-3500
bet. Columbus Ave. & Central Park W. on the Upper West Side
About to celebrate its 80th birthday, the artistry at this Country French
(mingled with self-described "bourgeois European") is not strictly
limited to the dancing nudes in the murals. This is a culinary experience
that is simply the standard for romantic elegance in the city. "A
prerequisite for living in New York," it's "a truly elevating experience,"
for brunch, "intimate" dinner—whatever, it's "worth the splurge." N.B.
Reserve well ahead of time, sometimes months, especially for holidays.

Cafe Des Sports

$29

329 W. 51st St. bet. Eighth & Ninth Aves./Clinton (212) 581-1283
While the "solid French food" is on the simple side (not much has change
in its thirty years), the "surly French staff" reminds older voters of "old
'50s New York." It doesn't, however, remind them of a great French
restaurant, and some suspect they "must survive on unwary theatergoers."

Cafe du Pont

$37

1038 First Ave. bet. 56th & 57th Sts./Midtown E. (212) 223-1133
Head due east to First Avenue to find this little Midtown Eclectic serving
light fare. A little French, a little Italian, a little American, a little
something for everybody. One of those places every neighborhood
should have to keep your group from arguing on street corners.

Cafe Español

$25

172 Bleecker St. (212) 505-0657
bet. MacDougal & Sullivan Sts. in the Washington Sq. Area
"The Sangria's the ticket" at this Spanish/Mexican Central Villager,
though the "best paella in the city" runs a close second, especially
in the "way too much" portioning here. While the "dimly lit"
atmosphere, somewhat down-at-heel, needs a face-lift, and the
weekend waits can take forever, you get "a lot for the buck,"
including "stellar shrimp in green sauce," and "great margaritas."

Cafe Español On Carmine

63 Carmine St. (212) 675-3312
at Seventh Ave. S. in the W. Village

$24

If you think your apartment makes you feel closed in, check out the "fabulous" "claustrophobic," Spanish goings-on here. It's a good thing "the paella can probably serve two," because if you order one for everybody, you might have to balance some on your nose.

Cafe Greco

1390 Second Ave. (212) 737-4300
bet. 71st & 72nd Sts. on the Upper East Side

Older diners appreciate the "quiet" atmosphere and "good value" prix fixe specials at this Upper East Side Mediterranean. A reliable "neighborhood" favorite, it's "unsurprising" and "never crowded."

Cafe Lalo

201 W. 83rd St. (212) 496-6031
bet. Broadway & Amsterdam Ave. on the Upper West Side

$14

Lots of traffic (usually from the nearby movie theater) is needed to swallow up the "largest dessert menu in NYC" at this Upper West Side breakfast, brunch and light food cafe. With occasional live music, a late-late menu, wines by the glass and even some Kosher options, this is the young crowd's "first-date after-movie hangout."

Cafe Le Figaro

185 Bleecker St. (212) 677-1100
at MacDougal St. in the W. Village

Open late, this West Village Italian Coffee and Dessert spot is a "great place for coffee and a chat." They have a "stay as long as you like" attitude. So, if you want some of the best espresso/cappuccino in town, or "just want to hang," stop by after dinner.

Café Loup

105 W. 13th St. (212) 255-4746
bet. Sixth & Seventh Aves. in the W. Village

$33

Everyone raves about the setting at this "comfortable, not trendy," art-filled Village French Bistro, and no wonder: Café Loup pulls down very good scores for its room and staff. So much so, that our voters pay chef/owner Lloyd Feit compliments we don't usually see: "We always feel comfortable"; "friendly waiters"; "dependable and welcoming, like an old friend from way back"; "a good place for showing off NYC to guests," and perhaps strangest of all, "very good attitude French."

Café Luxembourg

200 W. 70th St. (212) 873-7411
at Amsterdam Ave. on the Upper West Side

$42

It may be "on the decline" from its "trendy" heyday, but for many this Upper Westsider is still a "standby" and the "only fun restaurant near Lincoln Center." The "basic bistro" fare satisfies most who are well-acquainted with service that's often too "smug," tables that are always "too close," and a room that is "too noisy."

FOOD ROOM STAFF COST

Cafe Mona Lisa

282 Bleecker St. (212) 929-1262
at Seventh Ave. S. in the W. Village
"Just stop by and you will stay" at this West Village coffeehouse.
It's not just because the "service is a little slow" either. It has "cozy
chairs" and "desserts and salads galore." For parties keep in mind
they have "the best birthday song presentation ever."

Cafe Mozart

154 W. 70th St. (212) 595-9797
at Broadway on the Upper West Side
75 "scrumptious" desserts and soothing classical music make this
Upper West Side coffeehouse a "comfortable" place to linger. Late
hours keep it busy after a nearby movie or concert at Lincoln Center.

Cafe Nicholson

$53

323 E. 58th St. (212) 355-6769
bet. First & Second Aves. in Midtown E.
A strange location (hard by the bridge entrance) makes this unusual
American both elusive and exclusive. The room is beautiful and
quiet, and takes "top billing" over the "old-fashioned" American
food. Desserts are "excellent" at this "unique" place that's "like
eating in a curiosity shop."

Cafe Noir

$29

32 Grand St. (212) 431-7910
at Thompson St. in SoHo
It "feels like North Africa" or the "home of Bertolucci" in this
atmospheric newer pan-Med. Cafe Noir gets more praise for its
"laid-back" "sophistication" and "comfy mixed Euro scene"—"no
poseurs or stuffed shirts" here—than for its trendy mix of "friendly"
French, Spanish, and American "tapas," but then again, this is
SoHo, so "bring on the hookahs!"

Cafe Nosidam

$39

768 Madison Ave. (212) 717-5633
at 66th St. on the Upper East Side
Think fast: Junior's fitting at Barney's took WAY too long, and you
and the kids have the low-blood-sugar blues. So, what do you do?
This Italian/American is convenient for Madison Avenue shoppers
and Fifth Avenue museum-goers, especially since it's open through
teatime hours and welcomes parents with young children. And, after a
day of exhausting the credit cards up and down the block, you may
want to "try the great bargain prix fixe dinner."

Cafe Orlin

41 St. Mark's Pl. (212) 777-1447
bet. First & Second Aves. in the E. Village
A "neighborhood standard," this "sweet, small" East Village cafe is
popular with "students" and an "artistic crowd." A "good place to chat,"
it offers "tasty" Continental fare and sidewalk seats. No credit cards.

≣ = SUPERIOR ≡ = EXCELLENT ≡ = V. GOOD ═ = GOOD

Cafe Pertutti

2888 Broadway (212) 864-1143
bet. 112th & 113th Sts. in Harlem
This "nice space" offers "cheap, plentiful" Italian food—Cafe Perutti is a "good choice for the Columbia U. Area." How do you feel about "the best Caesar salad" or "fabulous desserts?" High chairs, kids' menus—bring in the menagerie.

Cafe Picasso

359 Bleecker St. (212) 929-6232
at Charles St. in the W. Village
The West Village is loaded with little beauties like this one. The Picasso hangs its hat on homemade pasta, salads and "original" brick-oven pizza. It's "old-world European" and reasonably priced.

Cafe Pierre

 $55

Hotel Pierre, 2 E. 61st St. (212) 940-8185
bet. Fifth & Madison Aves. on the Upper East Side
Ahh, the Pierre. Though this East Side French restaurant earns very good to excellent marks all around, it's not on everyone's A-list for special occasions, or even business dining spots. Why? The price tag, though high, is no higher than other similarly rated places, even on the same block. Perhaps it's the fact that Cafe Pierre is low key—no need for publicity—there are plenty of hotel guests and other rich tourists ready to take a meal here.

Cafe Reggio

119 MacDougal St. (212) 475-9557
bet. Bleecker & W. Houston Sts. in the Washington Sq. Area
This "cappuccino museum" on Washington Square is an Italian coffeehouse favorite for reviewers who wrote in to praise the "beautiful old room filled with antiques"—the "feel of Europe." It's open until 2 a.m. for coffee and a light bite, but bring cash.

Cafe Riazor

 $23

245 W. 16th St. (212) 727-2132
bet. Seventh & Eighth Aves. in Chelsea
"For lovers on a budget" is about the nicest thing anyone had to say about this Chelsea Spanish, sister to Cafe Rio Mar and specializing in Tapas at the bar. "Small and simple" translates to "dungeon" ambiance to many, who "wonder why it's so busy?" Hell—sometimes dumps like this are just plain "fun."

Cafe San Martin

 $35

143 E. 49th St. (212) 832-0888
bet. Third & Lexington Aves. in Midtown E.
Little known among our reviewers, this Midtowner serves up an eclectic mix of Spanish ("excellent paella"), French and Italian fare in a setting that is less hectic than others in the area.

▬ = FAIR   [blank] = POOR   ▤ = NOT RATED

FOOD *ROOM* *STAFF* *COST*

Cafe Torino

139 W. 10th St. (212) 675-5554
bet. Greenwich & Seventh Aves. in the W. Village
It may be a little "short on ambiance" but the "impeccable service and food, and the "large portions," combine to make this one of the "best kept secrets in the Village." Besides, it's "affordable and you can wear jeans." Check out the "nice garden."

Cafe Trevi $35

1570 First Ave. (212) 249-0040
bet. 81st & 82nd Sts. in Yorkville
You feel "good" about a restaurant where the chef and owner are the same person; ditto: this Upper East Side Northern Italian. "You always feel welcome" here with "super" "personalized service." "Great food," "crazy atmosphere," and a late menu (till 12 a.m.).

Cafe Un Deux Trois $30

123 W. 44th St. (212) 354-4148
bet. Sixth Ave. & Broadway in Midtown W.
The heavy pre-theater crowd is as loud in here as they are at the box office lines. The food receives a walloping "straightforward" "run-of-the-mill" as the "Times Square version of French cuisine," but the "loud decibel rating" probably dulls the taste buds. Most "love the crayons on the table" for the kids and the Theater District location. Judging from the staff scores, you may see your waiter at a matinee.

Caffe Bondi $32

7 W. 20th St. (212) 691-8136
bet. Fifth & Sixth Aves. in the Flatiron District
"Not a red-sauce place," this Flatiron Italian specializes in Sicilian dishes in a "relaxed, cheery atmosphere." The "owners give a sincere effort," and many voters consider the service top-notch. Desserts are a standout, including "great gelato."

Caffe Buon Gusto $21

236 E. 77th St. bet. 2nd & 3rd Aves./U.E. Side (212) 535-6884
1009 Second Ave. bet. 53rd & 54th/Midtown E. (212) 755-1476
71 W. 71st St. bet. Columbus & CPW/U.W. Side (212) 875-1512
151 Montague St., bet. Clinton & Henry/Brooklyn (718) 624-3838
Folks like these unsophisticated, "fresh and inexpensive Italians," for the atmosphere ("trendy" to some is "yuppie" to others) . The real draw is the "good homemade" pasta that is a real "bang for the buck."

Caffe Grazie $31

26 E. 84th St. (212) 717-4407
bet. Fifth & Madison Aves. on the Upper East Side
An unenthusiastic (and light) response to this Upper East Side Italian shows it to be part of the Metropolitan tourist pocket. Good "for post-Met sustenance," there are better Italians around.

Caffe Lure $29

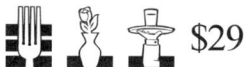

169 Sullivan St. (212) 473-2642
bet. Houston & Bleecker Sts. in the Washington Sq. Area
The hook at this SoHo French is that, unlike many area spots, it is a
"great value," with a nice, "down-to-Earth" feel. Ideal for a first
date, though this bistro doesn't have the most impressive
surroundings, prompting some decor snobs to ask "what's all the
to-do about?" Simple: "The price is right."

Caffe Med $24

1268 Second Ave. (212) 744-5370
bet. 66th & 67th Sts. on the Upper East Side
This little two-year-old Italian is in the shadow of other Italian
restaurants nearby. In fact, for such a sunny name, everything is
shadowy, from the "dark and cozy" atmosphere (some feel is
"sophisticated") to the only "fair" food."

Caffe Rafaella

134 Seventh Ave. S. (212) 929-7247
bet. Charles & W. 10th Sts. in the W. Village
This West Village Italian has some of the "best desserts in town." It does
year-round after-dinner service, "beautifully decorated" for coffee and
dessert "on a snowy night" or "for sidewalk people watching."

Caffe Rosso $26

284 W. 12th St. (212) 633-9277
at W. 4th St. in the W. Village
This little cobblestone street corner Italian is "charming and quiet,"
except maybe for the tables outside. While unadventurous, it's
mellow, especially for the West Village, and has "fresh pasta
dishes" and "excellent lasagna." No reserving.

Cajun

129 Eighth Ave. (212) 691-6174
bet. 16th & 17th Sts. in Chelsea
Oh I wish I was in Dixie, well not really, and fortunately New York
has "lively" "big portion" "spicy Cajun" places like this Chelsea
spot. All meals come with live New Orleans Dixieland music.

Caliente Cab Co.

61 Seventh Ave. S. (212) 243-8517
at Commerce St. in the W. Village
21 Waverly Pl. (212) 529-1500
at Greene St. in the Washington Sq. Area
If you haven't seen enough yellow for one day, check out the
"overpriced" food at this super trendy Mexican duo "for the bridge
and tunnel mindset or masochistic women." Large screen TVs for
mobile couch potatoes.

	FOOD	ROOM	STAFF	COST

California Pizza Kitchen

$16

Savoy Bldg., 201 E. 60th St. (212) 755-7773
bet. Second & Third Aves. on the Upper East Side

One astute observer remarks: "definitely not New York pizza." What tipped you off? The name of the restaurant? Still, this Left Coast chain manages to please with zillions of toppings, though it may not be as healthy as the name implies. "Finally, a New York restaurant with pineapple and Canadian ham pizza." Hmm.

California Tacqueria

$10

355 Ave. of the Americas (212) 229-0999
bet. W. 4th St. & Washington Pl. in the Washington Sq. Area

"Huge portions" of "cheap," "seemingly healthy" eats make this "better than Taco Bell" and "terrific for those in a hurry," but more demanding types bash "rude servers" and "really bland food." "There are definitely better burritos out there."

Cal's

$34

55 W. 21st St. (212) 929-0740
bet. Fifth & Sixth Aves. in the Flatiron District

The telltale comment, "a neighborhood favorite," is a signpost pointing diners to the simpler side of this Flatiron American's (with Continental and Mediterannean influences) menu. Though the room's "attractive," even "pretty" to some, the "tiny tables" annoy voters, unless they're outside in nice weather.

Campagna

$44

24 E. 21st St. (212) 460-0900
bet. Broadway & Park Ave. S. in the Flatiron District

Mark Strausman's Country Italian hot spot attracts a "who's who" of "record biz" types and "beautiful people," but our respondents part ways on whether this is "a great Italian restaurant experience" or simply "too hot for mere mortals." Sophisticated, "attentively prepared" food and a surprisingly "quiet" atmosphere make this "upscale Elaine's" a "nice place for business."

Campagnola

$40

1382 First Ave. (212) 861-1102
bet. 73rd & 74th Sts. in Yorkville

Like the Italian bicycles of the same name, the quality at this Yorkville restaurant is "very good," and the "service is tops." Plus, you can "sit up front and watch the world go by," The piano bar and "great antipasto" are highlights, and, again like the bikes, it's somewhat pricey.

Can

$32

482 W. Broadway (212) 533-6333
at Houston St. in SoHo

Whether you consider this SoHo French/Vietnamese "wonderfully inventive" or merely "average" is a matter of taste. Fans call the food "exceptional" and the prices "very reasonable," but phobes call it "overpriced" and "not especially memorable." "Clueless" service certainly doesn't help.

Candle Cafe · $17

1307 Third Ave. bet. 74th & 75th Sts./U.E. Side (212) 472-0970
It's a winning combo: "Good tasting, guilt-free food" and an
"extremely relaxing atmosphere" has propelled this macrobiotic Upper
Eastsider into Romac's Top 10 Vegetarians. Though some
"non-vegetarians don't like it," it's a popular neighborhood choice for
a "good meatless meal." Regulars advise that, like a lot of vegetarian
food, it can be "pretty bland," but "the sauce transforms it." While the
food ratings are somewhat inconsistent, all agree that the staff is great,
and the "veggie bacon double cheeseburger" is worth a try.

Canton · $34

45 Division St. bet. Bowery & Market/Chinatown (212) 226-4441
Satisfied voters can't say enough about the "superb," innovative fare at
this Chinatown Cantonese. For many, it's "possibly the best" in NYC
with a "homey" atmosphere and welcoming staff. The only gripe: It's
"expensive" and some would "go more often" if it "took credit cards."

Canyon Road · $27

1470 First Ave. bet. 76th & 77th Sts. in Yorkville (212) 734-1600
"All the beautiful people" head to this Yorkville "date place" for
"potent margaritas" and "surprisingly good" Southwestern fare.
Though "good" food at this tag is "overpriced," expect solid
service, authentic decor and tons of "preppy" twentysomethings.

Capsouto Freres · $46

451 Washington St. at Watts St. in TriBeCa (212) 966-4900
Some diners go for good French food "to brush against the
possibilities of a more sublime, perfect universe." So when they find it
in an "unpretentious," terribly romantic spot on "a desolate corner, it's
all the more satisfying. It's "an open secret" that this TriBeCa
favorite's "soufflés to die for," "orgasmic eggs Benedict," and "perfect
salmon" make for a "bit of France." Voters say it's "worth the search"
for a place that's "always on target." The room is "beautiful" so take a
date. Brunch earns raves and the prix fixe lunch "is a bargain."

Captain's Table · $37

860 Second Ave. at 46th St. in Midtown E. (212) 697-9538
Ahoy matey! This Midtown East seafooder serves "the best fish"
with a smile and doesn't bite off an "arm and leg." But, "if you
order whole fish, don't have it boned—eat one side and flip it over."
Participants call this place "old reliable" and advise that you reel in
some "great take-out," although you'd miss the "very pretty" decor.
Hop onto the boat for a pre-theater catch.

Caravan of Dreams · $17

405 E. 6th St. bet. Ave. A & First Ave./E. Village (212) 254-1613
"For hard-core organic, there's no equal," because some place has to
have "interesting and tasty offerings for the vegan in your life."
"Crunchy," "mellow," and "casual" ring chimes at this East Village spot.
But it's not all groovy. Moans arise that its a little pricey for "Spartan
portions" and its "a little bit on the fascist side, but otherwise a lovely
place to go for clean, healthy food in a foul, polluted universe."

FOOD ROOM STAFF COST

Caribe

$21

117 Perry St. (212) 255-9191
at Greenwich St. in the W. Village

"Bring a machete and a big appetite" to this "exotic" West Villager. The "evocative," "jungle" setting makes some Romac Reporters feel like they're on "vacation" while the "huge plates" of "flavorful," "spicy" Caribbean fare satisfy even "the big eater." Too bad the "flamboyant staff" is on a permanent holiday.

Carino

$26

1710 Second Ave. (212) 860-0566
bet. 88th & 89th Sts. in Carnegie Hill

To arms, to arms, the locals are coming, the locals are coming. The Upper East side is packed with "neighborhood feel" spots like this "reasonable" Italian. The food rates fair, the room scores fair, and it's good if you're recognized because the service is "nonexistent if they don't know you."

Carlyle

$59

Carlyle Hotel, 35 E. 75th St. (212) 744-1600
bet. Madison & Park Aves. on the Upper East Side

"Great food, wine, service and of course Bobby Short" launch this Upper East Sider into the pantheon of "great NYC hotel dining." A dressy room and ultraprofessional staff put the Carlyle in the Romac Top 50 for both categories, with a special-occasion price tag that's expensive but worth it. The circa-1930 New York setting simply oozes elegance, with little need to update across the years. Reservations are essential, but if you're like us and prefer your Cole Porter sung in falsetto, you may want to come early and hope there's a wait.

Carmine's

$25

2450 Broadway (212) 362-2200
bet. 90th & 91st Sts. on the Upper West Side
200 W. 44th St. (212) 221-3800
at Broadway in the Theater District

Huge, family-style portions are the trademark of these ballroom-sized, megapopular Southern Italians. Placing high on many Romac Tops lists, they're among the noisiest restaurants in New York and are top rated for dining with large parties, being crowded on weekends, and reportedly, have the Best Caesar Salad in Town. Faint of breath need not apply: it's a "garlic lover's dream and a vampire's nightmare. Where else do they have mouthwash dispensers in the bathrooms?"

Carnegie Deli

$20

854 Seventh Ave. at W. 55th St. in Midtown W. (212) 757-2245

It's an "overpriced tourist trap." The "decor is nonexistent." It's the "best deli in NYC." It's a "madhouse" with "unpleasant crowding." "Like dining in Socialist summer camp," "they seat you right on top of the other patrons." It's "an annoying experience" aided by the "surliest waitstaff in town." The "Flintstone-sized portions" are "so huge they take three people to finish." It's "what New York is: a rude waiter and a great pastrami sandwich." Ahh, everybody's got an opinion.

Carola

115 E. 60th St. (212) 644-1432
bet. Lexington & Park Aves. on the Upper East Side
Chef Deborah Aranoff's creations at Carola are eclectic, although
the cigar choices on the menu and the disco music hitting the ears
certainly contribute to the randomness. This is a place that must be
experienced to believe.

Casa Di Pre

 $25

283 W. 12th St. (212) 243-7073
at W. 4th St. in the W. Village
The owners have just introduced a new menu at this West Village
Northern Italian. "Romance will stay alive in this pleasant restaurant,"
and so will the household budget: You "can't beat the 5-7 p.m. dinner
special." The "homey, friendly staff" is also appreciated.

Casa La Femme

150 Wooster St. (212) 505-0005
at Prince St. in SoHo
"Go with the one you lust" to SoHo for exotic Pan
Mediterranean fare under a "unique" personal tent. It's "very
romantic" and there are lots of "beautiful people." Belly
dancing on Mondays. Film screenings on Wednesdays. Late
Menu until 3 a.m., Wed.-Sat.

Casani's

 $30

54 E. 1st St. (212) 777-1589
bet. First & Second Aves. in the E. Village
Hankerin' for French? Try this "mini Bistro" in the East
Village that "makes you feel like you're in France." So it's a
little "cramped"—okay, a lot. But, according to our reporters
it's "exactly what a bistro should be," with exceptional food
and "rude service." Soak up some rays at a sidewalk table for
weekend brunch.

Cascabel

 $42

218 Lafayette St. (212) 431-7300
bet. Spring & Broome Sts. in SoHo
Brimming with boomers, (in a "quietly subdued ambiance")
punctuated by changing artwork, Cascabel's food ("rattlesnake" in
Spanish) (American cuisine with French and Italian influences)
"has a bite to it." That is to say, it is "flavorful and creative," with
"excellent fish dishes" as standouts.

Castellano

 $45

138 W. 55th St. (212) 664-1975
bet. Sixth & Seventh Aves. in Midtown W.
What isn't an office in Midtown is probably an Italian restaurant.
Here's another high-end spot on the West Side you might want to
try for a business lunch, "unless you're under 40," in which case
"the staff ignores you."

FOOD ROOM STAFF COST

Caviarteria

$44

Delmonico Hotel, 502 Park at 59th/Midtown E. (212) 759-7410
For "caviar without the frills," Midtown lunchers hit this little
gourmet food shop with "delectable bites in too-cramped
surroundings." Just because it's small doesn't mean a "caviar
heaven" can't be "elegant." The French doors are open to the street
and the champagne, wine or sake is ready to pour. The happy hour
special can bring that tab down a bit.

Cedars of Lebanon

$27

8 W. 38th St. (212) 391-1118, 1119
bet. Fifth & Sixth Aves. in the Garment District
Recently relocated to the Garment District, this "original" Lebanese
has been a Middle Eastern staple for several decades now. The
belly-dancing and live bands go a long way in making up for the
no-frills decor. "The all-you-can-eat lunch is excellent" and like
everything else here, it's affordable.

Cellini

$46

65 E. 54th St. (212) 751-1555
bet. Park & Madison Aves. in Midtown E.
At times Northern and Southern Italians don't get on well, but they do
here in East Midtown where their palates mix in a "consistently good and
sometimes surprising" menu that's been called "delicate and delicious."
The "elegant atmosphere and staff" and "above-average food" make for
a "charming" evening that you need reservations to enjoy.

Cendrillon

$30

45 Mercer St. bet. Grand & Broome Sts. in SoHo (212) 343-9012
You may "need an interpreter for the menu," but "take a chance";
the Filipino/Asian mix "here is really delish." The chef/owner can
be "very helpful" from the "nice open kitchen" and the solid staff is
a plus. Kids are welcome.

Cent'Anni

$40

50 Carmine St. (212) 989-9494
bet. Bedford & Bleecker Sts. in the W. Village
The West Village houses a trattoria known as "one of the best
haunts in New York." And guess what? It's "not trendy or
pretentious." It's not cheap either, but the "wonderful neighborhood
Italian" fare rates in the top 200. Stop by for the "best espresso" or
try one of the many daily specials.

Centro Vasco

$29

161 W. 23rd St. (212) 741-1408
bet. Sixth & Seventh Aves. in Chelsea
It's reasonably priced, so "the average man can dine on lobster." Besides
the "generous" portions of seafood there's Spanish fare for average and
above average people alike. There's not much to look at; actually, it's
"tacky" and "so noisy on weekends you can't hear your companions."

Century Cafe $29

132 W. 43rd St. bet. Bdwy & Sixth/Midtown W. (212) 398-1988
With only "fair" ratings to its credit, this 25-year-old Midtown West
American/Continental "should have retired 99 years ago." Good for
occasional actor spottings, it's still a "favorite for pre-theater," but is best
either "as a fallback when there's no place else for a Times Square
lunch" or "after work for a couple of margaritas and a law clerk or two."

Chanterelle $69

2 Harrison St. at Hudson St. in TriBeCa (212) 966-6960
Even with the ultra high expectations four stars from the *Times*
creates, voters rate this TriBeCa French "excellent" all around.
With a spectacular wine list, "exquisite," "ethereal" ambiance and
one of the most knowledgeable staffs in town, it's "one of the few
New York establishments that approaches Paris standards." Even
so, some still call it "underrated," and the "high temple of
gastronome." Though some find such excellence "somewhat
intimidating," "if you can afford it, do it."

Charlie Mom's

47 Seventh Ave. S. (212) 255-2848
bet. Bleecker & Morton Sts. in the W. Village
Reviewers wrote in to report "better quality" and "good service" at
this West Village "neighborhood Chinese." "Consistent" basics
make it a local favorite.

Charlton's $41

922 Third Ave. bet. 55th & 56th Sts. in Midtown E. (212) 688-4646
There aren't many rewards for braving the "dark and gloomy"
atmosphere at this "overpriced" East Midtown steakhouse. A bottle of
vino from the 240-bottle wine list may make the "okay" steaks and
Contemporary American fare easier to swallow. Perhaps puffing on a
cigar at noontime helps business lunchers tolerate the churlish service.

Chat 'n Chew $17

10 E. 16th St. at Fifth Ave. at Union Sq. (212) 243-1616
"Enormous portions" of "homey American cooking"—e.g.,
"high-fat" everything, from "excellent mac 'n' cheese" to "black
and white cake like Mom makes"—are served up in a "friendly,
funky" "faux-country" room. The food ranges from "tasty" to
"awful," but the service garners a consensus: "Less chatting from
the staff" would mean "more chewing for the customers."

Chaz & Wilson Grill $26

201 W. 79th St. (212) 769-0100
at Amsterdam Ave. on the Upper West Side
This is one of those places where everyone raves about the dinner
specials: So okay, they're $9.95 on Mondays, Tuesdays, and
Thursdays. They're an "unbelievable deal"— if you're happy
chowing down on trendy American fun food (coconut shrimp,
sweet-potato fries) in a raucous atmosphere, where live music
alternates with "sports, sports, sports" on the tube and the
"partygoers" are a constant.

FOOD ROOM STAFF COST

Chelsea Bistro & Bar $36

358 W. 23rd St. bet. Eighth & Ninth Aves./Chelsea (212) 727-2026
This "paradigm of a solid, dependable bistro" dishes up "good food, good vin" in a "romantic," "mildly elegant" 23rd Street location that features a cozy fireplace in winter and a beautiful garden patio when the weather's fine. It boasts "standout French food," "convivial surroundings," and—surprise!—a "wine list as big as the Paris phone directory."

Chelsea Brewing Co. $23

Piers 59-62 (212) 336-6440
23rd St. & Hudson River in Chelsea
Forget the food, which, except for the fisherman's platter is "bad, bad, and bad." Try, too, to forget the service, because it will forget you (it's "slow" at its fastest). What's left? A memorable setting, overlooking the Hudson, that makes this a "surprisingly fun" spot to relax at the bar (or in the separate cigar room—a "great place for a Saturday afternoon."

Chelsea Commons $21

242 Tenth Ave. (212) 929-9424
at 24th St. in Chelsea
"A nice neighborhood bar," it's the (beer in the) outdoor garden, (beer during the) live music events and possibly the (beer in front of the) fireplace in winter that keeps this historic spot afloat. It certainly can't be the "lousy service" or "poor food."

Chelsea Grill $22

135 Eighth Ave. (212) 242-5336
bet. 16th & 17th Sts. in Chelsea
Kick back in front of the fireplace at this carnivores' paradise in—surprise—Chelsea. It's touted as a "great place to hang out" with the "best burgers" and "waffle fries, too." Baby-boomers are less thrilled: "nothing to write home about." But if you're really hungry this may be some of the "best food for the money."

Chelsea Trattoria $33

108 Eighth Ave. (212) 924-7786
at 15th St. in Chelsea
A "warm, friendly and accommodating staff" (though occasionally "clueless") is the highlight of this "great, moderately priced Manhattan Trattoria." "Perfect before seeing a dance concert at the Joyce," the pasta fish specials are good, and a "good value."

Chez Brigitte $16

77 Greenwich Ave. (212) 929-6736
at W. 11th St. & Seventh Ave. S. in the W. Village
Zees tiny French kitchen holds only 11 people around its counter, qualifying it as a "charmer" or a "hole in the wall," depending on your fear-of-intimacy quotient. A fine spot for solo diners, omelette lovers, and anyone who craves "mother's cooking." "Consistency and constancy are its greatest virtues," and the food and mood couldn't be less pretentious. No credit cards.

Chez Jacqueline

72 MacDougal (Bleecker & W. Houston/W. Vill.) (212) 505-0727
"Catering to regulars," this "charming" West Village write-in boasts "lovely" Provençal cuisine and "very French" ambiance. Service can be "snooty" if you're not a local.

Chez Josephine

 $38

414 W. 42nd St. bet. Ninth & Tenth Aves./Clinton (212) 594-1925
Owner Jean-Claude "will treat you like family at his swank shrine to his mother," Josephine Baker. A top ranking favorite, here you can expect "good continental food," "elegant, beautiful piano music," a "courteous staff," and a "very romantic setting." The "incredibly fun atmosphere makes Chez Josephine the perfect place to take out-of- towners" (if they are sophisticated). "Josephine would have been proud."

Chez Laurence

 $20

245 Madison Ave. at 38th St. in Murray Hill (212) 683-0284
Though "noisy and crowded," especially at lunch (when it's also "hard to get reservations"), this straightforward Frenchie is a "pleasant" "taste of Paris in New York."

Chez Ma Tante

 $34

189 W. 10th St. bet. Bleecker & W. 4th Sts./W. Vill. (212) 620-0223
This French bistro specializes in West Village ambiance: Cozy in winter, open sidewalk in the summer, with a staff that, shall we say, does not suffer from lack of personality. The food is above average, but the "crowding" isn't for everyone. "Okay for a quickie."

Chez Michallet

 $46

90 Bedford St. bet. Barrow & Grove/W. Village (212) 242-8309
A "charming" French bistro featuring "pleasant," typical bistro fare in "nice" "little" "cozy"—some would say "cramped"— West Village quarters.

Chez Napoleon

 $32

365 W. 50th St. bet. Eighth & Ninth Aves./Clinton (212) 265-6980
Encore, encore. This Clinton, family-run bistro is described as the "best French value in the Theater District." Reasonable prix fixe and pre-theater menus, which slice a healthy third off the regular price, help make it such. "The owner makes you feel right at home" with "warm service." So brush up on your French and saché on in.

Chiam

 $38

160 E. 48th St. (212) 371-2323
bet. Third & Lexington Aves. in Midtown E.
Hong Kong Cantonese with cordon bleu ratings make this one of the city's "favorite upscale Chinese." "Sophisticated and chic," it is "starkly elegant" with "good presentation" and an "amazing wine list." "Recommend Peking duck"; okay, we shall.

FOOD ROOM STAFF COST

Chikubu

$40

12 E. 44th St. bet. Fifth & Madison/Midtown E. (212) 818-0715
The food at this Midtown Japanese is good enough that long lines form at lunch. Then again it's "not worth the higher price tag unless you're trying to impress a client," so be sure and dump the tab on the expense account credit card. The prix fixe lunch seems the best way to go.

China Fun

$16

246 Columbus Ave. bet. 71st & 72nd/U.W. Side (212) 580-1516
1239 Second Ave. at 65th St. in Midtown E. (212) 752-0810
While the food may be only "fair" at these Midtown/Upper West Side Chinese joints, they sure are popular enough. A big crowd tells us that, sometimes, "greasy" can be good (i.e. the favorite dumplings and spareribs). Be advised: "East is friendlier than West."

China Grill

$39

52 W. 53rd St. bet. Fifth & Sixth/Midtown W. (212) 333-7788
There has to be something special about an International restaurant that is one of the five noisiest places in town, and qualifies as a "pick-up joint." While the black rock "decor is gorgeous," the "excellent," "enchanting" food is the real draw here. It is so noisy, in fact, you may want to "bring some out-of-towners" you're not interested in talking with.

Chin Chin

$37

216 E. 49th St. (212) 888-4555
bet. Second & Third Aves. in Midtown E.
Comments are a bit mixed for this tres "upscale Chinese" near the U.N. It gets its name from owner James Chin and chef Chin Hin Kuen, not from the double chin you might acquire from the "top-notch" "gourmet Chinese" that some find to be "too rich." We suspect that naysayers suffer from high-expectations syndrome: "The most gracious of hosts" serve up the "best gourmet Chinese in the city," in an elegant if austere setting. Voters' advice: forget the cost, don't sit in the back room and "let the chef choose your meal" (especially if it includes the "fantastic" Grand Marnier shrimp).

Choshi

77 Irving Pl. (212) 420-1419
at E. 19th St. in Gramercy
You just can't argue with "darn good" "fresh, fresh sushi" in a "small, quiet, friendly atmosphere reminiscent of the Far East." (It's in the Gramercy in case you're booking a flight.) If it's too quiet, grab a table on the sidewalk.

Christer's

$45

145 W. 55th St. (212) 974-7224
bet. Sixth & Seventh Aves. in Midtown W.
Scandinavia comes to Midtown West in the form of Christer's, a "cozy," "minimal" restaurant. To our voters' delight, this spot specializes in salmon: "a salmon lover's dream," they rave, also appreciating the business lunch and pre-theater specials. The "supportive," "attentive staff is to be commended."

Christine's  $14

208 First Ave. (212) 254-2474
bet. 12th & 13th Sts. in the E. Village
"Hearty, no frills" Polish food (is there such a thing as frilly Polish food?)—pierogi, apple latkes, "pickle soup!"—served up by "waitresses who think their own way." Basically, "European home cooking and European attitude." No credit cards.

Christo's Steakhouse  $47

Doral Inn, 541 Lexington Ave. (212) 355-2695
bet. 49th & 50th Sts. in Midtown E.
What is "old-world charm" to some is "another dark restaurant" to others. This Steakhouse, with Italian specialties, has been creaking along from 11 a.m. to 2 a.m. every day in the Doral for nearly sixty years, and our voters feel it is in need of some updating. Still, there is a place in this world for a restaurant that always has (and always will) allow pipe and cigar smoking.

Chumley's

86 Bedford St. (212) 675-4449
at Barrow St. in the W. Village
"Only those who know go" to this "drinkers' hideaway" in a "cool" West Village location. Head over for a dose of vintage NYC in a "casual" atmosphere complete with a fireplace, decent American basics and plenty of beer on tap.

Ciao Europa  $29

63 W. 54th St. (212) 247-1200
bet. Fifth & Sixth Aves. in Midtown W.
The "wonderful waiters" will see to your every need at this Midtown Italian located one block from Radio City. In other words, no matter what you think of the food or Elizabethan-style decor, at least you'll be treated like family. Nothing fancy here, the regional cuisine is simple and fresh, which the pure of taste find just "joyful," thank you very much.

Cibo  $38

767 Second Ave. (212) 681-1616
bet. 41st & 42nd Sts. in Murray Hill
Around the corner from the Daily News, this Murray Hill seasonal American (with Tuscan influences) is "welcome in a neighborhood that has little else as good." A "friendly owner" and staff make it ideal for business lunch, though "service varies widely," as do voters' opinions of the food.

Ciccio & Tony's  $27

320 Amsterdam Ave. at 75th St. on the U.W. Side (212) 595-0500
Two major caveats: (1) "If you don't know Italian food, you'll like it; if you know anything, don't go." (2) "If you're middle-aged, you won't fit in." In other words, this "okay" Tuscan is a good spot for young families and roving bands of youths who crave "garlic in leaps and bounds."

	FOOD	ROOM	STAFF	COST

Cinquanta $41

50 E. 50th St. bet. Park & Madison/Midtown E. (212) 759-5050
Who knew this East Sider serves up creative Italian cuisine—with
the menu printed in Japanese and Portuguese of all things—in an
attractive four-story brownstone on 50th Street? Not our reporters,
certainly, who didn't exactly vote for this one in droves.

Cinque Terre $36

22 E. 38th St. (212) 213-0910
bet. Park & Madison Aves. in Murray Hill
Boasting specials from the Italian Riveria (read: Mediterannean) this
mid-size Murray Hill spot is coming up on its first birthday, and is
surely (if slowly) finding an audience of appreciative voters. "Inspired
food in a charming setting," they write, "a real find." Pastas and
pastries are truly "home-cooked," plus BYOB keeps the tab low.

Circa $31

103 Second Ave. (212) 777-4120
at 6th St. in the E. Village
A band called Live Vinyl plays here on weekends; get the picture?
Yes, it's the East Village, where what's "hip" to the under-30s is
"pretentious" to their future selves. The room, however, is
inarguably "lovely," with coppertop tables and mosaic floors, and it
way outshines the "American bistro" food, which is "nice" at best.
No one seems to care, anyway; they'd rather "sink into the
armchairs and philosophize"— food for the soul, man.

Circus $38

808 Lexington Ave. (212) 223-2566
bet. 62nd & 63rd Sts. on the Upper East Side
For businessmen who simply must lunch out every day, and who
are sick of the same-old same-old, this East Side Brazilian is a
"perfect" alternative. Being Brazilian, it's a "fun place," with a
"wonderful owner and staff."

Cité $49

120 W. 51st St. (212) 956-7100
bet. Sixth & Seventh Aves. in Midtown W.
The $49.50 prix fixe dinner with unlimited wine may be the "best buy
in the city," and a location "convenient to Radio City and the theaters"
(there's validated parking for the "Bridge and Tunnel set") guarantees
crowds at this "big," "noisy" French-accented steakhouse." Owned by
the same folks that gave us Park Avenue Cafe, Smith and Wollensky,
and Post House, it's been "much improved" in recent years. Best
advice: "Save room for the best wines, which come last."

Cité Grill $38

120 W. 51st St. (212) 956-7262
bet. Sixth & Seventh Aves. in Midtown W.
A theater-friendly French/American steakhouse that also caters to the
nonbloodthirsty, with everything from "great burgers" to pasta. Just your
basic "bridge and tunnel"-intensive "nice little place" with "fine service."

City Crab

 $31

235 Park Ave. S. (212) 529-3800
at 19th St. in Gramercy

A high volume of mostly younger voters has pushed and elbowed their way through this "noisy" Gramercy seafooder, and have come away with wildly different impressions: Some think the food is "wonderful" if "straightforward," especially the Top 5 raw bar, while others call it "very disappointing seafood" in "small portions."

Ci Vediamo

 $23

200 E. 81st St. (212) 650-0850
at Third Ave. on the Upper East Side
85 Ave. A (212) 995-5300
bet. 5th & 6th Sts. in the E. Village
1431 Third Ave., at 81st St. in Queens (212) 650-0850

The food at these top 200 favorite spots "have gone up and down over the years" but right now is" "cheap and delicious." Make sure that you "don't miss the garlic bread with pasta dipping sauce appetizer" at these Italian (one Downtown, one Up, one Queens) siblings. Attensione! The busy, attentive staff is on the move: "you take a sip of water and they refill it".

Claire

156 Seventh Ave. (212) 255-1955
bet. 19th & 20th Sts. in Chelsea

"Inexpensive seafood" or the just plain "tasty," "dependable" Key West/Caribbean menu "make it worth the trip" to Chelsea. "Gay friendly, excellent fish"—"reliable, after all these years."

Cloister Cafe

238 E. 9th St. (212) 777-9128
bet. Second & Third Aves. in the E. Village

"The food is decent, the yard is heaven" at this East Village Eclectic cafe that's a "great escape from NYC." Popular for "cappuccino and desserts," it wins converts with its "romantic" ambiance and bargain prices. No credit cards.

Club Macanudo

26 E. 63rd St. (212) 752-8200
bet. Park & Madison on the Upper East Side

This new Upper East Side American hangs its hat on—you guessed it—the cigar craze. A "bar with food" that offers everything from snacks to steak.

Coconut Grill

 $23

1481 Second Ave. (212) 772-6262
at 77th St. on the Upper East Side

The Mediterranean-tinged fun food at this brunch and late-night favorite plays understudy to the star attraction: the are-you cool-enough-to-sit-here? sidewalk tables. Here, in a prime "social posturing arena," the "twentysomething" crowd is tasteful, but the food only intermittently tasty—more often "mediocre."

FOOD ROOM STAFF COST

Coco Pazzo

$50

23 E. 74th St. (212) 794-0205
bet. Fifth & Madison Aves. on the Upper East Side
"The elegant room" just off the park attracts "beautiful people" to
this Upper East Side Tuscan, which earns solid marks for the decor
and staff. The food, while "good" overall, receives uneven
responses, from "wonderful" to "pretentious." Perhaps owner Pino
Luongo has "too many restaurants and not enough chefs." So what?
Put your glasses on and look up from the table: Whatever's on the
plate, there's always "good, high-powered people-watching."

Coco Pazzo Teatro

235 W. 46th St. (212) 827-4222
bet. 8th Ave. & Broadway in the Theater District
Pino Luongo's new offering is a comfortable Theater District
Italian, sib to the uptown Coco Pazzo. This one boasts old-style
tableside preparations by your waiter, and lower prices.

Coffee Shop

$23

29 Union Sq. W. (212) 243-7969
at 16th St. at Union Sq.
This Union Square "ultratrendy chichi joint" with "okay" food
"shows how important location can be." Making the top 20 hit list
in several categories proves that despite the "Calvin Klein model
rejects" "who don't know how to serve" and "should be in LA,"
this hot spot is doing a lot of things right. If seeing "the beautiful
people" is your bag, this is your place.

Coldwater's

988 Second Ave. (212) 888-2122
bet. 51st & 52nd Sts. in Midtown E.
"Fresh," "delicious" seafood and "low prices" make this East
Midtowner a "cozy" write-in favorite. Voters warm up to the
late-night menu and "great bartenders."

Col Legno

$27

231 E. 9th St. (212) 777-4650
bet. Second & Third Aves. in the E. Village
Aromatic wood cooking and a fireplace may sound both tasty and
cozy, but our Romac Reporters give the Italian fare mixed reviews
and call the atmosphere "as charming as Starbuck's." Of course, if
Starbuck's is your favorite place, pull up a chair and enjoy
"expensive mediocre food" and "grumpy waiters."

Colors

$33

Park Atrium, 237 Park Ave. (212) 661-2000
bet. 45th & 46th Sts. in Midtown E.
A jacket-and-tie Italian/Continental that's fine, if unexceptional,
across the board, with a soothing atrium garden setting.

▤ = SUPERIOR ▤ = EXCELLENT ▤ = V. GOOD ▬ = GOOD

Columbus Bakery

$14

474 Columbus Ave. (212) 724-6880
bet. 82nd & 83rd Sts. on the Upper West Side
"Fine bakery goods"—especially the bread—along with salads and other light, organically correct foods, served up along with a "cute atmosphere" and live music on weekends. Unfortunately, it's all served up by a "disorganized staff" that sometimes "bites and barks."

Coming or Going

38 E. 58th St. (212) 980-5858
bet. Park & Madison Ave. in Midtown E.
So it has a "stupid name." It still has "great food and service" according to voters, who say this little,"charming" Italian/American (south of the park) has "very good lunches" (though a bit hectic), and may be a tad "overpriced for dinner," no matter how quiet and romantic things get.

Commonwealth Brewing Co.

10 Rockefeller Plaza, 35 W. 48th St. (212) 977-2269
bet. Fifth & Sixth Aves. in Midtown W.
This new brewpub offers an array of home brewed beer, appetizers and the company and comments that only an upscale Rock Center beer hall can draw: "brews better than the food."

Community Bar & Grill

216 Seventh Ave. (212) 242-7900
bet. 22nd & 23rd Sts. in Chelsea
The nice, spacious downtown atmosphere, complemented by a great garden had lots of voters writing in about this friendly and casual American in Chelsea. The live DJ is "excellent," and the food "well-prepared," making for a comfortable experience for the whole family, especially for brunch.

Contrapunto

$29

200 E. 60th St. (212) 751-8616
at Third Ave. in Midtown E.
The owners call their fare "inspired Italian," whatever that means. Voters describe it as "good pasta" served in "new ways" at "unbelievably low prices"—a "great pre-movie" nosh. Still, some grumble that the place has "seen better days" (with a much bigger menu and gourmet aspirations). Ignore the so-so room and service and "watch the world below at Bloomies" while enjoying some "don't miss" homemade gelati.

Cornelia St. Cafe

29 Cornelia St. bet. Bleecker & W. 4th/Wash Sq. (212) 989-9319
This little Eclectic/American Cafe has been set in the short, but bustling Cornelia Street row for more than twenty years, and voters couldn't resist writing in. This is a real village holdout, "charming with great food," that's "always trustworthy, a solid bet" for seasonal dishes and sidewalk people-watching, weather permitting.

	FOOD	ROOM	STAFF	COST

Corner Bistro $15

331 W. 4th St. at Jane St. in the W. Village (212) 242-9502
Where can you get killer "oversized delicious" burgers or the "best chili" at 4 a.m.? Right here at this West Village "dive." "Who cares about the rest." "The Bistro Burger is as deliciously decadent as anything you can imagine." And, this place also stars "a great jukebox" joint (No. 1 rating) and "the world's nicest bartenders," which is fortunate since "this happens to be one of the most lively and hard-drinking bars in town."

Country Cafe $33

69 Thompson St. bet. Spring & Broome/SoHo (212) 966-5417
"Cozy" and "casual," this "cute" SoHo cafe charms surveyors with its authentic, "relaxed" atmosphere that's "like Paris." "Super good" French fare and "fantastic" service make it a "great find." No credit cards.

Cowgirl Hall Of Fame $21

519 Hudson St. at W. 10th St. in the W. Village (212) 633-1133
You get "decent Tex-Mex," ("don't eat the food until AFTER the drinks"), a "friendly bar and a kitschy atmosphere that doesn't get stale" at this Greenwich Village homage to them big-boned gals. Affiliated with the National Cowgirl Hall of fame, the memoriabilia is real, as are the "killer" "mason jar margaritas" and chicken-fried steak. Child-friendly, especially the corndog-eatin' kind.

Crab House $29

Chelsea Piers, Pier 61 @ 23rd St. (212) 835-2722
23rd St. & Hudson River in Chelsea
Seafood that's merely "average" does nothing to keep this "giant room" (part of a chain of equally big restaurants with locations all over the country) from becoming "jammed" and "noisy." It's got to be the spectacular setting, practically dangling off the end of the Chelsea Piers, with a feast-for-the-eyes view over the Hudson River. There's a big menu and a huge, all-you-can eat salad and raw bar, but it's strictly BYOB (bring your own boat) to the docks.

C3 $26

103 Waverly Pl. (212) 254-1200
at MacDougal St. in the Washington Sq. Area
"Highly underrated," and devotees want to keep it that way. This eclectic (American with Mediterranean/Italian accents) "oasis" near Washington Square offers "stress-free dining" thanks to a "hip and polite staff" and a "cozy setting." Augmented by a "terrific wine list," this "home-cooking treat" inspires the sentiment "I hope more people don't discover this sleeper."

Cub Room $41

131 Sullivan St. at Prince St. in SoHo (212) 677-4100
With a bar scene that's still "hot," this "trendy" SoHo storefront is "cool for drinks" and "packed after eight." Expect to find a "Euro" crowd "in comfortable surroundings" enjoying sometimes- "wonderful," always-pricey American cuisine. Service delivers, but it's the "beautifully designed space" and "beautiful people" that keep it packed.

Cub Room Cafe
$25

185 Prince St. at Sullivan St. in SoHo (212) 777-0030
Cub Room's more casual sibling, this SoHo American cafe attracts
a similar crowd who appreciate the "beautiful rooms" and "tasty
food." "Brain-dead service" makes it a challenge for some voters,
but lower prices keep it popular as a "girls' lunch out spot."

Cucina
$33

256 Fifth Ave., Brooklyn (718) 230-0711
bet. Carroll & Garfield Sts.
"Cucina's as good as any Italian restaurant in Manhattan, at half the
price." The "elegant and delicious" Northern Italian fare, especially
the "excellent pasta" and "wonderful osso buco" combine with a
"stylish" room and "hospitable" service" to make fans say, "Thank
God it's out of the way."

Cucina & Co.
$22

MetLife Bldg., 200 Park Ave. (212) 682-2700
at 45th St. in Midtown E.
Tucked away in the MetLife building, Restaurant Associates'
attractive, "convenient" Mediterranean-style cafe makes for a "great
lunch spot," albeit a little "crowded." But while it's best known for
"midtown biz food," Cucina & Co. is also a "best dinner deal,"
thanks to its "reasonably priced" $19.95 prix fixe dinner for two.

Cucina della Fontana

368 Bleecker St. (212) 242-0636
at Charles St. in the W. Village
The downstairs area is the attraction at this West Village Northern
Italian restaurant, self-proclaimed as "good for weddings" and our
voters agree: "Romantic atmosphere" includes a "delightful garden"
that voters peg as a "secret special spot." The "cheap price" makes
it all the more attractive.

Cucina Di Pesce
$20

87 E. 4th St. (212) 260-6800
bet. Second & Third Aves. in the E. Village
A "second home"—or even a "first home"—for the throngs who
call this "the best low-budget Italian" and seafood joint around.
Yes, the "tiny, cramped tables" and the "waiting and noise" are "a
pain," but complimentary while-you-wait mussels and the "always
fresh fish" and "huge portions" more than compensate. There's a
lovely garden out back, too. It's all swim, no sink: "good food, well
prepared" in a "fun atmosphere."

Cucina Stagionale
$20

275 Bleecker St. (212) 924-2707
bet. Sixth Ave. & Seventh Ave. S. in the W. Village
No matter how close they jam the tables together at this West
Village Italian BYOB, there's still usually a wait, ususally
outside, even in bad weather. But it's definitely "worth the wait
anytime," for "excellent value" and "good service" in an "old
New York" setting.

FOOD ROOM STAFF COST

Cuisine de Saigon

$24

154 W. 13th St. (212) 255-6003
at Seventh Ave. S. in the W. Village

This dinner-only West Villager is "not a great space, but wonderful spice." Some think the food is "good, but is surpassed by Chinatown Vietnamese," but, do other spots have "genuinely nice people" serving dinner?

Cupcake Cafe

$12

522 Ninth Ave. (212) 465-1530
at 39th St. in the Convention Center Area

"You can't look in the window and walk by," nor should you even try. "Arguably" (though there's no dispute among our voters) "the best cupcakes, cakes and muffins in NYC" await in this "dive with class" (a "health department's dream"). A Hallmark copywriter couldn't say it better: "Their cakes make any occasion special and a special occasion unforgetttable."

Cupping Room Cafe

$23

359 W. Broadway (212) 925-2898
bet. Broome & Grand Sts. in SoHo

We don't know how much cupping they do here, but here's what the "cheery" room is like: A skylight brightens up the wood floors, exposed brick walls and antique bar while a potbellied stove heats up the patrons (though, with weekend crowding, the extra warmth is hardly needed). The "fantastic weekend brunch" is one of the five best in the city, and the American/Continental fare comes "fresh and delicious."

Curry in a Hurry

119 Lexington Ave. (212) 683-0900
at 28th St. in Murray Hill

This Murray Hill write-in delivers exactly what it promises: "fast-food" Indian eats that are "great if you're in a hurry." It's "consistently mediocre" but the "friendly" staff knows how to hustle and it's "cheap" and "clean."

Cyber Cafe

$14

273A Lafayette (212) 334-5140
at Prince St. in SoHo

For Webaholics only. This "different and cool" hangout offers sandwiches and pastries, aka "stuff in plastic," fit for cyber geeks whose fanaticism "transcends any desire for real food."

Da Ciro

$32

229 Lexington Ave. (212) 532-1636
bet. 33rd & 34th Sts. in Murray Hill

Just over a year old, this little Italian tucked away on the dark blocks of Lexington Avenue in Murray Hill is still relatively undiscovered, and that's the way the locals like it. Pizza from the wood-burning brick oven is "excellent," and the other "great food" (and low patron volume) make it a "wonderful neighborhood place."

≣ = SUPERIOR ≣ = EXCELLENT ≣ = V. GOOD ═ = GOOD

Dakota

$30

1576 Third Ave. (212) 427-8889
bet. 88th & 89th Sts. on the Upper East Side

The fact that the bar, not the kitchen, is the focus here doesn't bother our voters who call Dakota a "somewhat elegant," "fun place." Most call it "overpriced for what it is," saying it's packed with a "yuppie crowd that doesn't realize the '80s ended six years ago."

Dallas BBQ

27 W. 72nd St. bet. Columbus & CPW/U.W. Side (212) 873-2004
21 University Pl. at 8th St. in the Wash. Sq. Area (212) 674-4450
132 Second Ave. at St. Mark's Pl. in the E. Village (212) 777-5574
1265 Third Ave. bet. 72nd & 73rd Sts./U.E. Side (212) 772-9393

"Cheap and decent food" tells much of the story at these Barbecue spots that specialize in rotisserie chicken. "Lots of food," is more like it, with gigantic margaritas of many colors and side dishes that are bigger than Buddy Ebsen's head. The sodas are big, too, so why not go and get stuffed?

Dalton Coffee

$8

(many locations)

Folks find the coffee "average" and the light fare not good at this chain of convenient, if somewhat "sterile" coffee stands.

Danal

$26

90 E. 10th St. (212) 982-6930
bet. Third & Fourth Aves. in the E. Village

With "charming ambiance," ("like visiting friends in the country") this East Village French serves "delicious" "beautifully presented food" in a "romantic setting." A "great first date place?" You'd better be sure: "It achieves just the right mood"—"we got engaged in the garden." Looks like the food's not the only thing that will "leave you humming."

Da Nico

$24

164 Mulberry St. (212) 343-1212
bet. Grand & Broome Sts. in Little Italy

A relative newcomer to the dwindling Little Italy area, Da Nico has distinguished itself as a "fine Little Italy spot." The "very good" food (especially the pizza and gnocci, with "good Italian veggies") is "great and cheap for lunch," and though the atmosphere is a bit "too bright" and somewhat "tacky" in places, it's darker and cozier in back.

Daniel

$68

Surrey Suite Hotel, 20 E. 76th St. (212) 288-0033
bet. Fifth & Madison Aves. on the Upper East Side

It's "phenomenal." This "top-notch" French on the Upper East Side makes good on all it promises. Expect "superlative dining" (food ranked third overall in our survey) with "breathtaking presentations" and "unintimidating," knowledgeable service. A favorite of the "upper crust," it's got prices to match and tables that can be "a bit tight." Still, voters have only adulation for the "warm," "relaxing" atmosphere and the "genius" of chef/owner Daniel Boulud.

FOOD   ROOM   STAFF   COST

Darbar

$37

44 W. 56th St. bet. Fifth & Sixth/Midtown W. (212) 432-7227
One of the "best" in the city, this Midtowner delights diners with "a real taste" of traditional Indian favorites. Solid scores for service and an upscale atmosphere make it a favorite for business lunches and the pre-theater crowd. It's relatively pricey at dinner, so join the suits and try the prix fixe lunch and remember: This isn't Sixth Street.

Da Silvano

$43

260 Ave. of the Americas (212) 982-2343
bet. Houston & Bleecker Sts. in the W. Village
Snag a sidewalk table and "watch the crowds" at this West Villager that's known for A-list "star-spotting." A "professional and personable" staff (they "treat you like a prodigal child") serves up "straightforward" Tuscan fare. The only real complaint: "too expensive."

Da Tommaso

$34

903 Eighth Ave. (212) 265-1890
bet. 53rd & 54th Sts. in Midtown W.
Folks call this Midtown West Northern Italian "a well-kept secret: quirky, dated interior but utterly charming service and surprisingly good food." Family-owned and-operated, the "dark room" can be good for all kinds of things, though voters say to "take your clients."

Da Umberto

$46

107 W. 17th St. (212) 989-0303
bet. Sixth & Seventh Aves. in Chelsea
Judged a "spectacular restaurant from A to Z" by our reporters, this top-flight Chelsea Tuscan is "amongst the upper crust," with "old-fashioned waiters" serving "new Italian food" that is "second to none"—including the "best sweetbreads," "house antipasto," "sinfully good veal chop," and "incredible tiramisu." Don't worry: Da Umberto's "looks from the outside are deceiving"; this is where you go "when you really want to treat yourself."

Da Vittorio

$41

43 E. 20th St. (212) 979-6532
bet. Broadway & Park Ave. S. in the Flatiron District
Owned by Da Umberto's son, this Tuscan Italian yearling boasts a homey atmosphere but has some of the problems you get with a newly-opened restaurant: strange behavior from the staff, and an Amex-only policy. Whatever. The food is "very good," and this place is "very noisy," so someone must be enjoying it.

Dawat

$37

210 E. 58th St. (212) 355-7555
bet. Second & Third Aves. in Midtown E.
"Queen of Indian cooking" Madhur Jaffrey oversees the menu and the chefs at this "gourmet Indian," which offers "wonderful, elegant," and "immaculately prepared" food, "always accommodating" service, and tarot readers to boot. All this comes at "four times the price of East 6th Street," but for what many consider "the best Indian restaurant in town," a few extra rupees are a small sacrifice.

Decibel Sake Bar $22

240 E. 9th St. bet. Second & Third/E. Village (212) 979-2733
A "well-kept secret" (the joint doesn't even open until 8 p.m.) is
this very cool, very hip East Village saketeria, with its "unique sake
bar atmosphere," "amazing variety of sakes" to sip, and some
"challenging" selections on the small but "exotic menu." In short, a
"great place for friends to gather"—if your friends want an
"alternative to any regular bar."

DeGrezia $39

231 E. 50th St. (212) 750-5353
bet. Second & Third Aves. in Midtown E.
The focus of this "expense-account Italian" is on business dining,
particularly at lunch. The food's good, the atmosphere "great," but
entrees can be hit-or-miss, and pleasure seekers say it's "only for suits."

Delphini

519 Columbus Ave. (212) 579-1145
at 85th St. on the Upper West Side
This new Upper West Sider features big tastes from all over the
Mediterranean; the neighborhood needs this one. Amex only.

Demarchelier $38

50 E. 86th St. (212) 249-6300
bet. Madison & Park Aves. on the Upper East Side
Regulars rely on this Upper Eastsider for French brasserie standards
in a simple, old-style setting. It's a convenient stop after you've
walked the museum mile, but no-locals detect "too much attitude."

Deniz $38

400 E. 57th St. (212) 486-2255
at First Ave. in Midtown E.
Keeping "one step ahead," this Midtowner impresses diners with
unique seafood specialties and high-quality cuisine that "should put
Turkey on the culinary map." The reliable staff and loft-like setting,
complete with wall-side waterfall, make for a refreshing experience.
Try it for live Turkish music on the weekends.

Diane's

249 Columbus Ave. (212) 799-6750
bet. 71st & 72nd Sts. on the Upper West Side
Expect "excellent burgers" but "don't look for anything else" at this
Upper West Side write-in. A "dark" "haven," it's ideal for a quick,
"cheap" cholesterol fix. No plastic.

Dish Of Salt $36

133 W. 47th St. (212) 921-4242
bet. Sixth & Seventh Aves. in Midtown W.
Three words: ambiance, ambiance, ambiance. This "gorgeous space"
houses good "upscale Chinese" food in Midtown West/Theater
District. "Their Peking duck is to die for," though "overpriced." The
"American waiters" do their job and achieve "nice service."

___ = FAIR   [blank] = POOR   ≣ = NOT RATED

	FOOD	ROOM	STAFF	COST

Diva

$33

341 W. Broadway bet. Broome & Grand/SoHo (212) 941-9024
The owner's assertion that this "happening" hot spot is the place to see
and be seen may be one reason detractors call it "badly executed" and
"extremely predictable" for that hyper-trendy stretch of West
Broadway in SoHo. The Northern Italian menu makes no impression,
but the "guaranteed good time" does. If you must go, "bring earplugs."

Divino

$30

1556 Second Ave. bet. 80th & 81st Sts./U.E. Side (212) 861-1096
The Upper East Side has a rep for being too far away from
everything, but if you like trips to museums and solid meals at
reasonable prices, spots like this Italian work well for a casual date.
It offers "good food" and "better service" "in a relaxed atmosphere"
and the prix fixe is affordable even for the bohos who stray to this
part of town where supposedly nothing happens.

Diwan Grill

$32

148 E. 48th St. bet. Third & Lex./Midtown E. (212) 593-5425
A "good but busy lunch buffet" is the major draw to this "typical"
Midtown East Indian. "Fortune tellers every evening" and a cocktail
lounge attract only a small dinner crowd.

Dix Et Sept

$37

181 W. 10th St. at Seventh Ave. S./W. Village (212) 645-8023
"Why go to Paris?" ask some voters. For "reasonable steak frites"
and a "comfortable" "bistro atmosphere" this West Villager is
"reliable,""very French," and cheaper than Air France. For those
who wish to linger, or meet for drinks, the "charming bar" is a
"good" place to "hang out."

Docks

$36

633 Third Ave. at 40th St. in Murray Hill (212) 986-8080
2427 Broadway bet. 89th & 90th Sts./U.W. Side (212) 724-5588
"First-class fish at reasonable prices" only begins to tell the story at
these crowded (particularly at business lunch, though some say
they're "too noisy for business") seafooders. They also have a
"noisy and great weekend brunch" and the No. 2 rated raw bar in
the city. However, as with any spot this crowded, many voters hate
the mob scene, and the rushed feeling: "not the kind of place to go
if you want to linger and chat over coffee."

Dojo

$13

14 W. 4th St. (212) 505-8934
bet. Broadway & Mercer St. in the Washington Sq. Area
26 St. Mark's Pl. (212) 674-9821
bet. Second & Third Aves. in the E. Village
These "low-budget gems" have one of the favorite vegetarian plates
in town ("cheap and mediocre") and are top-rated for the unlikely
combination of closest tables and dining alone. The food is mainly
Asian/Eclectic, and the staff is the benchmark of surly. Though both
are dives, the original is better than Dojo West, a NYU fave the hip
say they "outgrew in high school."

Dok Suni

 $22

119 First Ave. bet. 7th & St. Mark's/E. Village (212) 477-9506
Expect the typical "funky" Gen-X crowd at this hip East Village
Korean. Some find it "too small" and somewhat "dark" but the
BBQ is "spicy," "hot" and "cheap" so it's "great for winter eating."
Too bad service is so "dismal." Cash only.

Dolce

 $30

60 E. 49th St. bet. Madison & Park/Midtown E. (212) 692-9292
A convenient Midtown location and "free happy-hour buffet" are
the big draw at this "iffy Italian." The after-work crowd reports that
"bland, boring pastas" and not-so-gentle service await should you
venture far from the bar.

Dolcetto

 $27

1378 Third Ave. bet. 78th & 79th Sts./U.E. Side (212) 472-8300
"Great value" on the prix fixe lunch and a $16 pre-theater menu
make this "always busy" but otherwise rank-and-file Italian popular
as an "early-dinner special."

Dominick's

 $29

2335 Arthur Ave. bet. 186th & 187th Sts./Bronx (718) 733-2807
Yeah, it's in the Bronx, and yeah, you have to share your table
with...whomever. But, "if you can stand the wait," it's one of the
best homestyle Italians in the five boroughs, and there is "no more
authentic." Go for the experience: Who knows, maybe your
tablemate will make you an offer you can't refuse.

Don Giovanni

 $21

214 Tenth Ave. bet. 22nd & 23rd Sts. in Chelsea (212) 242-9054
Would you like some pizza with your garlic? If you're a garlic
lover, here is a restaurant that's "not afraid" of it. Although you
might be afraid of the "slow" and "stuffy" service. If you're in the
mood for "great brick-oven pizza," this is a good stop for a
reasonable pre-theater meal. The rest receives only fair reviews.

Dosanko

 $13

423 Madison Ave. bet. 48th & 49th/Midtown E. (212) 688-8575
217 E. 59th St. bet. Second & Third/Midtown E. (212) 752-3936
These low-end Japanese restaurants have made an industry out of
cheap lunch specials and other noodle dishes classified by voters as
"Japanese fast food." "Good," "cheap," and "better than
McDonald's," "not bad for a Rock Center tourist trap."

Downtown

 $38

376 W. Broadway at Broome St. in SoHo (212) 343-0999
Giuseppe Cipriani (yep, same family) has recently opened this
SoHo offshoot to a very positive response, at least for the
yes-smoking policy, the "great bellinis," (a peach/champagne
drink), and lovely decor, including a terrace with good views. The
kitchen is having a harder time finding fans, and voters say it's "not
bad, but for the price you can do better."

FOOD ROOM STAFF COST

Duane Park Cafe

$44

157 Duane St. (212) 732-5555
bet. W. Broadway & Hudson St. in TriBeCa
Participants characterize this "serene" Contemporary American as "the best kept TriBeCa secret for fine mellow dining" and say "it doesn't get enough attention." Well, if voters keep giving the food and "efficient," top 100 service such good ratings, they can't exactly get pissed when it becomes a line-forming hot spot and that serenity flies right out the window, now can they? As with a lot of chef-owned spots, everything is "well-prepared." Stay for one of the "delicious desserts" or set aside a night for one of the seasonal wine-tasting dinners.

Due Restaurant

$28

1396 Third Ave. bet. 79th & 80th Sts./U.E. Side (212) 772-3331
Located well up Third Avenue, this little Northern Italian storefront has all the earmarks of the typical neighborhood spot: "Good people on staff" serve up "run-of-the-mill" pasta in a small dining room, or alfresco in nice weather. While it may not be a major destination, it suits undemanding locals.

Duke's

$20

99 E. 19th St. at Park Ave. S. in Flatiron (212) 260-2922
This "solid Southerner" is "cheap" for the upscale-restaurant-saturated Gramercy/Flatiron area, and here you get what you pay for. While it has "great ribs" at a "great deal" (read: "huge portions"), the sides are "boring," save the "killer onion rings." The "staff is nice as hell," but still this comfort food, with its lack of adequate veggies, served under satellite sportscasts, is called "low end" and may "not be fit for anyone over 30."

Dusit Thai

$22

256 Bleecker St. (212) 627-9310
bet. Sixth Ave. & Seventh Ave. S. in the W. Village
For "good," "inventive" fare and sound service, this "heart-of-the-Village" Thai is a "decent" value. It's small but "never crowded," perhaps due to the nondescript "coffee shop-like" decor.

E&O

$34

100 W. Houston St. (212) 254-7000
bet. LaGuardia Pl. & Thompson St. in SoHo
Wham! Though voters appreciate the "whimsical setting" of this SoHo Vietnamese/Thai, they slam the food, calling it "small portions" of "disappointing," "mediocre, overpriced eats."

Ear Inn

326 Spring St. (212) 226-9060
bet. Greenwich & Washington Sts. in SoHo
The "E" in "Ear" is formed by painting out part of the flickering neon that originally spelled "bar" at this 120-plus-year-old American on the outskirts of the West Village. "Great ambiance" is accented by an "old, old bar," and the simpler dishes—burgers, for example—are "yummy." This "good, dark dive" is in the city's Top 3.

East  $23

210 E. 44th St. bet. 2nd & 3rd Aves. in Midtown E. (212) 687-5075
251 W. 55th St. bet. Bdwy & 8th Ave./Midtown W. (212) 581-2240
354 E. 66th St. bet. 1st & 2nd Aves./U.E. Side (212) 734-5270
732 Seventh Ave. bet. 48th & 49th Sts./Th. Dist. (212) 265-8181
9 Barrow St. bet. W. 4th St. & 7th Ave./W. Village (212) 929-3353
9 E. 38th St. bet. 5th & Madison in Murray Hill (212) 685-5205
137 E. 47th St. bet. 3rd & Lex./Midtown E. (212) 980-7909
1420 Third Ave. bet. 80th & 81st Sts./U.E. Side (212) 472-3975
366 Third Ave. bet. 26th & 27th/Gramercy (212) 889-2326
The more formal side of the Teriyaki/Soba Noodle/Lunch Boy thing, these Japanese restaurants serve "consistently good" sushi at reasonable, in-and-out-the-door prices. "Best deals on Japanese food" can be had, especially the soup entrees, if you feel a little adventurous.

E.A.T.  $26

1064 Madison Ave. (212) 772-0022
bet. 80th & 81st Sts. on the Upper East Side
Everyone knows it's "bizarrely expensive" so if you're expecting a stereotypical NYC deli, "D.O.N.T." look to this Upper Eastsider. There's "no ambiance" and service is brusque, but "celebrities and tourists" know it's "trendy" and don't mind liquidating their assets for "delicious" soups and sandwiches that "melt in your mouth."

Eat & Drink  $32

148 Mercer St. bet. Prince & Houston Sts. in SoHo (212) 925-2477
Folks "prefer the cozy downstairs" lounge to the fancier dining upstairs at this just-SoHo Korean. Fancy fusion concoctions often fall flat, and those that are good come in "small portions." Simpler, traditional Korean dishes are your best bet.

Ecco  $36

124 Chambers St. (212) 227-7074
bet. W. Broadway & Church St. in TriBeCa
A "big Wall Street crowd" frequents the "somewhat cramped quarters" of this TriBeCa Northern Italian, who like the lunches, and also appreciate the live piano on Friday and Saturday nights. Either way, it's "a lot of fun in a great looking room."

Ecco-La  $22

1660 Third Ave. at 93rd St. in Carnegie Hill (212) 860-5609
Romac Reporters' #5 pick for a first date in town, this Carnegie Hill Italian has a "relaxing atmosphere," and "great pasta at good prices." Some prefer it for "just a quick bite," preferring fancier Italians further south for special occasions. "Ask to be seated in the back room" and bring cash.

Ecco L'Italia  $28

289 Bleecker St. at Seventh Ave. S./W. Village (212) 929-3355
With only "average food" and an average room to its credit, folks still call it a "fantastic West Village hideaway" featuring old time jazz artists on the weekends. The staff is "inconsistent" if they're not "slow," but you have to, like, get into the vibe, daddy-O.

	FOOD	ROOM	STAFF	COST

Edwardian Room

$57

The Plaza, 768 Fifth Ave. (212) 546-5310
at Central Park S. in Midtown W.

The room is in the name, and the room leads the ratings at this "very elegant," "pricey but wonderful" Continental in Ivana's very own Plaza Hotel. While the room places high in our Top 100, ER is not quite "fantastic in every way": Voters rate the food at just above average. P.S. Cornflakes-and-sweatpants types beware: Jacket and tie is required at all meals, including breakfast, and you simply must reserve, dahling.

Eighteenth & Eighth

$21

159 Eighth Ave. (212) 242-5000
at 18th St. in Chelsea

The quarters are tight and so are the "muscles" on the Chelsea "gym bunnies" at this "flirty," "ultimate gay" "casual" American. Breakfast and brunch are primetime so "expect a wait" for "tasty" "homestyle" fare and "great people-watching." As for decor, it's "nicer" since the "excellent renovation."

Eisenberg's Coffee Shop

$11

174 Fifth Ave. (212) 675-5096
bet. 22nd & 23rd Sts. in the Flatiron District

Who knew the "best tuna sandwich in NYC" was served at this "quintessential," "inimitable," "absolute original" of a "diner extraordinaire"? (They also specialize in pastrami, matzo ball soup, and a "helluvan egg cream"— not to mention "the oldest waitresses I've ever seen.") With the "best bad-for-you breakfast in town," this "inexpensive time warp" is definitely "worth the trip" to the Flatiron. The bottom line is, "if you're looking for this type of meal, why not go to the source?"

EJ's Luncheonette

$17

1271 Third Ave. (212) 472-0600
at 73rd St. on the Upper East Side
432 Sixth Ave. (212) 473-5555
bet. W. 9th & W. 10th Sts. in the W. Village
447 Amsterdam Ave. (212) 873-3444
bet. 81st & 82nd Sts. on the Upper West Side

"What's the fuss?" "Diners." "Why are they so popular?" "Good food," "fun menu and decor," "great pancakes and French toast," "the child-friendly" ("more strollers than the Upper West Side Barnes & Nobles") "places for breakfast." "Wait is extremely too long?" "Avoid at dinner and on weekends."

Elaine's

$37

1703 Second Ave. (212) 534-8103
bet. 88th & 89th Sts. on the Upper East Side

"Unless you're with Madonna" it's hard to get more than the once-over from "anti-hospitality" Elaine and her "star-conscious" crew. If you want to eavesdrop, head to this Upper Eastsider for "celebrity spotting" but be prepared for "mediocre" Italian fare and an "insiders-only" atmosphere.

= SUPERIOR = EXCELLENT = V. GOOD = GOOD

El Charro

$29

4 Charles St. (212) 242-9547
bet. Greenwich Ave. & Seventh Ave. S. in the W. Village
"The price is right" for "terrific paella" and other "consistent"
Spanish favorites at this one-time sleeper in the West Village. It's
"jammed" with diners who hunger for "huge portions" of
"authentic" eats but yawn that the "old-time ambiance" looks tired.

El Cid Tapas Bar

$28

322 W. 15th St. bet. Eighth & Ninth Aves./Chelsea (212) 929-9332
You must reserve a table for your tapas "or you'll eat at the bar" of this
charming, authentic Spanish establishment. The "great" tapas will
transport you to "tapas heaven"—if "the wait, the wait, the wait" and the
close quarters don't, that is. Great fun and sooo close to being in Spain,
El Cid Tapas Bar gets good marks for "intimacy" and authenticity.

Elephant & Castle

$20

68 Greenwich Ave. (212) 243-1400
at Seventh Ave. S. & W. 11th St. in the W. Village
Though the rest of the menu is "forgettable," taste buds will appreciate
the "tremendous" Caesar salad at this West Village American. A
"reliable" if "ordinary" brunch and "cozy" "pub-style" setting satisfy
herds of weekend "regulars." Service can be poky as a pachyderm.

El Faro

$28

823 Greenwich St. at Horatio St. in the W. Village (212) 929-8210
An "oldie and a goodie" opened in 1927, this venerated Spaniard
definitely has atmosphere, for better—"like stepping into Spain"—or
worse—make that worst, as in: "worst ambiance in the
world"—depending on your tolerance for hungry hordes, especially on
weekends (they don't take reservations). "Just when you thought it
couldn't get any more crowded—troubadours!" The sangria's great, and
the food, especially the paella, is just fine, and easy on the wallet too.

Elias Corner

$25

24-02 31st St., at 24th Ave. in Queens (718) 932-1510
"The best Astoria Greek" is this no-atmosphere storefront where
you get "gigantic portions" of simply prepared, "absolutely" fresh
seafood. There's "no menu," so you "pick fish from the cooler"
with the help of the "down-to-earth staff." Be prepared to wait in
line (no reservations), pay cash, and be "jammed in like sardines,"
but it's still "worth the trip to Queens" for an experience that's "like
popping down a rabbit hole for a mini vacation in the Greek isles."

Elio's

$41

1621 Second Ave. (212) 772-2242
at 84th St. on the Upper East Side
If the potentially "indifferent" service isn't a deterrent, expect to rub
elbows with "lots of famous people" at this "comfortable" and
"sophisticated" Upper East Sider. Elio dishes up "great,"
"always-reliable" Italian specialties but overlooked ordinary folks
claim "it's not fun if he doesn't know you." All this adds up to a
"quintessential NY eatery."

FOOD ROOM STAFF COST

Ellen's Cafe

$17

270 Broadway at Chambers St. in TriBeCa (212) 962-1257
The "dull" all-American chow can be as "tasteless" as the Formica
at this Financial District diner. Bulls and Bears in search of a
noontime sandwich note that the "friendly" staff and "cozy"
atmosphere make the experience more palatable.

Ellen's Stardust Diner

$17

1491 Broadway at 43rd St. in Midtown W. (212) 768-3170
1650 Broadway at 51st St. in the Theater District (212) 956-5151
1377 Ave. of the Americas at 51st/Midtown W. (212) 307-7575
"Good for tourists and kids," these Midtown '50s-style diners offer
"kitschy" decor and a "huge" menu of "luncheonette" standards.
"Service suffers for the singing" and most NYers have little
patience for eats that are as "plastic and artificial" as the
"mock-retro" environment.

El Parador Cafe

$33

325 E. 34th St. (212) 679-6812
bet. First & Second Aves. in Murray Hill
"Great Mexican food" is "a rare commodity in Manhattan," but this
Murray Hill old-timer clearly qualifies. "An old-fashioned kind of
NY Mexican," there's a large, seasonal menu and a huge array of
tequilas to choose from at the bar. "Relaxing atmosphere and good
food; I never get tired of it."

El Pollo

$14

1746 First Ave. bet. 90th & 91st Sts. in Yorkville (212) 996-7810
482 Broome St. at Wooster St. in SoHo (212) 431-5666
The "best" Peruvian roast "chicken under the sun"— and the
"cheapest"— is yours for the taking at this "good fast spot" located
in a tiny "hole-in-the-wall" in Yorkville (there's a more accessible
location on Broome Street, which diehards say is "not as good").
It's "weird but fun," and the "green hot sauce could melt your
fillings"—"YES!" El Pollo gets "high ratings for the chicken and
fries that are curly, but not for the staff who are surly."

El Pote Espanol

$30

718 Second Ave. (212) 889-6680
bet. 38th & 39th Sts. in Murray Hill
While it doesn't take una scientista des rockets to boil up "the best
two-pound lobsters" in el pote, this is one of the few Spanish spots
in the area. Older diners find it suits their pace.

El Quijote

$27

226 W. 23rd St. (212) 929-1855
bet. Seventh & Eighth Aves. in Chelsea
You "can't beat the lobster specials" at this "neighborhood institution"
in Chelsea. Voters tilt at an experienced staff and "1950s" red-velvet
room that could both use a "face-lift." Most are more quixotic and
praise "loads" of food at "easy-on-the-wallet" prices.

▤ = SUPERIOR ▤ = EXCELLENT ▤ = V. GOOD ▬ = GOOD

El Rincon de España $28

226 Thompson St. (212) 260-4950
bet. Bleecker & W. 3rd Sts. in the Washington Sq. Area
Don't let this "tourist dive" fool you, once inside you'll find
"authentic Spanish with serenades" at this no-reservations "corner
of Spain" in the "heart of the Village." Try the "unforgettable
paella" or the "delicious mussels in garlic sauce." "Great for a
romantic dinner"; it's family-run not fancy which means leave the
tie at home and put a rose between your teeth instead.

El Rio Grande $26

160 E. 38th St. at Third Ave. in Murray Hill (212) 867-0922
After work, swim on over to this Murray Hill Tex-Mex for "tasty"
margaritas but "skip the food." "Guys in ties" kickstart the weekend
here with "strong" drinks and a "great" "pick-up" scene and advise
visitors to stick to the bar, the "fun" stops at the border.

El Teddy's $30

219 W. Broadway bet. White & Franklin/TriBeCa (212) 941-7070
A sort of downtown wrought iron Pee Wee's Playhouse, this
TriBeCan is a hangout for the "fabulous people." Rating it as one of
the best after-work drink spots/Thursday nights out, diners are
pleasantly surprised by the "decent Mexican food," but most just
"stick to the drinks and the atmosphere."

Embers $33

9519 Third Ave., bet. 95th & 96th Sts. Brooklyn (718) 745-3700
Oooooh, valet parking! If you're a steak lover and you want "Peter
Luger's without attitude," this be the place. It rates the top 20 in the
steak category, so here's the rap: They serve "melt-in-your-mouth
steaks at a fraction of Manhattan prices," and the best part is the
"large portions." You can't make reservations which can be a
problem, especially when the crowds roll in on Friday and
Saturday. Children are welcome here.

Emilio's $36

167 E. 33rd St. bet. Third & Lex./in Murray Hill (212) 684-3223
"Hidden and out of the way," is just how some people like it. This
"pleasant" Italian in Murray Hill does as good or better than a lot of
little neighborhood spots. The food may be a little "over-pricey,"
but it pulls in a respectable rating and a pianist tickles the ivories
while you twirl your pasta.

Emily's $20

1325 Fifth Ave. at 111th St. in E. Harlem (212) 996-1212
Straight from the mouth of "a Southerner, this place has the best
BBQ and ribs in New York—smack, yum." It also has Jazz
Thursday, R&B Saturday, a late-night menu for the night owls,
breakfast and an early-bird special for the worm catchers, and
brunch on Sunday. If you're any where near Harlem, or even if
you're not, try this beautiful, "elegant and accessible" restaurant
with "great soul food" that is "one of the most pleasant dining
experiences" you'll have. Bring the kids.

Empire Diner

FOOD ROOM STAFF COST

$20

210 Tenth Ave. (212) 243-2736
at 22nd St. in Chelsea

Great people-watching after-hours and at Sunday brunch score
points for this trendy 24-hour Chelsea American/Eclectic, the top
diner in our poll. Too bad the food "sucks" and the service is
"snotty and slow," though a "nice piano bar," remade art deco
decor, and sidewalk seating satisfies the "lively, hip" clientele.

Empire Szechuan

$17

381 Third Ave. bet. 27th & 28th Sts.in Gramercy (212) 685-6215
1241 Amsterdam Ave. at 121st/Harlem (212) 678-2759
15 Greenwich Ave. (6th Ave. & W. 10th/W. Vill.) (212) 691-1535
2642 Broadway at 100th St. on the U.W. Side (212) 662-9404
193 Columbus Ave. bet. 68th & 69th/U.W. Side (212) 496-8778
173 Seventh Ave. S. bet. W. 11th & Perry/W. Vill. (212) 243-6046
2574 Broadway bet. 96th & 97th/U.W. Side (212) 663-6004
75 Second Ave. bet. 4th & 5th Sts. in the E. Village (212) 260-0206
251 W. 72nd St. bet. Bdwy & West End/U.W. Side (212) 496-8460
4041 Broadway at 170th St. in the Bronx (212) 568-1600

The "war is on" with many voters knocking these city-wide
Chinese/Japanese "generics" for their "nuisance" "menu tactics."
Others find fault with quality and service that vary widely by
location and warn: "use only in an emergency." In their defense,
"they'd deliver to Montreal" and prices are "reasonable."

Ennio and Michael

$32

539 La Guardia Pl. (212) 677-8577
bet. Bleecker & W. 3rd Sts. in the Washington Sq. Area

A "good neighborhood Italian" featuring "consistent quality and
consistent graciousness," this family-owned and family-friendly
purveyor of rigatoni alla ennio, and other Central Italian specialities
puts "love in every dish" and draws a loyal following for its
"friendly, concerned" attitude as much as for the "best veal."

Erizo Latino

$35

422 W. Broadway (212) 941-5811
bet. Prince & Spring Sts. in SoHo

Ex-Patria chef Alex Garcia serves Cuban/South American
"inventive and tasty" fare—seviche is a must. Those "excellent
flavors" are complemented by a "nice room," with live Latin music
and jazz on the weekends. Not cheap, though—the prix fixe lunch
will leave you staggering.

Erminia

$44

250 E. 83rd St. (212) 879-4284
bet. Second & Third Aves. on the Upper East Side

This Upper East Side Italian is as tiny as an ermine, and just as
luxurious. "Romantic, cozy and dark" it's "a jewel," "delightful in
every respect." One of "the most romantic places in town," the dim
lights and candles make this place strictly "for lovers."

= SUPERIOR = EXCELLENT = V. GOOD = GOOD

Ernie's

2150 Broadway (212) 496-1588
bet. 75th & 76th Sts. on the Upper West Side
Voters say this Upper West Side "institution" is still "noisy," "still big," and "still good." With a "huge selection" of Italian favorites, floor to ceiling windows, and a "great garden," it's a "casual," "spacious" write-in favorite.

Eros

 $38

1076 First Ave. bet. 58th & 59th Sts. in Midtown E. (212) 223-2322
The "dream decor" at this so-called gourmet Greek makes for a surreally splendid "cool summer evening date," but the food has voters saying "time to call it a day."

Esashi

 $20

32 Ave. A bet. 2nd & 3rd Sts. in the E. Village (212) 505-8726
It's a short hike from the subway stops in the East Village, but don't let that keep you from a terrific plate of sushi. Villagers are eating this one up at its "good-value" prices. "Very authentic," "absolutely the best," "don't miss the early-bird menu" served by an "extremely efficient" staff.

Ess-A-Bagel

 $8

359 First Ave. (212) 260-2252
at 21st St.in Gramercy
831 Third Ave. (212) 980-1010
bet. 50th & 51st Sts. in Midtown E.
These small storefronts have, to regulars at least, the "best bagels in NYC" (runs 2nd in our poll). The "quirky but fun" staff is "real New York," and so are the bagels with a huge assortment of flavored cream cheeses. So good, they're also No. 11 in town for breakfast, and in the Top 100 for food.

Est! Est! Est!

 $37

64 Carmine St. (212) 255-6294
bet. Bedford & Seventh Ave. S. in the W. Village
"Not as well known as it should be," this Northern Italian rates at least one, if not three, exclamation points for "really good" food in a soothing setting.

Estia Greek

 $26

308 E. 86th St. (212) 628-9100
bet. First & Second Aves. on the Upper East Side
The live music (from Wednesday through Sunday) and the "moderate prices" aren't enough to make voters fall in love with this Yorkville spot. Serviceable, not special.

Estoril Sol

 $36

382 Eighth Ave. at 29th St. in Chelsea (212) 947-1043
This Madison Square Garden variety Portuguese/Italian has, according to voters, the best Portuguese this side of Newark: You must reserve (hey—the Garden holds a lot of people) and folks "love this kind of fake stucco place."

FOOD ROOM STAFF COST

Etats-Unis

 $44

242 E. 81st St. bet. Second & Third/U.E. Side (212) 517-8826
With "tables close enough to participate in everyone's conversations," this teeny (30 seats) Upper East Side American has few, albeit fanatical, fans. Though it may be "hard to get in," the food is simply "excellent," particularly the "delicious breads and desserts" (the "chocolate souffle is heaven"). The "neighborhood spot" decor is on the "sterile" side, but they don't have room for anything fancy, and the food will transport you to another etat.

Evergreen Cafe

 $20

1288 First Ave. bet. 69th & 70th Sts./U.E. Side (212) 744-3266
Good dim sum (and "a staff that can tell you what's in it"), "fun dumplings," and "Grand Marnier prawns that keep you coming back for more" equal a "better than average" Upper East Side Chinese.

Fanelli's

 $18

94 Prince St. at Mercer St. in SoHo (212) 226-9412
Open since, you heard correctly, 1872, "this great old NY place" serves up "homey" food "with no fuss or attitude" in an "atmospheric neighborhood bar" that's archetypally "dark," "noisy," and "smoky." "The food isn't the greatest," but the "people-watching of the glitterless side of SoHo is." It's a "regular folks" type of place, y'know?

Farfalle Trattoria

 $26

680 Columbus Ave. at 93rd St. on the U.W. Side (212) 666-2431
If you throw a stone in New York City you're bound to hit an Italian restaurant. Here's one on the Upper West Side that holds up: good "traditional" Northern Italian with "great wine" in a wild, wonderful room, and service that gets the job done, all for a fair price. Weekend brunch with Sunday jazz. Patio dining.

Fashion Cafe

 $25

51 Rockefeller Ctr., 51st St. (212) 765-3131
bet. Fifth & Sixth Aves. in Midtown W.
One of the stranger entries into the amusement park restaurant scene, this Rock Center American draws ratings as thin as, oh, I don't know, its supermodel owners. They don't serve good food because they don't eat. It's as simple as that. Oh, and the ambiance? "Tourist trap for sex-crazed travellers who get off on leather-clad mannequins and scantily-clad waitresses."

Felidia

 $54

243 E. 58th St. (212) 758-1479
bet. Second & Third Aves. in Midtown E.
"Grandma never cooked like this!" or else she would have retired a rich woman. The "wonderful" and "outstanding" Northern Italian food is "a true favorite" with Romac reporters. Praise rolls in for Lidia Bastianich's "melt-in-your-mouth risotto" and "the best pasta, period!" Located in a "charming brownstone" a few blocks east of Central Park's entrance, this upscale beauty grabs high rankings in all categories. Better than Grandma? See for yourself.

Felix $38

340 W. Broadway (212) 431-0021
at Grand St. in SoHo

A "true Soho experience," you'll find "pretty girls and models at weekend brunch," "good views of West Broadway" and a "nice open room," plus the odd couple of standout items on the passable French menu.

Fellini $36

12 E. 49th St. (212) 832-2500
bet. Fifth & Madison Aves. in Midtown E.

This Midtown restaurant shoots for business diners but hits mainly tourists with its only "fair" International cuisine. While the room and ambiance are the best features here, it is still "loud and tight," and portions are "on the stingy side." Not quite la dolce vita.

Fifty Seven Fifty Seven $49

Four Seasons Hotel, 57 E. 57th St. (212) 758-5757
bet. Park & Madison Aves. in Midtown E.

Not a drop of rain on this parade: Contemporary American fare that's "the most delicious and beautifully prepared food ever" and a staff that "elevates service to a new plateau" add up to an experience that's "never a letdown." The martinis are sublime, and so is the I. M. Pei-designed dining room, a "beautiful people" hangout where a mere mortal can "feel like a queen." Even the bathrooms are tops. And oh, did we mention "the best orange juice in town"?

F. illi Ponte $46

39 Desbrosses St. (212) 226-4621
bet. West & Washington Sts. in TriBeCa

"The charm of what Little Italy used to be": simply put, "great Italian food" and warm, gracious service. "Wonderful views" of the Hudson and live jazz in the lounge make this a "great place to hang out" and affect a "mobster"-ish mein.

Fine & Schapiro $20

5 World Trade Ctr. (212) 775-7600
bet. Church & Vesey Sts. in the Financial District
138 W. 72nd St. (212) 877-2874, (212) 877-2721
bet. Columbus Ave. & Broadway on the Upper West Side

Though once the "ultimate in Jewish cuisine," these institutions have "lost some of their luster" in recent years. Though a few say they still turn out "decent" homemade gefilte fish, old-fashioned kishka, chopped liver, and chicken in a pot, this duo often disappoints, unless you enjoy "surly service."

Fino $41

4 E. 36th St. (212) 689-8040
bet. Fifth & Madison Aves. in Murray Hill

What's "wonderful, fresh" Northern Italian food to some is "overpriced and overrated" to others. The decor is inarguably elegant art deco, the staff intermittently "rude."

FOOD ROOM STAFF COST

Fiorello's $34

1900 Broadway (212) 595-5330
bet. 63rd & 64th Sts. on the Upper West Side
Pre- or post-Lincoln Center, the abbondanza antipasto bar at this
Northern Italian rates raves. Otherwise the peaks-and-valleys fare
never dips below "so-so," and the kitchen attains moments of
"great"-ness with its pizza and tiramisu.

Firenze $35

1594 Second Ave. (212) 861-9368
bet. 82nd & 83rd Sts. on the Upper East Side
"Gracious hosts" and "good, not-too-loud music" make this
"excellent storefront" on the Upper East Side a neighborhood
favorite that doubles as a "special occasion" spot. The "friendly
staff" is the real highlight of this "small and romantic" place.

First $32

87 First Ave. (212) 674-3823
bet. 5th & 6th Sts. in the E. Village
"Insufferably trendy" or "inventive" and "eclectic"? It's your
choice for "surprisingly good" "Upper East Side food at East
Village prices." Some suggest that the funky-chic,
"Gothic-edged decor" should win a "design of the year"
award, but poor scores for service indicate why "models
shouldn't be waitresses." Expect lots of "black," "attitude,"
and "amazing chocolate pudding cake."

Fish $23

2799 Broadway at 108th St./Columbia U. Area (212) 864-5000
To be as plain as the name of the restaurant's face, this is "the best
seafood in the Upper West Side, at extremely affordable prices."
The fish fare is "reliably fresh and tasty," the other choices
"uneven." But toss a great brunch and "cozy and stylish" setting
into the mix and you get "a godsend for this neighborhood."

Fishin Eddie $35

73 W. 71st St. (212) 874-3474
bet. Columbus Ave. & Central Park W. on the Upper West Side
Reel in "fresh fish and imaginative specials" at this north coast
seafood specialist in a "cozy but pricey " "Vermont inn" setting.
"Always fun," this "great date place" is "proof that the Upper West
Side offers its rewards."

Flamingo East $31

219 Second Ave. bet. 13th & 14th Sts./E. Village (212) 533-2860
"A fab place to linger in the waiting lounge," say voters of this East
Village, predominantly alternative lifestyle spot that's "just steps from
Dan Lynch's Blues Bar." "A different place to dine," the
Eclectic/Continental menu has a few fans, but it's the "zany people" that
folks call "warm and sweet" and tasty cocktails that are the real draws.

Flor de Mayo

2651 Broadway at 101st St./Columbia U. Area (212) 595-2525
Much more than just the usual Chino/Latino, this Spanish and
Chinese restaurant in the Columbia area has some of the "best
Cuban food off the Island." A more relevant comparison is a little
closer to home: Fans think it's even "better than La Caridad."

Florent

 $24

69 Gansevoort (212) 989-5779
bet. Greenwich & Hudson Sts. in the W. Village
Romac's Top after-hours dining spot, this diner-cum-French Bistro
serves until 4:30 a.m. While the food is "good," especially the "great
breakfast foods" and other "budget French food" ("the best frites west
of Broadway!"), the real lure is the "weird mix" of the "after-club"
crowd and graveyard shifters. "French flirts and men in skirts" and the
servers' "good sense of humor" make it a real Fellini scene.

Flowers

 $36

21 W. 17th St. (212) 691-8888
bet. Fifth & Sixth Aves. in Chelsea
The Contemporary American fare with international accents at this
"trendy" roof-top spot is interesting, but chewing can prove difficult
when your jaw has dropped. The models and other "beautiful
people" garner more attention than the tuna tartar with avocado
salsa or the teriyaki-glazed mahi mahi with veggie lo mein and
ginger lemon grass. But no one seems too distracted to notice that
even at these prices waiters "aren't pouring wine" and are "too
snooty for no reason." And yes, darling, reservations are essential.

Flying Burritos

 $17

165 W. 4th St. (212) 691-3663
bet. Sixth Ave. & Seventh Ave. S. in the W. Village
The "wacky decor," including hanging model airplanes, suits the
West 4th Street crowd, some who think the healthy Cal-Mex
cuisine is "better than Benny's." The large selection of tequilas at
the "good bar" may account for the name of the place. Sidewalk
dining is people-watching at its best.

Flying Fish

 $22

395 West St. (212) 924-5050
bet. Christopher & 10th Sts. in the W. Village
You can have your "fill of curry chicken with rice, peas, a variety of
Caribbean sides" and eclectic Spanish and West Indian fare at this
West Villager. That is if you're in the mood for so-so food in so-so
surroundings with so-so service and "great piña coladas."

Foley's Fish House

Renaissance Hotel, 714 7th Ave. (212) 261-5200
at 48th St. in the Theater District
The Renaissance Hotel just opened this seafooder, which boasts all
the features a hotel restaurant should; a piano bar, accomodations
for the kids, and a reasonable pre-theater menu. Tell us what you
think on your questionnaire next year.

FOOD ROOM STAFF COST

Follonico

$41

6 W. 24th St. bet. Fifth & Sixth Aves./Flatiron (212) 691-6359
Named for chef/owner Alan Tardi's Tuscan hometown, this
highly-rated Flatiron Italian is "truly unusual," but still "excellent for
all occasions, including business. The simple, terra cotta and
wainscoted room, tapestry-covered banquettes and large (seats 12)
refectory table give the place a down-to-earth elegance, matched by
the "very good" meats, pizzas, veggies and breads mostly prepared in
the wood-burning oven. "One of the finest haute Italians in town,"
fans rave, and add "the blood-orange granita cannot be surpassed!"

Food Bar

$21

149 Eighth Ave. bet. 17th & 18th Sts. in Chelsea (212) 243-2020
The "gayest place to dine in the city," this Chelsea cruisefest is
always a "high energy" party scene. Yes, the Eclectic/American
food "should be better," but the atmosphere "makes up for it"—"the
only restaurant in town where 'pork' is both a noun and a verb."
Blaring disco, an overabundance of mirrors, and a waitstaff that's
"hunky but inattentive" add up to a joint that's "loud and fun,
especially weekend nights; waiters will pinch your nipples."

Fortune Garden

$31

845 Second Ave. bet. 45th & 46th/Midtown E. (212) 687-7471
A fish tank and pond are better than TV for work weary eyes any
day. And who can say no to dim sum? This Midtown Easter offers
up Chinese fare with excellent service, and low traffic for a
meditative meal. It also offers a cheap prix fixe lunch.

44

$44

Royalton Hotel, 44 W. 44th St. (212) 944-8844
bet. Fifth & Sixth Aves. in Midtown W.
Most agree the American/Continental food is "wonderful," "great,"
hotel fare, but the focus here is atmosphere: If you have a craving to
"be seen" by "people most chic," then this "fab" "elegant, trendy"
spot is for you. If you enjoy "good people watching" where an
"indolent" (for a first-rate hotel) "too cool for life" staff "makes you
feel like you are in a play," then try it. If "ridiculously long waits"
are "not worth putting up with," stay away.

Four Seasons

$63

Seagram Bldg., 99 E. 52nd St. (212) 754-9494
bet. Park & Lexington Aves. in Midtown E.
"The ultimate in sophisticated dining," "you're definitely
paying for the flawless service, ambiance and food, but when
it's this good, it's worth it." "Don't go if you're under 35,"
the atmosphere and staff will seem "stuffy": Your future self
will find "gorgeous" Philip Johnson-designed "rooms,
gorgeous food, and gorgeous people." "First and only" are
two words that come up again and again: the first Seasonal
American, the only NYC restaurant designated an
architectural landmark (in Midtown's ominous Seagram
Building). Voted Tops for Business Lunch, and also on more
Romac "Tops by" lists than any other place, the Four Seasons
is "cool perfection: the gustatory equivalent of the MOMA."

= SUPERIOR = EXCELLENT = V. GOOD = GOOD

Frankie & Johnnie's $39

194-05 Northern Blvd., at 194th St. in Queens (718) 357-2444
269 W. 45th bet. Bdwy & Eighth/Theater District (212) 997-9494
Carnivores only need apply at this old Theater District speakeasy (with a
Queens sibling). The "huge portions" and "great steaks" make for a
"meat heaven in the old style," a "hideaway for the '90s." "Frankie and
Johnnie's stays in my mind as the perfect 1950s steakhouse—film noir,
misty night in Midtown, my father in a fedora."

Franklin Station Cafe $16

222 W. Broadway bet. Franklin & White/TriBeCa (212) 274-8525
Sidewalk seats and "tasty" French/Malaysian cuisine make this
casual TriBeCa bistro a reliable choice for lunch or dinner. With an
open kitchen, evening art slide shows and "pleasant" service, it's a
creative cafe that should be better known.

Frank's

85 Tenth Ave. at 15th St. in Chelsea (212) 243-1349
"Family-run" and "friendly," this "steak lover's steak joint" in the
Meat Packing District has been serving up "outstanding" beef since
1912. Expect a "casual," "beautiful new space," accommodating
service, and "top-notch" dining. Cigar-friendly.

Fraunces Tavern $34

54 Pearl St. at Broad St. in the Financial District (212) 269-0144
Yep, it's spelled right: back in 1762 when they first painted
the sign here, they used to say "purfuit of happineff," too.
And while "great for tourists," this place goes way beyond
vintage NYC, and is an utter "throwback to meat and potatoes
times." "Warm, cozy," and a "good place for a drink after
work," some say "it's a museum, not a restaurant." Hey, this
is a food guide. We've gotta be frank.

French Roast $18

2340 Broadway at 85th St. on the Upper West Side (212) 799-1533
78 W. 11th St. at Sixth Ave. in the W. Village (212) 533-2233
An oasis for caffeine freaks, these 24-hour West Village/Upper
West Side coffeehouses feature "okay brasserie food" ranging from
"decent" burgers and fries to "wonderful" desserts. The service is
glacial and the waitresses are "as unfriendly as they are pretty," but
the people-watching and eavesdroppping conditions are magnifique.
Still, those who aren't in the mood to "feel like a Euro-snob" say
"save your time and money and go to a diner."

Fresco $38

34 E. 52nd St. (212) 935-3434
bet. Park & Madison Aves. in Midtown E.
"Business lunch" for the power mongers keeps this contemporary
Tuscan restaurant in midtown invariably "crowded," despite "hefty
prices." Fresco has "fresh, hearty food," including robust pastas and
pizzas voters could eat "four times a day, seven days a week." The
requisite "caring and attentive" staff and "very pleasant room"
mean suited types "eat here too much but can't help it."

| | FOOD | ROOM | STAFF | COST |

Fresh Basil's $21

663 Lexington Ave. (212) 888-4292
bet. 55th & 56th Sts. in Midtown E.
Your "basic Italian" joint, good for midtown takeout, otherwise dangles
on the brink of "below average," begging the question "Why bother?"

Frico Bar $25

402 W. 43rd St. at Ninth Ave. in Clinton (212) 564-7272
While the "namesake dish (a stuffed Montasio cheese crisp) is the
best" at this Clinton Italian yearling, the rest of the menu is uneven.
"Sometimes great, sometimes greasy" they say, so that pounding in
your ears may be your heartbeat ("damn the cholesterol!") and not
the "blaring music."

Friend of a Farmer $22

77 Irving Pl. (212) 477-2188
bet. 18th & 19th Sts. in Gramercy
More than a little bit country and entirely non-rock-and-roll, this
Gramercy homestyle American has legions of fans, who love the
"wonderful baking" (giant cookies!, "dessert sharing is highly
encouraged"), "Vermont ambiance" and "almost too wholesome"
food including everyone's favorite, chicken pot pie. "It's like being
with the Amish" says one voter, though they have electricity, drive
cars, and say "you" instead of "thee."

Frontiere $41

199 Prince St. (212) 387-0898
bet. Sullivan & MacDougal Sts. in SoHo
"Very special indeed" coo fans of this southern French/Northern
Italian bistro. A "most attentive" staff—including "one of the nicest
maitre d's in New York" and a chef "who will cook you
anything"—always "make you feel at home." The food ranges from
"nice" to "wonderful," and the mood is consistently "charming."

Frutti Di Mare $20

84 E. 4th St. (212) 979-2034
at Second Ave. in the E. Village
"Sister" to Cucina di Pesce across the street, and "just as good," this
"decent Italian" with its "dimly lit" (if "a little crowded") ambiance
can be "insanely cheap for what you get." Though hardly
earth-shaking, it's a "great value" and a "cheerful" experience.
"Outdoor seating" on the sidewalk gets extra points—and so does
the "awesome tiramisu."

f.stop $31

28 W. 20th St. (212) 627-STOP
bet. Fifth & Sixth Aves. in the Flatiron District
No, it's not a telegram of a bad report card. "f.stop" celebrates the
Flatiron/Photo district. As a gallery, it does the job: "great photos"
are exhibited in a "spacious atmosphere," and there are plenty of
places to suck in those cheeks and look smashing. However,
photography is a visual medium, and (like some photos) voters find
the food "beautiful," but "curiously tasteless."

Fujisan of Chinatown

90 Baxter St. bet. White & Walker/Chinatown (212) 219-3331
What? Japanese food in Chinatown? Yes yes, say voters, who
enthusiastically wrote in to say they have "great sushi, a nice staff
and good portions." The "cooked Japanese" is also good, and one
Fujiphile went as far as to call it "impressive."

Fujiyama Mama

 $33

467 Columbus Ave. (212) 769-1144
bet. 82nd & 83rd Sts. on the Upper West Side
"The original trendy Japanese" features "the funkiest
atmosphere—complete with DJ" and "good" sushi." But "you've
got to be in the mood," or the flashing lights, blasting disco, and
"incessant birthday fests" can add up to an "Excedrin meal."

Fu's House

 $29

972 Second Ave. (212) 421-2322
bet. 51st & 52nd Sts. in Midtown E.
The Midtown lunch crowd likes this Chinese for its under-$10,
bargain prix fixe. It's appropriate that it's in Midtown since it's
mid-priced and middle-rated. Ask for the not-on-the-menu grand
marnier shrimp specialty and keep in mind that they serve dim sum.

Gabriela's

 $20

685 Amsterdam Ave. (212) 961-0574
at 93rd St. on the Upper West Side
Upper West Siders think this "authentic" Mexican neighborhood
spot is a real charmer. It's a "definite cut above the usual" for "good
non-burrito style" food and "great sangria," and most appreciate the
"earnest service." It's "kind of a dive" but the "sweet people" that
run the place are so friendly no one really complains. Prices are
reasonable but they "make you pay for extra salsa and tortillas,
which sucks." No smokes, no reservations.

Gabriel's

 $44

11 W. 60th St. (212) 956-4600
bet. Broadway & Columbus Ave. on the Upper West Side
The "interesting seasonal menu," consisting of pasta made fresh on
the premises and wood-grilled meats and game is "well-executed in
a comfortable environment." While the food remains
"unpretentious," the environment is still "sophisticated," though
some complain that "for an upscale restaurant," it's "very noisy and
hectic." In spite of the noise and the "good celebrity-watching,"
owner Gabriel Aiello doesn't have to blow his own horn: the "best
Italian fare on the West Side" is based on "simply good food."

Gage & Tollner

372 Fulton, Brooklyn (718) 875-5181
bet. Smith & Jay
"Still a classic" this 1879 "landmark" is "worth the trip" just to soak in
the old-time ambiance complete with an authentic mahogany bar and
original gas lamps. The "uneven" Continental/Steakhouse menu is in for
a change by a new chef: Go for a dose of "elegant," vintage Brooklyn.

FOOD ROOM STAFF COST

Galaxy

174 Eighth Ave. at 19th St. in Chelsea (212) 463-7460
While this Chelsea American has "good" (at least, life-supporting) atmosphere, its appeal is not exactly universal. What is "weird" to some is "trendy and stylish" to others, and the eclectic influences to the basic "diner food" are "interesting." Like most galaxies, it's still relatively "undiscovered."

Galileo

 $34

535 Hudson St. (212) 675-5252
bet. Charles & Perry Sts. in the W. Village
Any newcomer to the Village that earns an early rep as "friendly," cool, "first date place," and attracts an eclectic crowd, is in the running to stick around a while. Authentic Northern Italian fare and a "neat bar" doesn't hurt either. Outdoor dining lets you enjoy the neighborhood.

Gallagher's Steakhouse

 $43

228 W. 52nd St. at Broadway/Theater District (212) 245-5336
To call it "Peter Luger's with the right attitude and location" might be a little much, but in its first 70 years this Theater District Steakhouse has generated a core group of die-hard fans. Comments like "my favorite steak"and "I've been eating here for 45 years and nothing changes" keep diners coming back. While the steaks, the history (and its ranking in our Top 10 cigar spots) might make it a "real man place," some women find it "musty, dusty and crusty."

Gandhi

345 E. 6th St. (212) 614-9718
bet. First & Second Aves. in the E. Village
Some say this dark, Curry Lane spot "ranks with Mitali" for "best East Village Indian." "Not fancy, just plain good food" is this favorite standby, a relief from newer spots on the block that are getting more upscale. However, the tables are a bit "squashed together."

Garage Cafe

 $23

99 Seventh Ave. S. (212) 645-0600
bet. Grove & Barrow Sts. in the W. Village
It's one of the "newest hot spots" in the Village so boy does that make it "noisy." But who cares. The waiters are lots of fun at this Contemporary American and the bar is huge. They play jazz at the "great brunch," fire up the logs when old-man-winter rolls in and set up the sidewalk for people-watching when it's warm.

Garlic Bob's

 $12

508 Columbus Ave. (212) 769-2627
bet. 84th & 85th Sts. on the Upper West Side
1325 Third Ave. (212) 772-2627
bet. 75th & 76th Sts. on the Upper East Side
Rumor has it that they serve pizza with their garlic. If you love both, "this is the place." It's "a step above the normal pizza parlor fare," but compared with John's and Patsy's, it "sucks." Oh well. It's "fast" and serves up brick oven by the slice. There are two locations but neither has much in the way of service or ambiance.

Gascogne

 $43

158 Eighth Ave. bet. 17th & 18th Sts. in Chelsea (212) 675-6564
"A rare regional French that isn't Provençal," instead the menu at
this Chelsea bistro is from the Southwest. The food makes it one of
the "best French" places in the area, "charming and quaint" with a
"lovely garden" in back, and "waiters who smoke in the front."

Gene's

73 W. 11th St. bet. Fifth & Sixth/Central Village (212) 675-2048
Not only is this Central Village Italian and Continental restaurant a
landmark, it's also a "quiet, reliable neighborhood restaurant that's open
holidays." "Great lobster specials" rival the "excellent" $19 prix fixe.

Genji

 $26

56 Third Ave. (212) 254-1959
bet. 10th & 11th Sts. in the E. Village
"All-you-can-eat sushi" and "reasonable quality" add up to "okay"
Japanese—"not the best by a long shot."

Gennaro

665 Amsterdam Ave. (212) 665-5348
at 92nd St. on the Upper West Side
Lately, lots of talented young chefs are leasing small rooms, in
off-the-beaten path neighborhoods, and cooking the food they want
to cook. Case in point: Gennaro Picone, late of Bice and Barolo, has
opened this tiny new Upper West Sider: Support your local chef,
and vote on Gennaro next year.

Giambelli Fiftieth

 $47

46 E. 50th St. (212) 688-2760
bet. Park & Madison Aves. in Midtown E.
A Rip Van Winkle of a sleeper. this long-lived Italian rates high marks
across the board. Definitely "go when the truffles are in," but why wait?

Gianni's

 $32

15 Fulton St. (212) 608-7300
at Water St. at the South St. Seaport
This is Penny and Peter Glazier's (Monkey Bar, Tapika) first
restaurant, and though this glass-enclosed Northern Italian is often
called "one of the best in the Wall Street area," that ain't saying
much for the food. It's a good spot "to people watch at the Seaport"
or to smoke pipes and cigars on the outdoor terrace.

Ginger Man

 $27

11 E. 36th St. (212) 532-3740
bet. Fifth & Madison Aves. in Murray Hill
With 66 drafts and 120 bottles to choose from, this "old gents'
club" for the young and trendy ranks as a top beer drinker's
destination, and the cigar lounge wins it an award for "smokiest
place in town." Quaffing and puffing (and coughing) aside, the
merely hungry will find "fun" food that's "good for bar fare"—"if
you can eat while breathing cigar fumes."

FOOD	ROOM	STAFF	COST

Ginger Toon

417 Bleecker St. (212) 924-6420
bet. Bank & W. 11th Sts. in the W. Village
For "good" reliable Thai fare, locals head to this West Villager with a "great name." Expect solid service, modest prices and an unintimidating atmosphere.

Gino

780 Lexington Ave. (212) 758-4466
bet. 60th & 61st Sts. on the Upper East Side
Expect a "cosmopolitan" crowd and "big portions" of "solid" Southern Italian fare at this "classic old jet-set hangout" on the Upper East Side. Zebras on the walls make it a distinctive, sometimes "noisy" "gathering place" where the "elite sometimes eat." No plastic.

Giovanni $45

47 W. 55th St. (212) 262-2828
bet. Fifth & Sixth Aves. in Midtown W.
Just two years old, this Midtown Venetian/Northern Italian has sacrificed ambiance for volume: big restaurant, big wine list, big bar, but only normal-sized portions. We hear good things about the food, and with a private cigar room (with its own cigar menu, no less) and a reasonable pre-theater menu, it's worth a look.

Girafe $41

208 E. 58th St. (212) 752-3054
bet. Second & Third Aves. in Midtown E.
A "favorite for Midtown business lunches," this "old school" Northern Italian offers straightforwardly "good" dishes and an elegant, pampering atmosphere.

Girasole $42

151 E. 82nd St. (212) 772-6690
bet. Third & Lexington Aves. on the Upper East Side
Serving "delicious Northern Italian food in a pretty Upper East Side brownstone setting," folks find this restaurant's many game specialties somewhat "quirky." That's a good thing. An "adorable staff" and a large party room upstairs set Girasole apart from other area Italians.

Global 33 $28

93 Second Ave. (212) 477-8427
bet. 5th & 6th Sts. in the E. Village
Looking for an "airport cocktail lounge gone upscale," without all those pesky planes flying around? How about one with an Eclectic/International menu specializing in "good tapas"? The bar's the thing at this "trendy" new-to-the-scene East Villager, with a high-scoring bartender serving "fabulous martinis" in their shakers. The only baggage you need bring are some unresolved childhood issues.

▮ = SUPERIOR ▮ = EXCELLENT ▮ = V. GOOD ▬ = GOOD

Golden Unicorn

18 E. Broadway (212) 941-0911
at Catherine St. in Chinatown
Peking duck and dim sum are available at this very large Chinatown restaurant, but alas, no unicorn. No matter. Voters felt compelled to write in about this "excellent overall" Chinese, particularly for the "diverse variety" on the menu.

Gonzales y Gonzales

625 Broadway (212) 473-8787
bet. Bleecker & Houston Sts. in the Washington Sq. Area
We haven't figured out which one is Gonzales, but our voters say it doesn't matter: This "big," "fun place" has "great quesadillas" and a "unique atmosphere" that includes live music on the weekends. Too loud for some, most think it is "authentic," and worth the trip.

Good Enough to Eat $21

483 Amsterdam Ave. (212) 496-0163
bet. 83rd & 84th Sts. on the Upper West Side
"Almost too cute, but great comfort food" at this Upper West Side Top 10 Brunch and Breakfast spot. It's "like eating in the best restaurant in Burlington, VT," though unlike restaurants in the Green Mountain State, "expect long waits" on weekends.

Goody's $23

94-03B 63rd Dr., Queens (718) 896-7159
bet. Booth & Sander
Take a field trip to Queens for "rightfully famous little juicy buns" and similar "very tasty" Chinese chow, "caringly prepared" but carelessly served. The surrounding are "uninspired" at best, so takeout's the ticket. No credit cards.

Googie's

1491 Second Ave. (212) 717-1122
at 78th St. on the Upper East Side
When looking for a "comfortable" Italian American with a "good variety of food," "don't forget Googie's." This is a "solid diner" with "reliable food" at all meals, and the "garlic mashed potatoes are to die for." This is on the short list of places to take the kids on the Upper East Side.

Gotham Bar & Grill $50

12 E. 12th St. (212) 620-4020
bet. 5th & University in the Central Village
"An American classic" short-listed for "best restaurant in New York City," chef Alfred Portale's continental "class act" is a special-occasion favorite. The "heavenly" room is too airy for intimacy, meaning "it's not terribly romantic, which is welcome"—filling a niche for large parties, business diners, and older adults in search of sophistication sans froufrou. An expense account helps, but the "wonderful, imaginative" food makes for such a "fulfilling culinary experience" that "it's worth every penny." In sum: "superb."

FOOD ROOM STAFF COST

Gramercy Tavern

$52

42 E. 20th St. (212) 477-0777
bet. Broadway & Park Ave. S. in Gramercy

A trendy spot that promises to stick around for a long while, this Gramercy American is a Top 5 Favorite in the Romac Poll. "The best wine list," and a "very knowledgeable staff" (headed by owner/host Danny Meyer) fit beautifully into the "gorgeous decor," and though the "regular menu is somewhat limited, they have tons of nightly specials." "Always worth the trip," but the way everyone goes on about this place it might even be worth moving to Gramercy, just to be near it. Reservations extremely essential.

Grand Central Oyster Bar

$37

Grand Central Station, lower level (212) 490-6650
42nd St. & Vanderbilt Ave. in Midtown E.

Take a casual business client or out-of-town visitor to this "New York sight worth seeing" for "the freshest oysters in town"—at least 20 different types each day—"outstanding" lobster bisque, "luscious" clam chowder, and over 80 wines by the glass, along with "a feeling of New York as it was" (back in 1913, to be precise). The vaultlike room is "loud, loud, loud," and the food is "shamelessly overpriced, but what can you do? It has no peers in Manhattan."

Grand Ticino

$31

228 Thompson St. (212) 777-5922
bet. Bleecker & W. 3rd Sts. in the Washington Sq. Area

"You don't stay in business this long by accident" says one master of the obvious of this 75-year-old Village Italian: It's just "good, old-fashioned graciousness." "An impressive wine selection" and "good food" accompany the "quaint ambiance," that, though "somewhat faded," still works.

Grange Hall

$32

50 Commerce St. (212) 924-5246
bet. Seventh Ave. S. & Hudson in the W. Village

"Hip and homey," this West Village Organic American has updated its original speakeasy location as far as the New Deal of the 40s: It's nestled in a tree-lined cul-de-sac, and you get style, comfort and "excellent" cocktails in the bargain. "The perfect first date place," it's also many voters top pick for rehashing the evening over weekend brunch. P.S. Don't confuse "organic" with "healthy": While "all homemade, of course," the menu includes items like PB&J.

Gray's Papaya

$5

2090 Broadway at 72nd St. on the U.W. Side (212) 799-0243
402 Ave. of the Americas at 9th St./Cent. Village (212) 260-3532

"They're like soup kitchens where you have to pay, and I wouldn't want it any other way," is how most participants feel about these Central Village/Upper West Side dog and drinkers. Talk about cheap, "they fill your stomach (with 50-cent hot dogs!) when you're living on quarters till payday." And for speed, the "automaton-like professionals are capable of pumping out 470 servings an hour."

Graziella
$20

41 Greenwich Ave. (Charles & Perry/W. Village) (212) 255-5972
Any place voters refer to as "best value" and "inexpensive" for a
West Village Italian, you should jump at the chance to try it.
"Warm and cozy," its a "homey spot" for "a great simple meal"
"with friendly service." One drawback is that in a room this size,
the smoke gets in your eyes. Credit cards aren't a problem and they
serve beer and wine, so don't worry about lugging your own.

Great Jones St. Cafe
$19

54 Great Jones St. (212) 674-9304
bet. Bowery & Lafayette in the E. Village
Supplying "great hangover food" (they'll also supply the hangover),
this East Village Cajun/Creole (with Southern and Traditional
American fare) has quite a following for its 35-seat room. Voted
into the Top 20 Dives, the award-winning jukebox, ranked number
three in the book, is an attraction. The "cajun martinis will send you
to spice heaven," and the spinach quesadillas are also standouts.
"They're nicer to regulars, but it's worth becoming one."

Great Shanghai
$22

27 Division St. at Bowery in Chinatown (212) 966-7663
Kidnap a friend and take 'em to Chinatown for some "authentic,
Shanghai-style" Chinese food. The fare is "good but a little on the
greasy side," and it has possibly the "best Peking duck in NY."
Though the high-styling room is a bit down-at-heel, and the staff a
bit loutish, don't stop at the duck—"try it all."

Greenhouse Cafe
$28

NY Vista Hotel, Marriott World Trade Center (212) 938-9100
bet. Vesey & West Sts. in the Financial District
Hocus Pocus. A magician dazzles the kids on Sunday at this simple,
adequate American eatery in the Financial District. Its convenient
hours (and valet parking) make for easy access—breakfast is served
from 6:30 a.m. during the week.

Greenwich Cafe
$19

75 Greenwich Ave. (212) 255-5450
at Seventh Ave. S. & 11th St. in the W. Village
In two years, this "oddball" Village Eclectic has made its business
appealing to music lovers and night owls. "Always open when you
need them," it's "one of the few places you can enjoy at 4 a.m. on a
Tuesday." A "hip (but pushy) staff" pushes only so-so food.

Grifone
$45

244 E. 46th St. (212) 490-7275
bet. Second & Third Aves. in Midtown E.
A bit like classic jazz, Grifone has been noodling along for ten
years in its own "classy" way. Everything is "top-notch" and
"well-run," though mellow, making it "good for special business
lunches" (read: high prices).

FOOD   ROOM   STAFF   COST

Grotta Azzurra $33

387 Broome St. (212) 925-8775
at Mulberry St. in Little Italy
An Italian stalwart since 1908, this true-to-its-name blue den serves
up caveman-size portions of solid, standard fare—chicken
cacciatore, lobster fra diavalo, et al.—in a kitschy setting.

Grove $31

314 Bleecker St. (212) 675-9463
at Grove St. in the W. Village
One reason this West Village French/American Bistro places so high
on the outside dining list is that the outdoor space is partially enclosed
in winter. Another is that the "garden feels like a wedding reception"
(without all the pesky relatives). The best reason is the
seasonally-changing "good food, at bargain prices." Good brunch spot.

Grove Street Cafe $30

53 Grove St. (212) 924-8299
at Christopher St. in the W. Village
"Informal and elegant at the same time," this "born and bred
Village-ite" caters to late-night (till 2 a.m.) appetites with pasta,
steaks, soups, and other Continental fare. The food "makes you
swear you're home," but garden dining and live jazz give it a
"groovy" dimension Mom's may lack.

Gus' Place $31

149 Waverly Pl. (212) 645-8511
bet. Sixth Ave. & Christopher in the Washington Sq. Area
Here's a little bit of Greece in the West Village for lovers of "very
good Mediterranean" food. The "lovely space" invites "dancing and
music" so "Friday Greek night is a must." The pre-theater menu is
20% off, though "prices are going up." But the "menu is so
appealing" and the service "excellent," that diners keep coming
back to this "local treasure."

Habib's Place $10

438 E. 9th St. (212) 979-2243
bet. Ave. A & First Ave. in the E. Village
A "jazzy fast-food midget" (seating only eight!) that features very
good, very fresh Mediterranean/Middle Eastern eats, along with
"outrageously boss tunes," till 2 a.m. Watch for "pleasant
occasional visits by Iggy Pop," whose lust for life apparently is
matched by a lust for "the best falafel this side of Marrakesh."

Halcyon $44

Rihga Royal Hotel, 151 W. 54th St. (212) 468-8888
bet. Sixth & Seventh Aves. in Midtown W.
"Elegant" to a fault, this gorgeous room in the Rihga Royal Hotel
deserves more attention than it gets. The $32.50 prix fixe offers a
"great pre-theater value," and the "nice staff" will see that your
needs are properly accommodated. As for the innovative American
food, "there are always new items on the menu," and the quality is
"fabulous." Live nightly piano music is a suave added touch.

Hallo Berlin

$19

402 W. 51st St. at Ninth Ave. in Clinton (212) 541-6248
This "very nice" Clinton spot serves up authentic working-class
("fair") German food. "Sausage lovers" are encouraged to drop by
for a meal which will be "a remembrance hours after they leave."
Lower your expectations.

Hamachi

$27

34 E. 20th St. (212) 420-8608
bet. Broadway & Park Ave. S. in the Flatiron District
"Be sure and try a dinosaur roll" (sounds like a dance) at this
Gramercy/Flatiron-area Japanese. The "fresh sushi is served by the
friendliest chef" (how fresh is the dinosaur?). But beware, "the
prices change between lunch and dinner" for the same menu.

Hamburger Harry's

$17

157 Chambers St. (212) 267-4446
bet. Greenwich St. & W. Broadway in TriBeCa
145 W. 45th St. (212) 840-0566
 bet. Broadway & Sixth Aves. in Midtown W.
Burgers and burritos in faux-'50s settings make these the default for
many voters when they're "stuck in Midtown" or hanging out in
TriBeCa. While voters rated the burgers here No. 3 on the poll, not
everyone is impressed: Though "lots of toppings" are available,
they're a bit more expensive than other burger joints. "McDonald's
goes to graduate school."

Hangawi

$37

12 E. 32nd St. bet. Fifth & Madison/Murray Hill (212) 213-0077
"Simply divine," this "peaceful and refreshing," strictly vegetarian
Korean "dining experience" wows cognoscenti with its "lovely
setting," "unusual" and "exquisite" "Asian vegetarian" food, and
"attentive" service. Sure, you must "bend your knees and stoop at
strange tables," but this "serenely beautiful" "exotic" place is
"extraordinary, even for New York."

Harbour Lights

$34

Pier 17, South St. (212) 227-2800
at Fulton St. at the South St. Seaport
The "beautiful room" and "great views" of the Brooklyn Bridge and
Manhattan skyline are enough to keep this big room busy; well the
music and wine help too, but the American fare doesn't compare
report our voters. There's a new chef on board, John Loughran of
the River Cafe, and so change may be coming. In the meantime
stick with the "good seafood." Sure, it's pricey but people who visit
the Seaport can usually afford it.

Hard Rock Cafe

$23

221 W. 57th St. (212) 489-6565
bet. Seventh Ave. & Broadway in Midtown W.
"What more needs to be said?" It's a Hard Rock." Translation:
"overrated, overcrowded," with food that begs the question "why do
people pay for this?"

FOOD ROOM STAFF COST

Harglo's Cafe

974 Second Ave. bet. 51st & 52nd/Midtown E. (212) 759-9820
What does "New Orleans style" mean in NYC? At this
"comfortable" East Midtown Cajun, it means a "crowded bar up
front" and "mellow tables in back." "Unpretentious," it's a "good
place to take out-of-towners who are afraid of New York."

Harley Davidson Cafe

 $25

1370 Ave. of the Americas at 56th/Midtown W. (212) 245-6000
Documenting 90 years of Harley Davidson history in an interactive
environment using state-of-the-art audiovisual equipment (as
management is wont to describe it), this "interesting restaurant" is "an
acceptable backup when other theme restaurants are too crowded"
(yikes!) in a "kinky" setting stuffed with "real biker" memorabilia.
The "decibel levels are unmeasurable," the prices are a "wallet burn,"
and the place is a "tourist trap," so only "if the kids insist."

Harry Cipriani's

 $58

Sherry Netherland, 781 Fifth Ave. (212) 753-5566
bet. 59th & 60th Sts. in Midtown E.
"Great people-watching" and wonderful food is yours at this
"international classic" serving Contemporary Italian fare in the
Sherry Netherland Hotel. The handsome dining room and waiters
who "always seem like they actually care about you" tend to attract
a "sophisticated crowd." Cipriani's is one of the best places in
Midtown to meet for a drink. Harry has been "doing it right for
decades"—and it shows.

Harry's at Hanover Square

 $34

1 Hanover Sq. (212) 425-3412
bet. Pearl & Jones Sts. in the Financial District
"A manly kind of place," but women who appreciate a "great
history" like it, too. Long a "refuge for Wall Street traders," Harry's
pleases "testosterone" types with its "dark panelled bar,"
"stock-market ticker," and "cigar-smoking" "old-boys'-club"
atmosphere—the "basic" but "nonetheless satisfying" Continental
food" is beside the point. Detractors call it "stodgy" and suggest
that "Morton's will someday kill it."

Harry's Burritos

230 Thompson St. (Bleecker & W. 4th/Wash. Sq.) (212) 260-5588
241 Columbus Ave. at 71st St. on the U.W. Side (212) 580-9494
If Benny's is the benchmark, our voters say this Upper West Sider
is simply "better." Few seats, but portions big enough for two (the
"biggest damned burritos" are "healthy" if only average tasting),
with some of the "best salsa in town" ("but they charge you for it!).."

Hasaki

 $32

210 E. 9th St. bet. Second & Third/E. Village (212) 473-3327
"Be ready to wait in line" for "the best sushi in the East Village"—and
very likely 'the very best sushi you can afford without an expense
account." it's all "fresh, delicious" and "very authentic." When you
walk through the door, you "step down into heaven."

Hasta la Pasta

418 Sixth Ave. at W. 9th St. in the W. Village (212) 473-6608
With fast, "fresh pasta" and a "convenient location" this West Villager has its share of boosters. A popular write-in that's a "great lunch spot," it boasts "inexpensive specials" and a "relaxed atmosphere."

Hatsuhana

 $40

17 E. 48th St. bet. Fifth & Madison/Midtown E. (212) 355-3345
"Sushi so fresh" that "waiting for a table is worth it" at this "upscale Japanese place" that rates among the best in town." Though the ambiance is a little "antiseptic" and the prices a little high, Hatsuhana's many fans suggest that this is "the standard to measure" against the sushi and sashimi at any other restaurant in town.

Haveli

 $23

100 Second Ave. bet. 5th & 6th Sts./E. Village (212) 982-0533
"High-end Indian" food puts Haveli "a notch above" many other "Little India" contenders. Though it's "a little pricey," "nice surroundings" and an "eager to please" staff make this one "better than most."

Heartland Brewery

 $22

35 Union Sq. W. bet. 16th & 17th Sts. at Union Sq. (212) 645-3400
To the "young crowd," this "happening" Union Square "brewpub" is a "welcome addition to the neighborhood," offering "above average" "pub grub," "nice" "friendly" atmosphere, and a heartwarming selection of brewski (especially the "oatmeal stout"). Older types say "ho-hum," it's a "generic," "overrated," "wanna-be European." In any case, "the beer is better than the food."

Heidelberg

 $27

1648 Second Ave. bet. 85th & 86th/U.E. Side (212) 628-2332
Who would have thunk it? They give good sausage at this Yorkville joint—"one of the last old-time Germans." It's a "good time" kind of place: sample the "great beer selection," or try the chocolate fondue—"it's fab for two." Bring the kids, maybe they'll pick up a little German. Can you say strudel? "Need more be said?"

Helianthus

 $22

48 MacDougal St. bet. Prince & Houston/SoHo (212) 598-0387
The "weird menu" at this little SoHo spot is "creative and delicious," and consists of Chinese/Japanese-inspired Vegetarian dishes, served in a "beautiful sunflower decor," by a "very pleasant staff."

Henry's End

 $31

44 Henry St., at Cranberry in Brooklyn (718) 834-1776
If you find a trip to Brooklyn Heights exciting, wait till you try the menu at this adventurous American (located in a 100-year-old landmark building) featuring annual wild game festivals, elusive elk chops, and "an exotic beer for every exotic animal." The "terrific" food and "greatest staff on earth" make up for the "cramped" quarters and add up to "an amazing meal at an unassuming place."

	FOOD	ROOM	STAFF	COST

Hi-Life

$23

477 Amsterdam Ave. at 83rd St./Upper West Side (212) 787-7199
1340 First Ave. at 72nd St. on the Upper East Side (212) 249-3600
A cocktail lounge theme and "Hollywood booths" attract party people to these chrome-and-neon spots, and their throbbing heads inspire low ratings. Their advice: "Sit outside," especially on weekends, keep it simple and have "low expectations." Only then might the American fare, served in "grungy surroundings," be a pleasant surprise.

Home

$32

20 Cornelia St. (212) 243-9579
bet. Bleecker & W. 4th Sts. in the Washington Sq. Area
"The best small American restaurant in NYC," say voters of this teeny, 10-table Village spot that doubles in size when the weather's nice and the garden is open. The one complaint: "too damned small! The food was incredible but I got stuck in the booth!" Go with "local place" expectations, and your meal will be "too good to be true." "One of the best brunches you'll ever have" is accompanied by "homemade bloodies with freshly grated horseradish."

Honest Food Cafe

$22

100 W. 67th St. (212) 496-4000
bet. Broadway & Columbus Ave. on the Upper West Side
With cafeteria-style service, custom-made pizzas and mosaic-tile decor, Honest Food elevates itself to an upscale hole-in-the-wall. While the food may be "good," some find the Mediterannean salads and other cuisine "overpriced," especially for takeout.

Honmura An

$45

170 Mercer St. (212) 334-5253
bet. Prince & Houston Sts. in SoHo
The "healthy" handmade soba is the draw at this "elegant" and "romantic" SoHo Japanese and the catalyst for its vault into our Top 200. The abundant menu with vegetarian choices doesn't hurt either. Voters say the "beautiful" and "tranquil" room is "a different world." What's not so different are the SoHo prices which many say are "overpriced" especially for noodles, but fans say its "money well spent."

Hosteria Fiorella

$36

1081 Third Ave. (212) 838-7570
bet. 63rd & 64th Sts. on the Upper East Side
"Consistently good," "fresh and inventive" Northern Italian food (heavy on the seafood specialties) and a "great antipasto" make Hosteria Fiorella an "Upper East Side gem." The "friendly" staff and cheerful, comfortable dining room make for a "good dining experience," and it's especially "wonderful" for weekend brunch.

Hot Tomato

676 Ave. of the Americas (212) 691-3535
at 21st St. in Chelsea
This new Chelsea offering serves American comfort food till the wee hours. Let us know what you think on next year's poll.

= SUPERIOR = EXCELLENT = V. GOOD = GOOD

Hourglass Tavern

$24

373 W. 46th St. (212) 265-2060
at Ninth Ave. in Clinton

Ah, Romance. An American/Italian in Clinton that's touted as "a perfect place for a first date" must pass the Romac Reviewers' adjective test: how about: "enchanting," "unique, old New Yorky," "quaint." The prix fixe lunch and pre-theater menus are cheap and the food is "fresh," but the catch is the hourglass in the name; "they throw you out in 60 minutes." Well, you won't miss the show.

House of Vegetarian

68 Mott St. at Canal St. in Chinatown (212) 226-6572

It's soybean central at this Chinese Vegetarian write-in. A "large menu" with "many many choices" of "interesting fake meat dishes" served in a "dim, comfortable" atmosphere makes it a Chinatown favorite for "jury duty" and a "gotta-try for vegetarians." No credit cards.

HSF

$21

46 Bowery at Canal in Chinatown (212) 689-6969

You can strike up dinner conversation about what those letters stand for as you eat at this Chinese dive. The beef is that this is a place for "good dim sum" and the "Mongolian hot pot is a deal." The "language barrier keeps the waitress away" so bring a native if possible. It's "gone downhill" but in general it's a "reliable choice."

Hudson Bar & Books

636 Hudson St. bet. Horatio & Jane Sts./W. Vill. (212) 229-2642
(See review for Beekman Bar & Books.)

Hudson Corner Cafe

570 Hudson St. (212) 229-2727
bet. W. 11th & Perry Sts. in the W. Village

Sidewalk seats, "solid food," and "friendly" service make this West Village Italian/American a "perfect neighborhood" cafe. Locals appreciate the "varied menu," "great prices" and casual atmosphere where customer art lines the walls.

Hudson Grill

$27

350 Hudson St. (212) 691-9060
at King St. in SoHo

Multi-level, SoHo, microbrews, corporate parties, poetry readings, comedy nights, theme nights, cigar and pipe smoking... whew! That's a lot to go through just for a burger or a taco for lunch.

Hudson Place

$23

538-40 Third Ave. (212) 686-6660
at 36th St. in Murray Hill

This Midtown East/Murray Hill "neighborhood hangout" is "always packed," but it's the crowd that actually puts the fun and friendly atmosphere over the top. "Good reliable" Italian/American food "in a nice setting...and so cheap!"

FOOD	ROOM	STAFF	COST

Hudson River Club $51

4 World Financial Ctr., 250 Vesey St. (212) 786-1500
at West St. in the Financial District
"The food, the service, and the view are equally spectacular" at this favorite spot for expense-accounting business lunchers and lavish lovebirds alike. Chef de cuisine James Porteus recently took over the kitchen: Let's hope he continues the "extraordinary" tradition. He will be helped by "glorious" water views and "wonderful" service, which inspire a nobody-does-it-better cheer: "Go, New York, go!"

Hue $18

210 E. 23rd St. bet. Second & Third/Gramercy (212) 696-4779
"Ample portions" of "tasty and fresh" Vietnamese food at "budget prices" make this "simple" little spot a "great" addition to the "neighborhood." "Low key" means "so so" food, and the room and ambiance is defined by the "formica setting."

Hunan Balcony $18

1417 Second Ave. at 74th St. on the U.E. Side (212) 517-2088
2596 Broadway at 98th St. on the U.W. Side (212) 865-0400
Wildly diverse comments about these joints prove that quality is in the mouth of the chopstick holder. Some think these spots are the "best all-around Chinese," while others say they're "run-of-the-mill," and call eating there "feeding—not dining."

Hunan Garden $25

1 Mott St. at Bowery in Chinatown (212) 732-7270
Some voters have been frequenting this Chinatown standby since they were "old enough to remember birthdays." With a row of solid scores, it's a reliable choice for Chinese standards.

Hunan Park $16

721 Columbus Ave. at 95th St. on the U.W. Side (212) 222-6511
235 Columbus bet. 72nd & 73rd Sts./U.W. Side (212) 724-4411
From a large field of contenders in the Upper West Side Szechuan sweepstakes, Hunan Park emerges with scores that are neither here, nor are they there. Comments are generally favorable, especially for the "great lunch specials."

Hurley's $32

1240 Sixth Ave. at 49th St. in Midtown W. (212) 765-8981
This "great old bar" is "perfect for an after-work" drink, but it's not distinguished at all by the "average" American fare (heavy on the steak and seafood). The bottom line, Hurley's is a "hangout for Rockefeller Center media" types and a "nice place to meet friends and go somewhere else."

Ici $40

19 E. 69th St. bet. Park & Madison/U.E. Side (212) 794-6419
The "delightful," low-traffic environs make this Upper East Side French a nice place to sit and talk about the "interesting menu," but be warned, there's not much room" and "no waiting area."

Ideal $17

322 E. 86th St. (212) 737-0795
bet. First & Second Aves. on the Upper East Side
Sprechen zi Deutche? According to Romac Reporters the
"respectable decor at the new location lacks the authenticity and
character of the original." That goes double for the food and service.
Then again it's cheap.

Il Bagatto $22

192 E. 2nd St. (212) 228-0977
bet. Aves. A & B in the E. Village
"Brava!" say fans who "haven't had pasta like this since Italy." It's a
"favorite new restaurant" in "Alphabet City," with "quite authentically
Italian" food, "cool people," and a "hip atmosphere." "The entire
neighborhood has discovered it," making this one a tough res.

Il Buco $32

47 Bond St. (212) 533-1932
bet. Bowery & Lafayette St. in the E. Village
This "eclectic" Pan-Mediterranean restaurant-cum-antique store
with a five-page wine list may sound like it's biting off more than it
can chew. Noted as a "great place to seduce someone," it's rated in
the top 100 for its romantique, antique, candle and kerosene
ambiance, which one voter attributes to "a date that changed my
life." If the former doesn't clinch the evening, the "great,"
"thoughtfully prepared food" should. Hey, if you're not hungry, go
antique shopping! Yes, they're for sale.

Il Cantinori $46

32 E. 10th St. (212) 673-6044
bet. University Pl. & Broadway in the Central Village
The "warm," "wonderful" rustic Tuscan setting and "outstanding"
food make this "very classy," "very elegant" Northern Italian
restaurant on a tree-lined street in the Village a "fabulous place to
take an out-of-town client." Though a few suggest that it's "gone a
bit downhill lately," Il Cantinori still gets "really good" marks
across the board. Patio dining in warm weather is a plus.

Il Corallo $22

172 Prince St. (212) 941-7119
bet. Thompson & Sullivan Sts. in SoHo
"A little cramped, but the food" at this SoHo Italian is "so good,
and the prices are terrific." "Tight tables" make for a "noisy" room,
but "for the price, this is a wonderful informal restaurant." In all,
folks find this more than just an okay Corallo.

Il Cortile $37

125 Mulberry St. bet. Canal & Hester/Little Italy (212) 226-6060
"Ask for the back room" when you "make a reservation" at this
"top-notch" Northern and Southern Italian. Not many spots in Little
Italy have chefs trained at the Culinary Institute, and chef Michael
DiGiorgio brings a fresh level of creativity that inspires some guests
to call it "the best Italian, period!"

FOOD ROOM STAFF COST

Il Fornaio
$24

132-A Mulberry St. (212) 226-8306
bet. Grand & Hester Sts. in Little Italy
Sidewalk dining and a "homey atmosphere" at this Little Italy joint are just part of the story. The traditional Southern Italian food is downright "excellent," including delicious pizza and baked ziti that's "the best in town." All this and "good, cheap lunches," too—what more could you ask?

Il Gabbiano
$37

232 E. 58th St. (212) 754-1033
bet. Second & Third Aves. in Midtown E.
"Rather old world" and "somewhat stuffy," it's true, but this "quiet and intimate" Midtown Italian is good to know about "if you're in the neighborhood." "Very tasty food," "attentive" service, and a "romantic atmosphere" get good marks, but the fact that it's "not overly busy" make Il Gabbiano worth a try.

Il Giglio
$50

81 Warren St. (212) 571-5555
bet. W. Broadway & Greenwich St. in TriBeCa
Open for lunch and dinner, this classy and understated TriBeCa Italian is tasty but "expensive for what it is." With the same owners as Il Mulino, it has a lot to live up to. Underwhelmed surveyors say it's "unspectacular" and "disappointing."

Il Menestrello
$43

14 E. 52nd St. (212) 421-7588
bet. Fifth & Madison Aves. in Midtown E.
Ssshhhhhh. Rumor has it this East Midtown is a top sleeper. With excellent ratings across the board, it's a great bet for a quiet evening of spectacular fish and pasta prepared Italian style. Credit cards Si!

Il Monello
$48

1460 Second Ave. (212) 535-9310
bet. 76th & 77th Sts. on the Upper East Side
This very highly rated Italian gets surprisingly few comments from our supporters—perhaps a function of the steep prices. Too bad, it has some of "the best" Contemporary Italian food around, with an interesting menu showcasing the specialties of Tuscany, plus elegant, flower-filled quarters, and an excellent staff. A "good bet," to say the least.

Il Mulino
$54

86 W. 3rd St. (212) 673-3783
bet. Sullivan & Thompson Sts. in the Washington Sq. Area
The top Italian in our book, Il Mulino wows fans with its "heavenly Italian food" and ambiance "so traditional you feel like part of the family." "Plan on a long wait," "fabulous" service, and "unbelievable" prices, but for such a "magnificent dining experience," it's "worth it." Complaints center on "cramped" quarters and a certain attitude about "reservations." Dress up.

Il Nido $52

251 E. 53rd St. (212) 319-6122, (212) 753-8450
bet. Second & Third Aves. in Midtown E.

This East Midtown Northern Italian is "superb but expensive." The quiet dining room is a "great space," the service is "exceptional," and "the food is so good you'll want to order everything," "you must go." Il Nido has been around since before the Italian invasion and practice, in this case, has made perfection.

Il Tinello $49

16 W. 56th St. (212) 245-4388
bet. Fifth & Sixth Aves. in Midtown W.

If every restaurant were as hospitable as this Midtown Northern Italian, New York might be able to kick the rudeness rep. The "amazingly attentive service" complements the delicious food and quiet ambiance. It's "a great lunch spot," a less expensive way to try this "sleeper."

Il Toscanaccio $49

7 E. 59th St. (212) 935-3535
at Fifth Ave. in Midtown E.

Pino Luongo conquers the post-Crate and Barrel shopping scene (and a whole lot more) with this informal Tuscan remake of Amarcord. It's a "pretty spot," with its bleached-wood floors and pots of herbs on the walls, with suave service and a well-executed, homey-sophisticated menu heavy on the interesting pastas. All in all, this "jewel" is a "great find."

Il Vagabondo $30

351 E. 62nd St. (212) 832-9221
bet. First & Second Aves. on the Upper East Side

The food, to most, is only "average," and the staff could stand to be "more attentive." So what's the attraction? The indoor bocce court. You can play "before, during and after your meal," and while the ambiance is "homey," bocce attracts all kinds and the crowd can sometimes get "weird."

Inagiku $45

Waldorf-Astoria, 111 E. 49th St. (212) 355-0440
bet. Park & Lexington Aves. in Midtown E.

Special kudos for the service that help make this an "all around fine dining experience." Some call this "the place for tempura" but "other dishes" are "also very good" and the sushi is "extra fresh."

Indian Oven $22

200 W. 84th St. (212) 874-6900
bet. Broadway & Amsterdam Ave. on the Upper West Side

This little Indian, miles north of Little India, has been cooking "good," "authentic" Indian cuisine for 21 years. While undistinguished, it's reliable and the closest thing to Bombay north of 58th Street.

FOOD ROOM STAFF COST

India Pavilion
$20

240 W. 56th St. (212) 489-0035
bet. Broadway & Eighth Ave. in Midtown W.
While this Midtown West Northern Indian cites value quotes from press over the years, our voters call it "greasy," and say "you get what you pay for." "Overpriced" for Indian food, it will never take the place of a quick trip to Sixth Street.

INdiGo
$31

142 W.10th St. (212) 691-7757
bet. Sixth Ave. & Seventh Ave. S. in the W. Village
A popular food magazine recently named chef Scott Bryan the best in the City; while our reviewers are fond of his creative cooking, they instead choose to laud the "fair prices," but note that seating is tight and the menu is "limited." And while the food and service are "lovely," the trendies have latched on: "almost laughably hip."

Indochine
$39

430 Lafayette St. (212) 505-5111
bet. E. 4th St. & Astor Pl. in the E. Village
"Just another scene" to some (though past its trendy prime), everyone agrees you should "go for the sights" but can't come to a decision on the French/Vietnamese cooking. The East Village crowd (in the tropical decor) overcomes the slipping kitchen and "small portions," so you leave "hungry but happy."

In Padella
$21

145 Second Ave. at 9th St. in the E. Village (212) 598-9800
The manager won't take credit cards or reservations at this romantic East Villager, but the kitchen will dish out "standard" Italian food in a "nice atmosphere" atmosphere. Service can be "very erratic," but sidewalk seating and reasonable prices make it popular with Gen Xers and good for dates.

Intermezzo
$22

202 Eighth Ave. (212) 929-3433
bet. 20th & 21st Sts. in Chelsea
"Great lunch deals" at "very reasonable" prices (check out the "salads" and "penne al pomodoro") are the attractions at this attractive little Italian storefront in an up-and-coming Chelsea location. "Sit in front" and "watch the boys go by" at what voters call "a great deal."

Internet Cafe
$18

82 E. 3rd St. (212) 614-0747
bet. First & Second Aves. in the E. Village
"Good networking" is the appeal to wonks who like to combine "two favorite things": "surfing the net" and "stuffing" their faces. The "bland" American cafe food is beside the point for this crowd—the "helpful staff" is "good if you need guidance," and the computer set-up is "internationally acclaimed." But as someone pointed out, what's the purpose of going out if you're only going to "lose yourself in a computer screen"?

▮ = SUPERIOR ▮ = EXCELLENT ▬ = V. GOOD ▬ = GOOD

Ipanema

 $27

13 W. 46th St. (212) 730-5848
bet. Fifth & Sixth Aves. in Midtown W.
"Try the steak with the fried egg on top." If you're in Midtown and
you're homesick for Portugal or Brazil or even if you aren't,
"wonderful, superb, original food," served by "delightful waiters,"
in a "pleasant and relaxing atmosphere," can't be all bad. Of course,
that depends on what you think of: "a bit pricey, but worth it."

Isabella's

 $31

359 Columbus Ave. at 77th St./U.W. Side (212) 724-2100
This "people-watching" paradise on Columbus reminds voters why
they "don't live Uptown," but if "lively" is your thing, Isabella's is
your place. The service "depends on the waiter" and the "imaginative"
Italian food is all over the block ("surprisingly delicious" to "boring.")
"Every blind date I've had has taken me here": Since there are "no
quiet intimate dinners," at Isabella's, you might want to give a copy of
the Romac Report to your matchmaker, dahling.

Island Spice

 $22

402 W. 44th St. bet. Ninth & Tenth Aves. in Clinton (212) 765-1737
"Tiny" and "pretty," this "authentic," theater-periphery "gem"
serves up "Caribbean flair," including Jamaican specialties and
"jerk the way it was meant to be." Naysayers feel it's "interesting
for one visit," but the "food won't sustain your attention."

Iso

 $33

175 Second Ave. at 11th St. in the E. Village (212) 777-0361
Fans say you "can't get better sushi for the price" than at this "tiny," way
"hip" East Village specialist in "fresh." "Be prepared for a wait," a
"cramped" table, and busy "rude" waitstaff—but the "fish is wonderful"
and you can "afford the prices." That's all that matters, right?

Ithaka

 $31

48 Barrow St. (212) 727-8886
bet. Seventh Ave. S. & Bedford St. in the W. Village
It "feels like you're in Greece" from a table in the "beautiful"
glassed-in garden greenhouse or the dark, atmospheric bar. The food is
"satisfyingly authentic," but is it "the best Greek food in Manhattan?"
No, say voters, who are "disappointed after all the raves."

I Tre Merli

 $36

463 W. Broadway bet. Houston & Prince in SoHo (212) 254-8699
Look at this name enough and it morphs into something akin to
Itchy Mary. Voters are itchy: "People don't go for the food!" Okay,
okay! "You're paying for the atmosphere" at SoHo's "Eurotrash
central." It's "a stylish place" that "feels like a party in a cellar"
(note the wall to wall wine racks), but it's much too noisy and
overcrowded unless you're there for the "trendy crowd," and the
"lousy service." If you're desperate to check out this "SoHo scene"
it's "best in summer when the doors open up to the outside," or go
for the "wine, wine, wine."

I. Trulli

	FOOD	ROOM	STAFF	COST

I. Trulli — $43

122 E. 27th St. (212) 481-7372
bet. Lexington Ave. & Park Ave. S. in Gramercy

I. Trulli is "a real find" for "nicely prepared," "fresh" Southern Italian food, with a "delightful" garden, "romantic" fireplaces, and a "truly caring, knowledgeable staff" under the alert direction of owner Nicola Marzovilla. Interesting "Sardinian specialties" and a well-informed wine list mean this one "really clicks." In short, this place that "takes you out of the city" "could be your home."

Jackson Diner — $15

37-03 74th St. (718) 672-1232
bet. Roosevelt & 37th in Queens

Decor-wise, the "best in Queens" redefines the word "plain," but withhold judgment until you dive into the "delicious homestyle Indian food." It used to be a diner; the owners kept the name and lack of look and simply changed the kitchen. The cheap prices are the real deal for huge helpings including plenty of veggie options, and a "killer lunch buffet." So "forget East Sixth Street Indian dives, this is the place."

Jackson Hole — $17

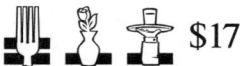

517 Columbus Ave. at 85th St. on the U.W. Side (212) 362-5177
6935 Astoria Blvd., at 70th St. in Queens (718) 204-7070
232 E. 64th St. bet. 2nd & 3rd Aves./U.E. Side (212) 371-7187
1611 Second Ave. bet. 83rd & 84th Sts./U.E. Side (212) 737-8788
1270 Madison Ave. at 91st St. in Carnegie Hill (212) 427-2820
521 Third Ave. at 35th St. in Murray Hill (212) 679-3264

The original location in Murray Hill wins New York's Best Burger crown, and the rest of these American ersatz '50s diners are consistently good, too. Their expectations having been lowered by the word "hole" in the name, voters are pleasantly surprised by large portions (though thick patties are not to everyone's taste). Beer by the pitcher and a good jukebox make these joints cosmopolitan Beefsteak Charlie's.

Jai Ya Thai — $22

396 Third Ave. at 28th St. in Gramercy (212) 889-1330
8111 Broadway, at 81st St. Queens (718) 651-1330

"Crowded (but rightly so)," these Thai restaurants are consistent from one to the next, though the newer Gramercy location is even more "claustrophobic." The food is "very good," "one of the best Thais in New York," though we get a lot of spice warnings here: "keep a water pitcher on the table" seems the best advice.

Janine's — $26

302 Columbus Ave. (212) 501-7500
bet. 74th & 75th Sts. on the Upper West Side

"Satisfactory" homestyle American food (pot roast, roast chicken, and lemon pound cake) at prices that love the family makes this spiffed-up luncheonette a "welcome newcomer" to the Upper West Side. Service is "lackadaisical," but Janine's has got a nice, comfy neighborhood feel.

= SUPERIOR = EXCELLENT = V. GOOD = GOOD

Japonica $31

100 University Pl. (212) 243-7752
at 12th St. in the Central Village
This gem is pricey, but it boasts some of the freshest "out of this world" "butteriest" sushi in the city. To avoid weekend crowds "get your out-of-town client to take you" during the week. If you do have to wait, do it outside (weather permitting) and watch the Village-ites who are as exotic as the fish "flown in daily from Japan."

Jaraf $37

720 Second Ave. bet. 38th & 39th/Murray Hill (212) 696-1654
Coming up on its second birthday, this "rustic and elegant" American bistro specializes in hearty food and cordial service. Located in the northern section of Murray Hill, it's "relaxed and homey," with "intimate" ambiance. Closed Monday.

Jean Claude $32

137 Sullivan St. bet. Prince & Houston in SoHo (212) 475-9232
Close quarters and a "crowded and smoky" room only enhance the "left bank feel" of this SoHo French: It's "unpretentious," the "staff is funky" and the food is simply "excellent." Some say the menu could "change more often," but that you "can't go wrong with the breaded skate" and the "excellent meat dishes." Dinner only.

Jean Lafitte $45

68 W. 58th St. at Sixth Ave. in Midtown W. (212) 751-2323
"Classic French bistro fare" that captures "solid" ratings is still the appeal of this West Midtown boite. There are a couple of good prix fixe deals, and it's handy to Carnegie Hall.

Jekyll & Hyde $23

1409 Ave. of the Americas (212) 541-9517
bet. 57th & 58th in Midtown W.
91 Seventh Ave. S. (212) 989-7701
bet. Barrow & Grove Sts. in the W. Village
"The bathroom behind the bookcase is worth it" to some, who find these kitschy, Gothic American theme park restaurants (sisters to Night Gallery) a first choice for tourists. They rank high for such features as out-of-towners, beers on tap and exotic experiences, but a taste of the food turns our voters into snarling beasts. Special effects and character actors make them "a little piece of Orlando, right in Manhattan. Ugh!" "My 16-year-old cousin from Jersey loves these places. Enough said?"

Jerry's Diner $25

101 Prince St. bet. Mercer & Green Sts. in SoHo (212) 966-9464
While maintaining the feel of the former coffee shop space, Jerry Joseph updated the concept of American diner food ten years ago, and now has something of a following. "Too upscale for a diner," it's "definitely a spot to celebrity watch," though "long waits for brunch" and spotty staff detract from the SoHo cool.

FOOD ROOM STAFF COST

Jewel of India

$30

15 W. 44th St. (212) 869-5544
bet. Fifth & Sixth Aves. in Midtown W.
"Fancy Indian" food make for a "great pre-theater" alternative to the area's Continental/Italian standards. The "beautiful," "classy" setting (call it "Mogul/bordello") and "quick" service are welcome attributes. There's also an early-evening cocktail hour and lunch specials that make Jewel of India "a great deal for business lunches."

Jezebel

$38

630 Ninth Ave. (212) 582-1045
at 45th St. in Clinton
"Upscale Soul Food" in a "funky," "pretty," "Southern fantasy" atmosphere make Jezebel a "really fun place." True to its name, it's the "sexiest place to eat in NY," all dark lighting and intimate seating. The great-looking staff, sporting everything from "dresses to leggings," is "friendly," and as for the food ("good ribs," "great she-crab soup," and "excellent collard greens and black-eyed peas"), it's jes' the "tastiest."

J.G. Melon

$23

1291 Third Ave. (212) 744-0585
at 74th St. on the Upper East Side
You want a "great burger?" Go to J.G. Melon. You want other food, go to another restaurant, there are plenty in New York.

Jimmy's Neutral Corner

$22

125 W. 43rd St. (212) 764-2366
bet. Sixth Ave. & Broadway in Midtown W.
Fans say this Midtown "hangout" "has potential" but weak scores keep it on the ropes. Fun bartenders save it from a TKO.

Jimmy Sung's

$32

219 E. 44th St. (212) 682-5678
bet. Second & Third Aves. in Midtown E.
Too new to have attracted much notice, this elegantly appointed "classy Chinese" located on a convenient block offers a sophisticated Cantonese/Hunan menu, plus free evening and weekend parking, a piano bar, and various good-value prix fixe menus. The "downside is the price."

Jing Fong

20 Elizabeth St. (212) 964-5256
bet. Bayard & Canal Sts. in Chinatown
With perhaps the "largest dim sum selection" in Chinatown, this Chinese has "long lines on weekends," that can make the wait to get in up to an hour on Sundays. "Authentic," with "okay" atmosphere," it's "huge" and good enough that voters feel "lucky they have an English menu."

▤ = SUPERIOR ▤ = EXCELLENT ▤ = V. GOOD ▬ = GOOD

Jo-An Japanese

 $35

2707 Broadway (212) 678-2103
bet. 103rd & 104th Sts. in the Columbia U. Area
This Columbia U. Area Japanese is a "sleeper," with "the right attitude." It will be "very good" if it "tries a little harder."

Joe Allen

 $29

326 W. 46th St. (212) 581-6464
bet. Eighth & Ninth Aves. in Clinton
"Noisy and fun," this Theater District standby is "good for stage celebrity-watching" after a show, and has what some call the "best Caesar salad." Stick to the "dependables": salads, burgers, fries, drinks, meatloaf and soup. "Expensive for what you get."

Joe Babbington's

202 Ninth Ave. (212) 741-2148
bet. 22nd & 23rd Sts. in Chelsea
This historic Chelsea spot was once Dutch Schultz's speakeasy, but for the past six years has been serving "large portions" of "good Southern home cooking." The "good neighborhood" feeling is increased by special bargain meals and especially good barbecue.

Joe's Fish Shack

 $22

520 Columbus Ave. (212) 873-0341
at 85th St. on the Upper West Side
"Not so good" is one of the kinder cuts aimed at Joe's. Hey, read the sign. This is a "good juke joint." Daniel ain't called "Danny's Sauce Hut," now, is it?

Joe's Shanghai

 $18

9 Pell St. (212) 233-8888
bet. Bowery & Mott St. in Chinatown
13621 37th Ave., at Main St., Queens (718) 539-3838
"Ask the waitress for the authentic stuff" so you can get a taste of the "great Shanghai food," including "excellent steamed crab dumplings," shredded pork with bean curd, steamed buns, noodle dishes, and turnip cake. It's nothing to look at, and we'll see if voters think Joe's is "the most delicious restaurant of its kind in the five boroughs": There's a "new location in Chinatown." "Get there early," because there's "usually a wait."

John's of 12th Street

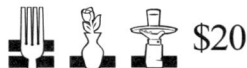 $20

302 E. 12th St. (212) 475-9531
at Second Ave. in the E. Village
With six-foot candles adorning the back room, you might think it's St. John's the Divine, but the "cozy," ancient tavern decor is anything but. This is the old stuff: Heavy Italian food with old-fashioned linen apron service and some of the "best brick oven pie in NY." This is the East Village's "Italian/American nostalgia spot."

FOOD ROOM STAFF COST

John's Pizzeria

$17

278 Bleecker St. at 7th Ave. S. in the W. Village (212) 243-1680
408 E. 64th St. bet. York & First/Upper East Side (212) 935-2895
48 W. 65th St. bet. Broadway & CPW/U.W. Side (212) 721-7001
"Can pizza" fired in a coal burning oven "get more perfect?" We could fill this entire book with the "best thin crust pizza on earth" comments. The uptown locations are "full of children," so singles say "stick with Bleecker St." N.B. The "salad with house dressing is excellent, enough for 2-3 people to share."

Jo Jo

$50

160 E. 64th St. bet. Third & Lex./U.E. Side (212) 223-5656
"Oh, the rapture that is Jo Jo," Jean-Georges Vongerichten's eponymous showplace. "Consistently good food" with "interesting variations" is yours for the taking at this "favorite" Upper East Side restaurant, with its "very, very satisfying" Contemporary French food and surefooted staff. True, the "tables are too close together" and the place can get "too noisy," but otherwise it's "the perfect place when you want to impress."

Josephina

$29

1900 Broadway bet. 63rd & 64th/U.W. Side (212) 799-1000
Folks love the "stunning," "beautiful decor" that includes giant hand-painted murals; the "courteous, concerned staff"; and a "large, bustling" atmosphere. It's "the only place a vegetarian can get a fair shake on the Upper West Side."

Josie's

$27

300 Amsterdam Ave. at 74th St. on the U.W. Side (212) 769-1212
From the fresh-wheat shots at the bar to the chemical-free milk paint on the walls, this dairy-free, free-range Upper West Side American is plenty PC, and voters, especially vegetarians, love it. Though "a bit loud," it's "like healthy, man," "a welcome alternative to the West Side pasta ghetto," and the cute and "comfortable atmosphere," though "crowded," makes it an ideal first-date spot.

Jubilee

$39

347 E. 54th St. bet. First & Second/Midtown E. (212) 888-3569
Sutton Place has a recommendation for something "cozy on a cold winter night." How about a "lovely" French bistro with offerings like "delicious mussels" and a "good veggie plate," and competent servers to boot? It can be "too dark," but that could also mean "romantic." Live jazz on Thursdays, smoking permitted.

JUdson Grill

$40

Equitable Building, 152 W. 52nd St. (212) 582-5252
bet. Sixth & Seventh Aves. in Midtown W.
Voters advise: "catch this rising star on the way up." Another giant Equitable Center spot, this New American, with 40-foot ceilings, is at once "sleek and professional" and "warm and inviting." The food is "very eclectic," and folks tell us "don't be fooled by the location: this is a serious chef with great potential." Service can be wonderful but is sometimes uneven, but JUdson will soon lose the new restaurant blues.

▤ = SUPERIOR ▤ = EXCELLENT ▤ = V. GOOD ▬ = GOOD

Jules $30

65 St. Mark's Pl. (212) 477-5560
bet. First & Second Aves. in the E. Village
"Watch out for the crazy accordion player" who "rules" at this
"very-French, country-inn-style" restaurant. Try the "clams and
white wine," or if you're looking to end a liaison dangereuse the
"pungent moules will keep you loveless for a week." But be
prepared for a "typical French place, typical French staff," because
"hey! They're rude just like real French waiters!"

Julian's $27

802 Ninth Ave. (212) 262-4800
bet. 53rd & 54th Sts. in Clinton
Can't decide whether to go Northern or Southern Italian? Do both at
this "great Ninth Avenue pre-theater spot," that boasts a "romantic"
setting, with "totally satisfying," "fresh Mediterranean cuisine," and
"moderate prices." Our under-40 voters are fonder than others,
calling it "a gem in the neighborhood," and encourage you to "bring
a date" to this "soothing and intimate" place.

Junior's

386 Flatbush Ave. Ext. (718) 852-5257
at DeKalb Ave. in Brooklyn
This landmark restaurant represents "the spirit of old Brooklyn and
the best cheesecake" to most voters, who simply wouldn't let us
leave it out of the poll. "Still, the best cheesecake in America," the
"wannabe actor staff is also very entertaining."

Kabul Cafe $23

265 W. 54th St. (212) 757-2037
bet. Broadway & Eighth Ave. in Midtown W.
Serving Middle Eastern, Afghan and Persian dishes, this little Clinton
restaurant is a "favorite" with local diners and worktime lunchers. "Great
food, and cheap too" make this "never crowded" spot "a real find."

Kang Suh $24

1250 Broadway (212) 564-6845
at 32nd St. in the Garment District
"Your clothes will remind you" of the meal at this well-rated
"Korean barbecue," where the delicious food is "grilled right at
your table." Westerners may find the ambiance lacking and the
service a little "scary," but in light of the "good," "solid Korean
food," it hardly matters.

Kan Pai $25

1482 Second Ave. (212) 772-9560
bet. 77th & 78th Sts. on the Upper East Side
According to regulars, "quality has gone down somewhat" at this
Upper East Side Japanese. Some find a "really nice atmosphere"
while others pan "makeshift decor." All agree that service could be
smoother, though late-night and sidewalk dining compensate.

FOOD ROOM STAFF COST

Karyatis

$32

35-03 Broadway, Long Island City (718) 204-0666
bet. 35th & 36th Sts.

Though a "bit run down," this Astoria Greek is "what Greek food is truly about." Award-winning lamb stew and other authentic dishes make this place "worth the trip," even if it is "swarming with children" at times. Would it be too much to ask to get a place like this in Manhattan?

Katsuhama

$25

11 E. 47th St. (212) 758-5909
bet. Fifth & Madison Aves. in Midtown E.

Tired of the diet? Japanese deep fry sound enticing? This Murray Hill spot offers "heavy and oily" food fit for an emperor, for a "reasonable price," in a not so hot room, with less than geisha service. The kids' menu is a novelty at a Japanese restaurant. Japanese wine and beer, of course.

Katz's Deli

$14

205 E. Houston St. at Ludlow St./Lower East Side (212) 254-2246

Infamous site of Meg Ryan's "I'll have what she's having" scene, this "NY legend" is also known for "heavenly hot dogs," huge "hand-carved" pastrami sandwiches, egg creams, and "undisputed" "schtick." Though many mutter that it's not the equal of "the Carnegie" or Second Avenue Deli, Katz's is the "ultimate" "Lower East Side" "institution," despite—or, more likely, because of—its "shockingly bad" "cafeteria-deli" decor, "sleazy" characters, and "authentically grumpy waiters." Oy.

Keens Steakhouse

$37

72 W. 36th St. bet. Fifth & Sixth/Garment District (212) 947-3636

Everything old is, well, old, but some of the traditions that put this place in business 110 years ago have come back into style. Like "absolutely classic cool pipes" and cigar smoking, and a relaxed "dark" "boy's-club" atmosphere, "but, sometimes, boys know how to eat." A "great place for the guys: good meat and scotch," it's a civilized after-Garden or pre-wedding place.

Keewah Yen

$33

50 W. 56th St. bet. Fifth & Sixth/Midtown W. (212) 246-0770

"Friendly" staff, "elegant" quarters, and "high-quality food" are just enough to recommend this Midtown Chinese that "time has passed by."

Kelly & Ping

$20

127 Greene St. bet. Prince & Houston Sts. in SoHo (212) 228-1212

Who would have guessed that a Pan-Asian grocery and noodle shop, that shoots for Shanghai ambiance, would become "trendy?" Or that like being in a Bangkok open-market would "add to the comfortable charm?" Some think this "no-frills" Thai, Japanese, Korean, Vietnamese and Chinese is an "exotic experience," "like a movie set for Colonial Asia."

= SUPERIOR ≣ = EXCELLENT ≣ = V. GOOD ➖ = GOOD

Khyber Pass
$19

34 St. Mark's Pl. (212) 473-0989
bet. Second & Third Aves. in the E. Village
"One of the first Afghans in NYC and still one of the best," this "authentic" East Villager remains a "dark," low-key favorite for many. "Excellent" appetizers and St. Mark's people-watching are big draws, and no one complains when the check arrives.

Kiev
$13

117 Second Ave. at 7th St. in the E. Village (212) 674-4040
"Borscht + peirogies" = "down-home" "Eastern European food, cheap and open 24 hours." That's the formula for this top 200 favorite, super popular (= congested, so expect to wait 80% of the time because you can't make reservations) top 20 dive that's "a classic in the East Village." Though it also ranks high for all sorts of things ranging from breakfast and the late menu, to dining alone and eavesdropping, it "has nothing to offer" in the way of decor, or service ("reluctant staff"). But if you're into "late night weirdo watching," you're home. Bring your own beer.

Kiiroihana
$29

23 W. 56th St. (212) 582-7499
bet. Fifth & Sixth Aves. in Midtown W.
The lunch special is a "good" choice for business diners looking for "reasonably priced" Japanese fare in Midtown.

King Crab
$27

871 Eighth Ave. (212) 765-4393
at 52nd St. in Midtown W.
No crabbing about the "interesting variety of seafood," "great" seafood platters, and Alaskan crab legs at this "romantic, relaxing" crustacean palace. If you're a penny "pincer," check out the prix fixe lunch and dinner.

Kings' Carriage House
$40

251 E. 82nd St. (212) 734-5490
bet. Second & Third Aves. on the Upper East Side
Put on that elbow-patched tweed jacket you never admit to owning and sink into the "sublimely romantic" English manor-style dining and sitting room at this year-old "very elegant" upscale Upper East Side Continental. The food shows promise and the waiters are gaining experience. Try the traditional Sunday roast dinner or leave work early one day and make a reservation for afternoon tea.

King's Plaza Diner
$16

4124 Ave. U, Brooklyn (718) 951-6700
bet. Hendrickson & Coleman
"It's a diner"—a "real diner, with real diner food"—and for some folks that's plenty. "Late hours," "awesome breakfast," and an "endless menu"—all that and "generous and kind" waitresses who will "give you anything you want" make it "quintessential." As one philosopher notes, it's a "community thing." So the food is "typical?"—it's a diner, get it?

	FOOD	ROOM	STAFF	COST

Kin Khao

$30

171 Spring St. (212) 966-3939
bet. W. Broadway & Thompson Sts. in SoHo
"Pad Thai that will make you sing": "Beautiful food" makes Kin Khao "the barometer for all Thais." "Stylized decor" and "beautiful people" are par for the course in SoHo—so, too, "noise," "crowds," and "waits"—"but the food is good."

The Kiosk

1007 Lexington Ave. (212) 535-6000
bet. 72nd & 73rd Sts. on the Upper East Side
In its first year, this Upper East Side French incarnation of Nell Campbell (yep, she's the same Nell of Nell's on 14th Street) has been slow to find its true foodie audience. Sure it attracts an entourage of trendies and model-types but let's not kid ourselves; they're more interested in striking a pose then eating the food. However, the few voters rating the food say it's "inventive," and like the place for its "Downtown atmosphere."

Kitchen Club

$31

30 Prince St. (212) 274-0025
at Mott St. in SoHo
A core group of regulars have mixed feelings about our writing up this "friendliest restaurant in the city": On the one hand, they want to keep its "really great" Japanese/European menu a secret, but on the other they love it so much they want to see it succeed.

Knickerbocker

$32

33 University Pl. (212) 228-8490
at 9th St. in the Central Village
"NYU students and their parents" converge on this "clubby, comfortable" steakhouse that's "reliable rather than great." A live jazz band brings it up another octave.

Kodnoi Thai

$29

208 E. 60th St. (212) 688-9885
bet. Second & Third Aves. in Midtown E.
There's no boom of Thai places in East Midtown, so try this one after shopping or the movies. The kitchen cooks to order (for all you nit-pickers) and offers daily specials for the experimental types. It's mid-priced but not much on service. Smoking and credit cards permitted.

Kokachin

$51

Omni Berkshire, 21 E. 52nd St. (212) 355-9300
at Madison Ave. in Midtown E.
"Excellent for a hotel restaurant," say voters, and surprise—"even New Yorkers eat there." The Mediterranean/Seafood menu has decidedly Japanese undertones, and a high percentage of Japanese diners—presumably guests of the Omni. While it "hits more than misses," it does occasionally miss, with "unexciting results," in a room that feels a bit "like a hotel lobby." More and more, business diners are finding it convenient for lunch.

Korea Palace

$30

127 E. 54th St. (212) 832-2350
bet. Lexington & Park Aves. in Midtown E.

There are a lot Korean restaurants around the city and this Midtowner is a solid choice on all counts. "Try out Korean food for business" or for "large groups of people," in a "slightly upscale" atmosphere. The prix fixe lunch is a good deal—it should be, you provide the labor, grilling your own food at your table.

Kosher Tea Room

$37

193 Second Ave. (212) 677-2947
at 12th St. in the E. Village

Our reporters are divided on whether they "love the idea" of "kosher Russian" here or would rather "go to Le Marais" when they want "expensive kosher food." For the record, the gourmet cooking "does not taste kosher," and it has "music and caters to a small crowd." With few upscale kosher choices in town, this one's worth a first look.

Krispy Kreme Donuts

265 W. 23rd St. (212) 620-0111
bet. 7th & 8th Aves. in Chelsea

Will the coffee invasion be followed by the donut invasion? This southern chain specializes in the hot glazed variety: When the red light in the window is lit, the donuts are fresh from the vat.

Kurumazushi

$52

18 W. 56th St. (212) 541-9030
bet. Fifth & Sixth Aves. in Midtown W.

This Sushi-only, Midtown Japanese has been serving traditional sushi pieces for 20 years, and has withstood (and ignored) the trends that have beset the discipline, prevailing with "very good" if "ridiculously overpriced" food. Hey, "if it's good enough for Yoko, it's good enough for me."

La Boheme

$36

24 Minetta Ln. (212) 473-6447
at Sixth Ave. in the Washington Sq. Area

French Provençal fare dished out in a casual setting that's convenient for Village theatergoers. The bistro menu includes French-accented brick-oven pizzas, soups, and other unpretentious fare. And now it's time to roll out our favorite French bistro adjectives: "romantic" and "charming."

La Boite en Bois

$40

75 W. 68th St. (212) 874-2705
bet. Columbus Ave. & Central Park W. on the Upper West Side

"If you can squeeze in," this "small" but "terrific" place is "the cutest ever" for "quiet," "intimate French dining." You may "feel like a sardine," but the food's "delicious," the service is "good," and there's a cheap pre-theater menu.

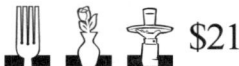

FOOD   ROOM   STAFF   COST

La Bonne Soupe
$21

48 W. 55th St. bet. Fifth & Sixth Aves./Midtown W. (212) 586-7650
French for "The Good Soup," this Midtown Bistro has a big lunch crowd that appreciates the "easy in, easy out" atmosphere and simple dishes like onion soup, salads, omelettes, and crème brûlée. The "adorable decor" ("sit in the balcony") is offset by some of the closest tables in town, complaints that "the soup deal is getting too expensive," and service that can slow to an escargot's pace.

La Bouillabaisse
$26

145 Atlantic Ave., bet. Henry & Clinton/Brooklyn (718) 522-8275
This little Brooklyn Heights BYOB is "like visiting your French family," that is, if that family has a line out the door, makes you wait to sit down, has "terrible decor" "but who cares for food this great?" (including, of course, "terrific bouillabaisse"). No credit cards, no smoking, no reserving.

La Boulangere
$18

49 E. 21st St. (212) 475-8772
bet. Broadway & Park Ave. S. in the Flatiron District
Here's something different, a reasonably priced French/American cafe with organic produce in Flatiron/Gramercy. It's a good "place for a quick lunch out of the office." The room won't feel like a vacation and the service probably won't smile, but the "bread," "salads" and "desserts" are "great." Breakfast seven days.

L'Absinthe
$43

227 E. 67th St. bet. Second & Third/U.E. Side (212) 794-4950
Resembling nothing so much as an authentic, fin-de-siecle Parisian brasserie, this attractive Upper East Side spot showcases chef/owner Jean-Michel Bergougnoux's contemporary French sensibility (salmon with couscous, curried mussels, and so forth). There's a sidewalk cafe that appeals to the Chanel set, and a small but sensible little wine list. Few know it; more should.

L'Acajou
$34

53 W. 19th St. bet. Fifth & Sixth/Flatiron District (212) 645-1706
"Good without pretension" characterizes this "reliable" Flatiron bistro with many "devoted followers." Housed in a "former luncheonette," L'Acajou is a little "quirky," but even at its "noisiest," the dark little dining room is "a pleasant and charming place to be." Staff is "friendly," the traditional bistro fare can be "delicious," and there are a number of interesting two-week food and wine "festivals" throughout the year to keep things interesting.

La Caravelle
$60

33 W. 55th St. bet. Fifth & Sixth/Midtown W. (212) 586-4252
Consistently one of the top draws in New York, this "big money" Midtown spot "keeps rolling along" with "impeccable service" and "excellent" French fare, and a new chef, Cyril Renaud (ex-Bouley). The ambiance, complete with fresh flowers on every table, accents what supporters call "the paradigm of haute cuisine." The only grumble is that sometimes the smoke wafts from the bar to the dining area. Dress up.

La Caridad

$12

2184 Amsterdam Ave. at 68th St. on the U.W. Side (212) 568-4294
The owners call it "International," but our voters call it one of the
best Chino/Latino diners in town. A Top 20 dive (also for dining
alone) it's the Upper West Side's 24-hour place to beat: there are
better, but none with such convenient hours and location.

La Casalinga

$15

120 First Ave. (212) 979-1246
bet. 7th & 8th Sts. in the E. Village
Not the casa to linger in unless you're seeking "unimpressive"
(some say downright "bad") Italian food and atmosphere to
match, and "rising prices."

La Colombe d'Or

$43

134 E. 26th St. (212) 689-0666
bet. Third & Lexington Aves. in Gramercy
After a two year absence, the original owners have returned to this
Gramercy Provencal, to serve "rich" and "tasty bistro fare." Its
"grand dining sans the grand manner," and consistent in the
"always" category, as in "always beautiful," "always quaint,"
"always very good." Try "the best Dover sole in town" or try its
pre-theater menu for a cheap date. Otherwise, be prepared to pay
through the nose. Smoking is permitted.

La Côte Basque

$61

60 W. 55th St. (212) 688-6525
bet. Fifth & Sixth Aves. in Midtown W.
A bit "stuffy," yes, but this formidable Frenchie is "outstanding."
The food is simply "excellent," and comments like "very heavy"
"the competitors are more interesting" mean this is "classic" fare.
Those seeking "the best service ever" (better still if you're one of
the legion of devoted regulars), a "handsome setting" (great for
business lunchers—others prefer the less-hectic dinner hour) and
"classic" cuisine find this a "wonderful experience."

La Focaccia

$27

51 Bank St. (212) 675-3754
at W. 4th St. in the W. Village
You'll find a brick oven at this West Village Northern Italian, but
you won't find any pizza: The oven is used to cook strictly fish and
meat dishes. While there are better Italians nearby, the atmosphere
makes "you feel like you've been invited into someone's house."

La Folie

$31

1422 Third Ave. (212) 744-6327
bet. 80th & 81st Sts. on the Upper East Side
Reviewers "love the ambiance" at this warm Upper East Side
French bistro, which boasts a fireplace. Solid service and food back
up already solid ratings.

FOOD ROOM STAFF COST

La Fondue

43 W. 55th St. (212) 581-0820
bet. Fifth & Sixth Aves. in Midtown W.

Even if you didn't know the name of the place, your nose would tell you you're in a room filled with melted cheese. Still, you don't want to eliminate this Swiss/French from your list of "fun, reasonable and predictable" places. A silly change of pace, it could use La Renovation after 20 years.

La Goulue $43

746 Madison Ave. (212) 988-8169
bet. 64th & 65th Sts. on the Upper East Side

The "new location" gets solid marks for "better food" and a "prettier crowd," but the real attraction is the gorgeous fin-de-siecle bistro atmosphere, complete with mahogany walls and a chic little bar. There's also a little terrace, nice for Sunday brunch.

La Granita $25

1407 Second Ave. at 77th St. on the U.E. Side (212) 717-5500

It's only been around for about a year, but the "decent Italian food" at a decent price has made this another solid choice for Upper East diners. It's basically "formula style" but the brick-oven pizza, grilled vegetables and lobster ravioli stand out. It has two floors and a "great open-air atmosphere in the summer" which makes the so-so service less noticeable.

La Grenouille $63

3 E. 52nd St. bet. Fifth & Madison/Midtown E. (212) 752-1495

Here's one of New York's best: Classic Haute French has been lightened and updated with seasonal specialties, and the effect is "sublime"; the "opulent" setting, that includes a fireplace, attracts romantic diners and business lunchers on expense accounts, all dressed to the nines. The staff, headed by one of NYC's best maitre d's, is "marvelous." This "delicious corner of Paris" is "exceptionally good and agreeable," but if you want to make it for a "special occasion," call well in advance.

La Jumelle Bistro $28

55 Grand St. (212) 941-9651
at W. Broadway in SoHo

Reservations are essential at this small French gypsy bistro: After all, you're competing with the neighborhood regulars, who drop in two or three times a week for "the best endive salad So of Ho," and "wonderful steak." This "fun" spot attracts a cool, trendy, young W. Broadway crowd—a "motorcycle is a must."

La Luncheonette $33

130 Tenth Ave. (212) 675-0342
at 18th St. in Chelsea

Here's one way to please diners: Lower their expectations with the joint's name, then serve "wonderful" French fare in a "warm and funky" environment. The "owner is a great host," the service is on the money, and "the fun loyal regulars" make you feel at home.

La Maison Japonaise

$36

125 E. 39th St. (212) 682-7375
bet. Lexington & Park Aves. in Murray Hill
This Murray Hill French/Japanese has been in business "for over 20 years, and it's still wonderful." Some recommend it for "good business lunch," and the prix fixe specials are "great deals." The "interesting, well done menu" including items like Wasabi Steak, are good for "taste bud exploration."

La Mangeoire

$39

1008 Second Ave. (212) 759-7086
bet. 53rd & 54th Sts. in Midtown E.
It may be "a little tired," but most surveyors appreciate the "unassuming" ambiance and "authentic," "well-prepared" French fare at this Midtown "standby." Expect a "warm setting" with service that makes you "feel like a regular."

La Mediterranee

$32

947 Second Ave. (212) 755-4155
bet. 50th & 51st Sts. in Midtown E.
With a "great rustic, French country atmosphere" that's conducive to "important conversations," this Midtowner satisfies voters with "consistently good" bistro fare. Weekend dinner hours can be busy so regulars advise that it's "better during the week" or for a convenient business lunch.

La Metairie

$42

189 W. 10th St. (212) 989-0343
at Seventh Ave. S. in the W. Village
Self-billed as "International" cuisine, most voters think of it as mostly a mix of Southern and French New Orleans styles. Whatever the influences, voters "love the feeling of this small, crowded but charming place." With "tables incredibly close," "great, if you can handle 'intimate' dining."

La Mirabelle

$36

333 W. 86th St. (212) 496-0458
bet. West End & Riverside Aves. on the Upper West Side
Not the finest French in town, this Upper West Side bistro is inviting for its "country-home" atmosphere ("really nice people") and five small dining rooms. Many rooms make for easy-to-book private parties and parents who don't have to worry about the kids making a little noise.

Landmark Tavern

$29

626 Eleventh Ave. (212) 757-8595
at 46th St. in Clinton
This "classic," "old-world" New York tavern has become a bit of a "bar-baby hangout" thanks to its "romantic" decor and "nostalgic"—if merely "okay"—"pub food." "Soda bread," "pot pie," and "potato soup"—not to mention "Scotch eggs," English "bangers and mash," and the "best damn bloody Mary anywhere"—are the sort of "hearty" "favorites" that are the perfect antidote to the usual trend du jour.

FOOD · ROOM · STAFF · COST

Langan's

$31

150 W. 47th St. (212) 869-5482
bet. Sixth & Seventh Aves. in Midtown W.

The new menu should offset dismal food marks such as it "seems occasionally mass-produced at this Theater District Irish/American. No matter, the "good service" still draws in an undemanding crowd for business lunch and pre-theater.

Lanza

$23

168 First Ave. (212) 674-7014
bet. 10th & 11th Sts. in the E. Village

"Where native Lower East Siders" go when they want "classic," "basic" "old-style Italian dishes." The "tiny room" is "jammed" and the service can be "rushed," but the food is "reliable" and you really can't beat the "lunch and dinner specials"—the "after-9 p.m. prix fixe" (at $11.95) is quite possibly the "late-night deal of the century."

La Paella

$27

557 Hudson St. bet. Perry & W. 11th/W. Village (212) 627-3092
214 E. 9th St. bet. Second & Third/E. Village (212) 598-4321

Participants mean it when they say "killer sangrias" slide down the bar here. The "moderately priced, authentic Spanish fare" and central locations in the East and West Village has put these spots on the favorite list, though the "stingy," "chintzy" portions don't do much for anybody and "too much waiting" for a table or an order "makes some angry." Still, the inside is "charming and warm," and the paella and seafood tapas are "outstanding" .

La Petite Auberge

$36

116 Lexington Ave. (212) 689-5003
bet. 27th & 28th Sts. in Gramercy

If you're into that "European feel," one of those "best-kept secrets" is waiting for you in Gramercy. The "always consistent," "country-style" French fare makes this "small" but "comfortable" bistro a "great find." It also might just have the "nicest wait staff in NYC," which is saying a lot. Step in and try some of "the best soufflés" in town.

La Primavera

$38

234 W. 48th St. (212) 586-2233
bet. Broadway & Eighth Ave. in the Theater District

Hell's Kitchen is devilishly hot: check out the Northern Italian here, it's seven 'm' delish—mmmmmmm! In line with other "pre-theater spots, be on the lookout for "snob appeal"—"if you're nobody, they'll tell you."

L'Ardoise

$34

1207 First Ave. (212) 744-4752
bet. 65th & 66th Sts. on the Upper East Side

This "storefront French" has what Upper East Siders want: It's "as good as the snooty French restaurants, at half the price." A "fun place" with "eccentric owners," the great prix fixe bargains and calm, older-crowd atmosphere leads one voter to comment, "this place would make it in France!"

La Reserve

 $60

4 W. 49th St. (212) 247-2993
at Fifth Ave. in Midtown W.

"Very accommodating" is the consensus at this Rock Center
Contemporary French mainstay that many say is the "ultimate
special occasion spot. Divine!" The food is "excellent," and is
essential to a real New York diner's food vocabulary. And
while the "luscious food" may tempt you, save room for some
of the city's "best desserts." Most voters appreciate the "serene
atmosphere," though younger diners think the ambiance could
use some "updating," to catch up with the food. P.S. Don't
forget Les Reservations.

La Ripaille

 $51

605 Hudson St. (212) 255-4406
bet. Bethune & 12th Sts. in the W. Village

Another entry in the "romantic French bistro" sweepstakes. This
one's enhanced by a fireplace and a grandfather clock, marred by a
"smoke-filled room with little appeal" and "tables squished so close
together they deter romance." The simple and good food, however,
should do nothing to dampen your ardor.

La Rosita

2809 Broadway (212) 663-7804
bet. 108th & 109th Sts. in the Columbia U. Area

Old fashioned, real Cuban cooking includes the "best cafe con
leche" and "very affordable breakfast" at this Upper West Sider.
"Always crowded," it has the "best rice and beans," though "service
leaves something to be desired."

La Serre

33 E. 61st St. (212) 355-2900
bet. Park & Madison Aves. on the Upper East Side

Owned by Sylvain Fareri of La Metairie and Silvano Marcheto of
Da Silvano, La Serre is an upscale, small rustic French
neighborhood spot, which should be popular in these parts.

La Spaghetteria

178 Second Ave. (212) 995-0900
bet. 11th & 12th Sts. in the E. Village

Open for lunch and dinner, this inviting East Village Italian wins
fans with "reasonable" prices, "great specials" and a "friendly
staff." Desserts are often "awesome," but entrees are "average."

La Taza De Oro

 $13

96 Eighth Ave. (212) 243-9946
bet. 14th & 15th Sts. in Chelsea

This Puerto Rican West Villager recently celebrated its 50th
anniversary, so there's little chance of its BYO policy going away
anytime soon. That's fine with voters, who say they have the "best
inexpensive Puerto Rican food" in town. The "goat stew" is
"excellent," and you simply "haven't lived until you've had the soup."

FOOD ROOM STAFF COST

Lattanzi

$38

361 W. 46th St. (212) 315-0980
bet. Eighth & Ninth Aves. in Clinton
"Lovely, charming, elegant in all ways," about sums up this
Northern Italian "Clinton choice for a hit evening." Here's a
word: fireplace. And another: garden. Okay, that's two. Getting
the picture? A "lovely little restaurant oasis with a unique menu"
and top grub that "can surprise" and is "worth the trip just for the
garlic flatbread."

L'Auberge du Midi

$44

310 W. 4th St. (212) 242-4705
bet. Bank & W. 12th Sts. in the W. Village
For such a small French restaurant, this West Villager has a large
selection of cheese and wines, though the actual food preparation is
"overrated," to quote one of the kinder reviewers. Other features,
like a cruvinet and two fireplaces, give this place its appeal.

Laurita's Cafe Soul

311 Church St. (212) 941-0202
bet. Walker & Lispenard Sts. in TriBeCa
The sounds of '70s soul classics fill the air. The menu features
down home cookin' like barbecued chicken, deep-fried catfish and
seafood gumbo. Fans say "don't let out the secret" there's
"excellent everything here." Well, we won't.

Lavo Thai

$19

90 Third Ave. (212) 477-6955
bet. 12th & 13th Sts. in the E. Village
An interior decorator hasn't stepped foot in this East Village
Thai, but who cares: The "good value" meals make up for it.
Since they serve "good food in a place no one goes to," the
"pleasant" staff "doesn't push." The daily lunch special is a steal,
or call for a little spicy takeout after a long day at work. The
$10.95 prix fixe dinner is a steal.

Layla

$44

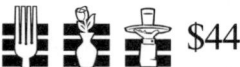

211 W. Broadway (212) 431-0700
at Franklin St. in TriBeCa
This "trendy" DeNiro/Nieporent offers "creative" "great" Middle
Eastern fare, but it's the over-the-top "exotic" atmosphere,
complete with live belly dancers ("keep them on later") that makes
Layla "a hoot." "Authentic," "only in new York."

Le Beaujolais

$33

364 W. 46th St. (212) 974-7464
bet. Eighth & Ninth Aves. in Clinton
While this Beaujolais isn't exactly nouveau, the calm atmosphere,
Classic French menu and inexpensive, anytime prix fixe options
have their appeals, particularly to an older crowd.

≣ = SUPERIOR ≣ = EXCELLENT ≣ = V. GOOD ═ = GOOD

Le Bernardin  $73

Equitable Bldg., 155 W. 51st St. (212) 489-1515
bet. Sixth & Seventh Aves. in Midtown W.
"The very best seafood restaurant in the world"? That's not going overboard for voters who succumb to rapture of the deep when it comes to this "superb" purveyor of French-accented seafood. You simply "can't get any fresher fish than this"; add "casual elegance" and "meticulous service," and there's "nothing to compare" to this "fish heaven" that tops out in all categories.

Le Biarritz  $40

325 W. 57th St. bet. Eighth & Ninth/Clinton (212) 245-9467
Looking for a high-end French place? It's nice to memorize them all so you don't have to jump in a cab to find one. This "tired" one's been around 30 years so somebody must be pleased. There's a kids menu so you can start the little rugrats on soufflé ASAP.

Le Boeuf A La Mode  $41

539 E. 81st St. bet. East End & York/U.E. Side (212) 249-1473
Never mind what the name means, this here's a classy French joint. It's a top 50 sleeper which means it's romantic and not too crowded; which also means not so noisy you can't hear the words: will you marry me? "Take advantage of the prix fixe." Break out the Armani jacket.

Le Chantilly  $54

106 E. 57th St. bet. Park & Lex./Midtown E. (212) 751-2931
Placing high in our "older adults" category, this East Side French typically serves "haute cuisine in plush surroundings" to a "super-elegant, ladies-who-lunch crowd." It has what an older crowd wants: "dependably fine dining," from a staff that is "professional all the way" (though some might disagree, as the "maitre d' makes you feel like he is in love with you"). This kind of pampering is "romantic," and the "pre-theater dinner is one of the best deals in town."

L'Ecole  $32

French Culinary Inst., 462 Bdwy. at Grand/SoHo (212) 219-3300
Don't worry, it's not like getting your hair cut at the barber college. "The students" at this French Culinary Institute restaurant "cook like old pros," and the "five-course prix fixe"is one of the city's fine-dining bargains. Lunch costs even less, and though the staff obviously changes around a lot, there are no complaints of inconsistency here.

Le Colonial  $42

149 E. 49th St. bet. Third & Lex. in Midtown E.(212) 752-0808
The period photos, soft yellow walls and ceiling fans are meant to evoke French colonial Vietnam of the early 1900s, and have the effect of creating one of the best looking rooms in town. Some say the "great bar on the second floor" is even better, though "overcrowding" can be a problem. While there are more authentic Vietnamese in the city, there are none as comfortable, and certainly no other SE Asian "power scene."

FOOD　ROOM　STAFF　COST

Leda

871 Seventh Ave. (212) 582-7500
bet. 55th & 56th Sts. in Midtown W.
This upscale new seafood restaurant gets its flavors from all over the Mediterranean—and gets its chef, David McKenty, from Kokachin. There are tapas, a raw bar, and a cheap bar menu from 3-5 in the afternoon.

Le Jardin Bistro $29

25 Cleveland Pl. (212) 343-9599
at Kenmare & Spring Sts. in SoHo
You might guess it from the name: The attraction at this easterly SoHo French Bistro is the garden. Folks find the food "not terribly French, " "average bistro food" that's "reasonably priced," and warn: in the colder months the "cozy" room can get "much too crowded."

Le Madeleine $33

403 W. 43rd St. (212) 246-2993
at Ninth Ave. in Clinton
Satisfy those pre-theater calf's liver cravings at this "casual, classy, romantic" bistro where they're "pros" at handling the eight-o'clock-curtain crowd. Perhaps a certain je ne sais quoi keeps the food from surpassing "nice"-ness, but the setting provides the missing elan; it's hard to believe you're in Hell's Kitchen when you're sitting in the "exquisite" glass-enclosed garden, "a lovely escape from the city noise."

Le Madri $47

168 W. 18th St. (212) 727-8022
at Seventh Ave. in Chelsea
Food can be "lusty" and "glamorous." Why not? That's what voters say of the pizza and pasta at this Chelsea Northern Italian. It's "pricey" but the "great space" in an "airy" "beautiful room" makes this a true favorite. And we can't forget the maitre'd—its nice to know you're welcome as soon as you walk in. For "a dream payday—Barney's, then Le Madri."

Le Marais $34

150 W. 46th St. (212) 869-0900
bet. Sixth & Seventh Aves. in Midtown W.
A French steakhouse that is, among other things, Kosher: it's "so good," however, "you wouldn't know it was." "Great food," is marred by the much-maligned "lousy" staff, which somehow manages to get you out the door in time for the show. "Jazz and cigar" night Mondays.

Le Max $34

147 W. 43rd St. (212) 764-3705
bet. Broadway & Sixth Ave. in Midtown W.
If you're in the Theater District you might want to try this French Bistro... or you might not. The food's fair and the fare's costly, but if you're a vegetarian smoker you're in luck.

Lemon
$34

230 Park Ave. S. (212) 614-1200
bet. 18th & 19th Sts. in Gramercy
A "beautiful place of the moment" whose moment is quickly passing; "the crowd is already bridge and tunnel," note alarmed observers of the "see-and-be-seen" scene. Behind the social scrim there is nothing: the fare is "a step above airline food," and "the service is worse." We'll let someone else say what begs to be said: "It's a lemon."

Lemon Grass Grill
$19

2534 Broadway (212) 666-0888
bet. 94th & 95th Sts. on the Upper West Side
It sounds distinctly unexciting, but the lure of "good Thai food at reasonable prices" draws throngs to this "reliable hangout." The "best pad Thai since Bangkok" wins multiple kudos, but connoisseurs say the "Americanized" fare "lacks the freshness necessary for Thai food." Oh, piffle: it's "yummy."

Lenge
$27

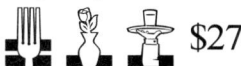

1465 Third Ave. at 83rd St. on the Upper East Side (212) 535-9661
202 Columbus Ave. at 69th St. on the U.W. Side (212) 799-9188
Larger and more popular, the Upper West Side version of these Japanese restaurants is also the better of the two, making it to the Top 15 for sushi in town on the strength of sheer traffic. Expect "long waits" and "tight packed" tables, occasional brusque service and "reasonable prices," especially for the area.

Lenox Room
$48

1278 Third Ave. (212) 772-0404
bet. 73rd & 74th Sts. on the Upper East Side
The cuisine served at this "more casual Aureole offspring" is far less daunting than the label "progressive American" might lead you to expect: It's unfussy, flavor-intensive, and often simply "excellent." The mood is understated and "grown-up," right at home on the Upper East Side, as is the "superior, albeit pretentious" staff and well-heeled atmosphere.

L'Entrecote
$39

1057 First Ave. (212) 755-0080
bet. 57th & 58th Sts. in Midtown E.
If you miss congeniality at your local French bistro, maybe you should make a reservation at this tiny spot, tucked away in Sutton Place for more than 20 years now: Though the environment is quite friendly, the back-to-basics French food is nothing special.

Leopard
$55

253 E. 50th St. (212) 759-3735
bet. Second & Third Aves. in Midtown E.
This French/Continental, um, spot holds only 30 diners, but each and every one seems to have left ecstatic. The menu is as "limited" as the seating, but the "wine is included" and it's a great place to "impress your date" or "impress your clients." "A secret joy: it does not get better than this. Don't tell anyone!" Yeah, okay.

FOOD ROOM STAFF COST

Le Parker Meridien

$42

118 W. 57th St. (212) 245-5000
bet. Sixth & Seventh Aves. in Midtown W.
Even features like high tea and live music don't impress surveyors
who cite "plastic plants, plastic food" at this Midtown Continental.
Scores suggest that the wants-to-be-upscale ambiance appeals to
some, but all agree that it's "overpriced" and service can be "snotty."

Le Perigord

$56

405 E. 52nd St. (212) 755-6244
bet. First Ave. & the East River at Sutton Pl.
This 62-year-old "bastion of old world French food" continues to
quietly wow its staid older audience with "fine food," "elegant" (if
a "bit cold") quarters, and a remarkably "good-humored staff."
Chef Pascal Coudouy has snapped up the cuisine lately with
Southwestern French dishes. If you find this kind of Sutton Place
restaurant "overpriced" and "snooty," stay away.

Le Pescadou

$39

18 King St. (212) 924-3434
at Sixth Ave. in SoHo
Serving "good" Provençal-style French seafood "on a sweet block
in SoHo," regulars say chef Sara Daniels' cooking is "imaginative
and resourceful," while most say it's at least above average.
"Friendly" and "pretty," the "cozy" environs is taken too far in one
respect: "the bathroom is ridiculously small."

Le Petit Hulot

$40

973 Lexington Ave. (212) 794-9800
bet. 70th & 71st Sts. on the Upper East Side
Though they enjoy the soufflé, the mostly older crowd is attracted
to "one of the nicest gardens" in New York at this Upper East Side
French. The food can be "lovely," but is outclassed by the
"romantic" ambiance and the "wonderful team" of servers here.

Le Quercy

$35

52 W. 55th St. (212) 265-8141
bet. Fifth & Sixth Aves. in Midtown W.
Twenty-years-old and feeling it, this somewhat "cramped,"
"quintessential French bistro" is still "reliable" to some, "tired" to
most. Still, to a sedate older crowd, it's "one of Midtown's best
bargains" with its twenty buck pre-theater menu.

Le Refuge

$45

166 E. 82nd St. (212) 861-4505
bet. Third & Lexington Aves. on the Upper East Side
Voters call this 20-year-old Classic and Contemporary French
Bistro "a calm oasis," filled with "mature (i.e. adult)" patrons who
enjoy the "quaint view of the brownstones" on East 82nd Street, not
to mention the "very good" food. While voted into the Top 50, the
staff seems "stuck up" to younger diners.

= SUPERIOR = EXCELLENT = V. GOOD = GOOD

Le Regence $58

37 E. 64th St. (212) 606-4647
bet. Madison & Park Aves. on the Upper East Side
"A very civilized experience," with "very good food and service" can be had at this classic French just off the Park on the Upper East Side. The room is the star, in the Top 25 on the Romac Poll, and is what voters can only try to describe as "gorgeous and elegant." Having trouble with the high price tag? "Welcome to the world of decadence, opulence and sheer regality." "Wow," "what a posh place!"

Le Relais $48

712 Madison Ave. bet. 63rd & 64th/U.E. Side (212) 751-5108
"Lively" and "well situated," this "very French" little bistro is famous for "people-watching" with its "curbside view" of the Madison Avenue scene. The menu offers up "authentic French flavor," attracting ladies who lunch and the "Euro-flash." If you're not either, go to Le Relais when you're "feeling European."

Le Rivage $35

340 W. 46th St. bet. Eighth & Ninth/Clinton (212) 765-7374
"The value is all" at this Clinton French, which serves "bourgeois food in a cozy setting, with efficient service at a decent price." "Always consistent," though it is not the finest French in town, many like it for the "convenience, before or after the theater."

L'Ermitage $42

40 W. 56th St. (212) 581-0777
bet. Fifth & Sixth Aves. in Midtown W.
Don't let the French name fool you: this 20-year-old, weekday-only Upper Midtown spot is strictly Russian and Eastern European, down to the balalaika players and Russian paintings. If you miss the bad food from the bad old days of the Russian Tea Room, this place will sate your wants. Oh, and hermits, beware: They have a reputation for "treating solo diners poorly."

Les Celebrites $73

Essex House, 155 W. 58th St. (212) 484-5113
bet. Sixth & Seventh Aves. in Midtown W.
"Polished elegance," including a Romac Top 10 menu that voters call "exquisite," and a Top 5 room described as "the epitome of deluxe," really describes the truly "superior" staff at this art-deco hotel restaurant just South of the park. Celebrity paintings (by the celebs, not of them) adorn the walls as do this place's many awards. It has such distinctive and characteristic charm, voters "want to get married just to have anniversaries here."

Les Deux Gamins $24

170 Waverly Pl. (212) 807-7357
bet. Sixth Ave. & Grove St. in the W. Village
This tiny West Village French bistro serves "good" (if "inauthentic") food, in an "unpretentious" "authentic" atmosphere. The sidewalk usually sports a few "hip" "chain smokers," sipping "great coffee" and making it feel "like Paris."

FOOD ROOM STAFF COST

Les Halles

 $36

411 Park Ave. S. bet. 28th & 29th/Gramercy (212) 725-6244
"Crowded and too noisy for conversation," this Gramercy Parisian bistro corrals a mostly over-30 crowd in cheek-to-jowl quarters for "adequate" steak and frites. To avoid "rude service" and claustrophobia, there's a "great butcher counter for home chefs."

Lespinasse

 $78

St. Regis Hotel, 2 E. 55th St. (212) 339-6719
bet. Fifth & Madison Aves. in Midtown E.
The crowned ratings tell the story: this Midtown French is the finest restaurant in New York. The top-rated room, food, and staff, aided by one of the finest maitre d's in town, make it "a total experience," "elegant, luxurious and special." The "creative cuisine" of "chef Gray Kunz is the best in town," voters tell us, and though the "bill may be dizzying, it's worth every cent." "Prix fixe lunch is a best bet," and of course there's a "great wine list," after all, Lespinasse is "splendid and perfect!"

Les Pyrenees

 $37

251 W. 51st St. bet. Bdwy & Eighth/Theater Dist. (212) 246-0044
A class act in the Theater District, this "reliable and comfortable" French standby offers "authentic" fare ranging from "good" to "wonderful," in a "quiet, romantic" setting complete with fireplace.

Les Sans Culottes

 $30

329 W. 51st St. (212) 838-6660
347 W. 46th St. (212) 247-4284
bet. Eighth & Ninth Aves. in Clinton
Folks call these Country French restaurants "a pig-out": when seated, a basket of fruit and vegetables, a selection of sausage and a dish of paté await you at your table (be careful to "watch your intake")."Always reliable," they "continue to keep prices modest" and remain "great fun" with a "lovely staff."

Le Taxi

 $41

37 E. 60th St. (212) 832-5500
bet. Madison & Park Aves. in Midtown E.
Oh, the generation gap. The younger crowd think the French fare here is "innovative," while those comfortably settled into middle age find "nothing to rave about." The latter probably doesn't know what to think when "Eurotrash meets the Upper East Side," but that's life in the big city. Everyone agrees that it's "bright and airy" and the service lags.

Letizia

 $37

1352 First Ave. (212) 517-2244
bet. 72nd & 73rd Sts. in Yorkville
A good but par-for-the-Upper-East-Side-course classic Italian, with "an atmosphere defined as that of a teller machine" and an all-over-the-Italian-map menu to match. But it's got two perfect swings: the staff, which is "attentive, playful and knowledgeable" and "treats you as if you have a million dollars." And equally important—if not more so: "the best broccoli rabe in town."

Le Veau D'Or $38

129 E. 60th St. (212) 838-8133
bet. Lexington & Park Aves. in Midtown E.
Sure, Le Veau D'Or has "traditional French Bistro food," and
ambiance that couldn't be anything but "old-fashioned": The place is
60 years old. All agree the food is only "fair," and in need of an update.

Lexington Bar & Books

1020 Lexington Ave. at 73rd St. in Carnegie Hill (212) 717-3902
(See review for Beekman Bar & Books.)

Le Zoo $33

314 W. 11th St. *at Greenwich St. in the W. Village (212) 620-0393*
Some say "must go" and others say "overrated" about this trendy bistro
on a "charming" but "out-of-the-way" West Village corner. Service with
a smile helps balance out the "pretentious" "cell phone"-using clientele.
Then there are the crowds and inconsistent food which ranges from "no
comment" to "worth it," but prices are "so reasonable," especially the
prix fixe brunch which is a good deal. No reservations.

Life Cafe $16

343 E. 10th St. at Ave. B in the E. Village (212) 477-8791
"Support your local Boho" at this Cal-Mex/Vegetarian/American
that was "immortalized in Rent" for its rotating art show and
Downtown ambiance. "The food is plentiful," including the "best
nachos in the East Village" and plenty of non-dairy soy alternatives.
"The kids," though, "have an attitude."

Limbo $11

47 Ave. A bet. 3rd & 4th Sts. in the E. Village (212) 477-5271
"Pull up a board game and relax with a friend" at this little East
Village trendy throwback, a classic (though updated) coffeehouse with
"living room ambiance" and the usual poetry and other readings. "A
great place to read and write in peace," the sandwiches and soups are
"average," the "chocolate cake is great," and the staff has "attitude."

Limoncello

The Michelangelo Hotel, 777 Seventh Ave. (212) 582-7932
at 51st St. in Midtown W.
If you, or someone you know, is staying at the Michelangelo Hotel,
then this upscale Italian is the obvious choice—it's right there.
"Okay food, after work crowds" can be found at this Midtowner.

Lincoln Tavern $29

51 W. 64th St. at Broadway on the U.W. Side (212) 721-8271
In the site of the old Zachary's, this American tavern is "a great
late-night spot for drinks and a nibble," but when it comes to more
elaborate dinners, the food is only "fair." The "chic space" is good for
lunch, though the room "competes with Sardi's for closest tables."

FOOD   ROOM   STAFF   COST

Lipstick Cafe

$19

885 Third Ave. bet. 53rd & 54th/Midtown E. (212) 486-8664
Named for its Midtown building, not the makeup, fans say the
"interesting" American fare is perfect for a "quick lunch on stools":
"Too bad it's not open for dinner or on weekends," "less expensive
than you might expect," and in the morning the "good" pastries and
coffee are outclassed by the "best jelly doughnuts!"

Live Bait

$21

14 E. 23rd St. (212) 353-2492
at Madison Ave. in the Flatiron District
"Have a beer and move on" is the best strategy for this "loud,"
"crowded," "popular bar" that just happens to serve what some call
"solid, Southern-tinged dishes," but others rate merely "mediocre."
The "semi-surly" staff of "wannabe models" are "beautiful" and
they know it, but it's "good for after work" or "lunch"—if you're
still part of the "lost generation."

Lobby Lounge
Four Seasons Hotel

$34

57 E. 57th St. (212) 758-5700
bet. Park & Madison Aves. in Midtown E.
For just three years now, this comfortable little lounge, with its own
piano player and "excellent" ambiance, has been serving "very
good" Continental food in the lobby of the Four Seasons. Usually
populated by out-of-town hotel guests, they only take reservations
for lunch, and have a lovely afternoon tea.

The Lobster Club

$49

24 E. 80th St. (212) 249-6500
bet. Fifth & Madison Aves. on the Upper East Side
Gunning for "upscale comfort food," Anne Rosenzweig's recent entry
into the Upper East Side dining scene may be a "nice neighborhood
restaurant," but early reports say the food "disappoints"" Maybe it
received "too much press." Voters say the signature club sandwich is
"tasty" but they "wouldn't name a restaurant after it."

Lola

$34

30 W. 22nd St. (212) 675-5544, (212) 675-6700
bet. Fifth & Sixth Aves. in the Flatiron District
"There is no brunch like gospel brunch at Lola's": live gospel singers
light up a dressy Sunday morning crowd. Otherwise, it's "always
pleasant," with live music on Wednesday and Saturday nights, a long,
hopping bar ("home of the 'Lola'—cocktail of the year") and pretty
decor that includes "cool black bathrooms." The Eclectic seafood
menu is "good," with "spicy fried chicken" a standout.

Lombardi's

$20

32 Spring St. (212) 941-7994
bet. Mott & Mulberry Sts. in Little Italy
With all those "old originals" and "famous" pizzerias around, this Little
Italy brick oven is not only "first rate," it's the first one. That's right,
America's first licensed pizzeria may be the "best in New York," and
"the closest thing to Italian pizza" "this side of the Atlantic."

▤ = SUPERIOR ▤ = EXCELLENT ▤ = V. GOOD ▬ = GOOD

Lotfi's Moroccan

 $24

358 W. 46th St. (212) 582-5850
bet. Eighth & Ninth Aves. in Clinton
The "superb," "always reliable, tasty" Moroccan fare here is "a major find." With a "beautiful interior" and service that "gets you to the theater on time," this place is on it's way. You might even say it's "a Moroccan on a roll."

Louisiana Community Bar & Grill

622 Broadway (212) 460-9633
bet. Bleecker & Houston Sts. in the Washington Sq. Area
This "commercial Cajun experience" is good for "lots of southern fun," marked by "not-so" "cajun food" (including "pecan pie that's rich and satisfying") and "great bands." In fact, LCB ranks in the top 10 for live music in the city, making it a "down and dirty Dixie" bar in a "spacious," downtown setting.

Lucky Cheng's

 $28

24 First Ave. bet. 1st & 2nd Sts. in the E. Village (212) 473-0516
An entire waitstaff of men in geisha drag (though not nearly as polite as geishas) propel this big East Village Pan Asian to the top of our "exotic experience" list (aka "trendy nonsense"). "Small portions" make the food "overpriced," especially for what voters dub "middling Californian/Asian." This is "alternative dining" at its alternativiest, "shock your mom from Minnesota."

Lucky Dog Diner

 $16

167 First Ave. bet. 10th & 11th Sts./E. Village (212) 260-4220
A few dissenters call this East Villager a "faux diner," perhaps because it's so "cozy and clean." Even they, however, admit that it has "decent," "authentic diner food" and deserves its place in the Top 5 Diners. The price is right, too: free seconds on the blue plate special makes the Lucky Dog "downright Midwestern."

Lucky Strike

 $27

59 Grand St. (212) 941-0479
bet. Wooster & W. Broadway in SoHo
"The crowded bar makes the scene" at this French/American bistro that's so carefully downscale, "it's almost a dive." A "good beer selection" and the "best mashed potatoes in town at 1a.m." turn this "smokers' paradise" into "the kind of place you might hate to admit liking, but do."

L'Udo

 $32

The Colonnade Row, 432 Lafayette St. (212) 388-0978
bet. E. 4th St. & Astor Pl. in the E. Village
Here's a spot where the "great" garden is the draw. As for the French and Italian country food, it's "okay" and reasonably priced but the under-30 crowd likes it considerably more than other participants. No one's hog wild about the service: They treat you "like tourists." It's located in NoHo across from the Public Theater, so if you're wandering the streets downtown, this one's easy to find.

___ = FAIR   [blank] = POOR   ▦ = NOT RATED

	FOOD	ROOM	STAFF	COST

Luma

$36

200 Ninth Ave. bet. 22nd & 23rd Sts. in Chelsea (212) 633-8033
Chef Scott Bryan's American cuisine has created this destination in Chelsea, aided by an excellent wine list and some of the city's favorite vegetarian options. "Good for those way-off Broadway pre-theater dinners," it is surprisingly reasonable, and well-run: "Luma proves that quality dining can be delicious, yet relaxed and efficient." Try the early-bird specials before catching a flick at the Chelsea Googleplex.

Lumi

$40

963 Lexington Ave. at 70th St. on the U.E. Side (212) 570-2335
This Upper East Side regional Italian has earned a reputation as "sedate" and "graceful" since opening just over a year ago. While not a major destination, area residents call it "a nice addition" with sidewalk seating and roaring fireplaces, but warn that the wine list, though reasonably priced, is not always well-stocked.

Luna Park

$26

Union Sq. & 16th St. (212) 473-8464
at Union Sq.
Why create an interesting outdoor setting when you've got Union Square Park? That seems to be the reasoning behind this slapdash Mediterranean, ranking high on our outside dining list and even higher for having the surliest staff. "Packed on Thursdays," the people-watching and the bar are the real attractions. No reserving.

Lundy's

$32

1901 Emmons Ave., Brooklyn (718) 743-0022
at Ocean Ave.
"Welcome back to Brooklyn," cry fans of this once and future seafooder, restored to "a good enough likeness to the original" to put the raw bar in the Top 10, after only one year since reopening. Whether "it's not the original Lundy's," or it's "better" is for you to decide, after you've tried "large portions" of "simple fish dishes." "Waiting for a table seems contrived" at this huge seafood outpost.

Lusardi's

$40

1494 Second Ave. (212) 249-2020
bet. 77th & 78th Sts. on the Upper East Side
Though traffic is light, owner Luigi Lusardi would still prefer that you reserve at this "good, reliable, local" Northern Italian on the Upper East Side, about to celebrate its 25th anniversary.

Lutece

$66

249 E. 50th St. (212) 752-2225
bet. Second & Third Aves. in Midtown E.
Former chef/owner Andre "Soltner is gone, but the tradition lives on" at this "grandaddy" of "superb" modern French restaurants. While they no longer "break any boundaries, the preparation is flawless," served by a knowledgeable if "intimidating" staff. Of course the wine list is great, the maitre d' is great, and you'll feel more comfortable dressed up. While "Soltner is missed: Lutece is still wonderful, just different."

Mackinac Bar & Grill

 $29

384 Columbus Ave. (212) 799-1750
bet. 78th & 79th Sts. on the Upper West Side
"The Great Lakes meet the Upper West Side" at this Italian/American,
and we're not sure who wins. Food prep is on the old-fashioned side,
with "succulent steak and fries" and creamed spinach standards. The
warm atmosphere is an "excellent place for the elderly or
out-of-towners," "bring Dad and other tweedy pipe-smoking types."

Madame Romaine de Lyon

 $27

132 E. 61st St. (212) 758-2422, (212) 759-5200
bet. Park & Lexington Aves. on the Upper East Side
The service is "friendly" and the pianist "awesome" at this Upper
East Side French/Continental, but the recommendation on
everyone's lips is for the "best omelettes in New York City." In
fact, some think they should nickname Lyon "omelette city."

Mad Fish

 $34

2182 Broadway (212) 787-0202
bet. 77th & 78th Sts. on the Upper West Side
The Upper West Side has long waited for its culinary ship to come
in. This "welcome addition" to the neighborhood brings a haul of
"very fresh fish," creatively prepared, and a "great raw bar" that's
among the city's best. Landlubbers beware: The nonfish entrees are
only "so-so." The "great martinis" will help soften the "unbearable
din" that leads some to remark, "happy fish . . . mad diners."

Main Street

 $26

446 Columbus Ave. (212) 873-5025
bet. 81st & 82nd Sts. on the Upper West Side
Beep! Passing through the Upper West Side on the look out "for a
good old fashioned American meal?" Enter the "cavernous dining
room" and dive into a "bottomless mashed potato bowl." Bring the
whole family "in for a little communal eating," because with the
"mammoth portions" served, this is "a great place to go with a large
group." It's also "great for new parents."

Malaga

 $30

406 E. 73rd St. (212) 737-7659
bet. York & First Aves. in Yorkville
You'll find "paella heaven" at this family-run spot that proves Spain
is "more garlicky than Italy." Though the surroundings are "worn,"
Malaga gives "good value" on "tasty neighborhood fare," leading
some to "hope nobody else discovers this place."

Malika

210 E. 43rd St. (212) 681-6775
bet. Second & Third Aves. in Midtown E.
Malika is a large, banquet hall-like U.N.-area restaurant that
promises "exclusive Indian cuisine." If you're looking for that
ethnic food experience in midtown, the few voters who have found
this new spot say "try the excellent lunch buffet."

FOOD ROOM STAFF COST

Maloney & Porcelli

37 E. 50th St. (212) 750-2233
bet. Park & Madison Aves. in Midtown E.

This American serves large portions (same ownership as S&W) of its offerings in interesting presentation styles: little pots, pails, bags and bowls. Drop by for a big meal, and you'll bring home leftovers.

Mama's Food Shop $11

3rd St. & Ave. B in the E. Village (212) 777-4425

They have a "great approach to food" at this East Village Southern Home Cooking spot. "It's great, and inexpensive, as long as you don't mind helping to make it yourself": That is, once you order you might have to pop it in the microwave, in the shop or at home.

Manatu's

340 Bleecker St. (212) 989-7042
bet. Christopher & W. 10th Sts. in the W. Village

"Friendly," "accommodating" and "always busy," this 24-hour Continental serves up "glorified diner food" in a "gay positive" atmosphere. Popular for late night "cruising" in the West Village, it boasts a "huge menu" and "fast service."

Mandarin Court $20

61 Mott St. at Canal St. in Chinatown (212) 608-3838

"In the heart of Chinatown," you can find "great dim sum" 8-3 p.m., seven days, plus a regular (and excellent) Hong Kong Chinese menu the rest of the day. The "overcrowding" is a tipoff to the superior quality of the food, and there's "no decor, no service" here.

M & R Bar $24

264 Elizabeth St. (212) 226-0559
bet. Prince & E. Houston Sts. in SoHo

"Cozy" and unpretentious, this Little Italy liquor store-turned-bar-turned-eatery is a "find." The casual Italian/American menu features "great Caesar salads and French fries with lemon" and "awesome fried chicken," but the "cool," laid-back" atmosphere is the real draw.

Manganaro's Hero Boy $14

492 Ninth Ave. (212) 564-1442
bet. 37th & 38th Sts. in the Convention Center Area

"Great for office affairs" of the culinary kind, this self-proclaimed inventor of the six-foot hero proffers "great party sandwiches" and standard Italian steam-table fare in "ohhh, what portions."

Mangia $18

16 E. 48th St. (212) 754-0637
bet. Madison & Fifth Aves. in Midtown E.

Serving lunch only (and a good one, at that), smack dab in the heart of Midtown, this "great Italian buffet" is usually purchased for takeout, and (in the opinion of most voters) constitutes "gourmet on the go." It's usually "convenient," but the staff can get harried.

Mangia e Bevi  $22

800 Ninth Ave. (212) 956-3976
at 53rd St. in Clinton

Party time! At this "Italian carnival" the "maitre d' welcomes you
like you're his long-lost brother." What?! Huh?! This one's top 5 in
the noise category and some say come only if you like "tambourines
with your tomato sauce." The hawklike waitstaff that "stands over
you until you leave" doesn't go over well with those who don't
want to be "pressured into gulping down their meals hurriedly."
Most agree this is "terrific food and a great deal" though it may be
"difficult to get a table in the evening," lunch could be "your best
bet." Of course then you'd miss the "conga line."

Manhattan Cafe  $44

1161 First Ave. bet. 63rd & 64th Sts./U.E. Side (212) 888-6556

"Wanna splurge?" "Forget S&W" (Smith & Wollensky to you, dear
reader) and "feed here" on the "best steaks around," plus "the
freshest seafood" and "excellent pasta dishes." Fans say it's got "the
best lobster in the city"—and "no one knows it"—not to mention
"attentive service" and "beautiful decor" that may put you in mind
of "George Bush's country club." All in all, Manhattan Cafe is
"worth the high $$$" for a "great experience in dining."

Manhattan Ocean Club  $53

57 W. 58th St. bet. Fifth & Sixth Aves./Midtown W. (212) 371-7777

"The Dover sole is almost better than sex" at this "seafood paradise"
located in spacious quarters as pretty as an "art museum" in West
Midtown. "Delicious, fresh seafood," "excellent service" and a
first-class wine list make MOC a "great location for business meals."

Man Ray  $29

169 Eighth Ave. bet. 18th & 19th Sts. in Chelsea (212) 627-4220

A "great spot before the Joyce," this Contemporary American bistro
is "a beautiful nostalgic riff on the art-deco train/steamer thing."
But while the design is "overkill trendy" to some, everyone agrees
the food is "consistently good," with a "good selection," though
waits can be long. A prime pick for brunch.

Maple Garden

236 E. 53rd St. bet. Second & Third/Midtown E. (212) 759-8260

Confused Canadians take note: this UN Area restaurant is strictly
Peking-style Chinese, with little more than a few antiques to elevate
it above the corner noodle shop. What's the use of "lots of food,"
when it's "as mediocre as this?"

Mappamondo  $20

11 Abingdon Sq. at Bleecker in the W. Village (212) 675-3100
581 Hudson St. at Bank St. in the W. Village (212) 675-7474

"There must be a thousand restaurants just like these," so why are
these globe/map themed Italians so popular? "They're cheap." As in
"cheap bottles of wine" and "cheap date." Get it? Tons of people do.
The tables are too close, the music is too loud, the waiters are too busy
to give you too much attention.

| | FOOD | ROOM | STAFF | COST |

March

$64

405 E. 58th St. (212) 754-6272
bet. First Ave. & Sutton Pl. at Sutton Pl.
"Another spot to break in the corporate card," this "impressive" but "subtle" New American in Sutton Place is "unbeatable for that special occasion." "Delightful combinations" of "innovative" fare and an "intimate, romantic setting" complete with fireplace and garden make it "excellent" across the board. Service is spectacular, too.

Marchi's

$39

251 E. 31st St. (212) 679-2494
bet. Second & Third Aves. in Murray Hill
"Come hungry" to this decades-old, ivy-covered brownstone, where you can expect "quaint atmosphere," "friendly service," and "fair prices" for "heavy portions" of well-prepared, "authentic" Northern Italian food. No bells and whistles, just "comfortable" and "nice," "like eating at home."

Marguery Grill

133 E. 65th St. (212) 744-2533
bet. Lexington & Park Aves. on the Upper East Side
A new menu and chef Gerard Hayden, who has been sous chef at Aureole, Park Avenue Cafe and TriBeCa Grill, helps this "pleasant" spot (ex-Lex) transform into Marguery Grill.

Marichu

$36

342 E. 46th St. (212) 370-1866
bet. First & Second Aves. in the UN Area
With "very good" food from the Basque region of Northern Spain, this UN-Area Spanish is "a well-kept secret." That's a good thing: this place is small, but doubles in size when the garden is open.

Marion's Continental

$26

354 Bowery (212) 475-7621
bet. E. 4th & Great Jones Sts. in the E. Village
For "cool" "cocktails" in a room that reeks of retro "chic," try this "laid-back" East Villager that was built for socializing. The martinis and cosmopolitans are more "delicious" than the "limited" but competent Continental fare so drink up and soak in the Downtown "atmosphere."

Mark's

$51

The Mark Hotel, 25 E. 77th St. (212) 879-1864
bet. Fifth & Madison Aves. on the Upper East Side
The "old-English gentlemen's" club decor and "superb, individualized service" appeal to a sedate clientele who appreciate the "beautiful" hotel setting and solid, seasonal Contemporary French/American food. Plus they've got the "best bartenders in NY" at the wonderful "after-dinner bar."

Marlowe
$31

328 W. 46th St. (212) 765-3815
at Eighth Ave. in Clinton
The American Fusion menu is good, but the many ambient extras, including candlelit tables, two fireplaces, a garden and sidewalk dining are the main attractions. "Quick, if you want to get in and out to see a show," it's "almost never crowded," and has a competent staff and cheap pre-theater deal, making it more a restaurant of convenience than of necessity.

Marnie's Noodle Shop
$14

466 Hudson St. (212) 741-3214
bet. Grove & Barrow Sts. in the W. Village
This Pan Asian noodle shop may have "fresh" food, but the "tiny, cramped" atmosphere, indifferent service and varying quality make it "fair, but nothing special."

Martini's
$33

810 Seventh Ave. (212) 767-1717
at 53rd St. in Midtown W.
A "wonderful open space," and one of the best martinis in town doesn't compensate for Italian/Mediterranean cooking that is "an embarrassment" at this West Midtowner.

Marti Turkish
$20

1269 First Ave. (212) 737-6104
bet. 68th & 69th Sts. on the Upper East Side
"Good food at a good price." That's Marti's, an Upper East Side Turkish that offers a different taste for you spice hounds. On weekends, they have live Turkish musicians. Playing live Turkish music, that is.

Mary Ann's
$19

116 Eighth Ave. (212) 633-0877
at 16th St. in Chelsea
2452 Broadway (212) 877-0132
at 91st St. on the Upper West Side
1503 Second Ave. (212) 249-6165
bet. 78th & 79th Sts. on the Upper East Side
86 Second Ave. (212) 475-5939
at 5th St. in the E. Village
Though "healthy Mexican" sometimes tastes more Tex than Mex at this noisy, crowded citywide chain, it's still a New York favorite. They keep the cost of your meal down by cramming in lots of tables and refusing all credit cards. Folks agree, the Chelsea location's the best.

Mary Lou's

21 W. 9th St. (212) 533-0012
bet. Fifth & Sixth Aves. in the Central Village
"Low key, quiet and comfortable," this West Villager is "another smokers' refuge" that also serves notably good Continental food, specializing in seafood dishes. With a "good wine list," folks call it "a fancy place for a good price."

FOOD ROOM STAFF COST

Mary's

$31

42 Bedford St. (212) 741-3387
bet. Seventh Ave. S. & Bleecker St. in the W. Village
"Superb, yet unpretentious food in a romantic, relaxed setting," say voters of this very West Village American, located in a "charming and elegant" 19th-century townhouse that includes fireplaces and a "great bar." N.B. Bizarrely, the private room pays homage to none other than "Big Bad Mama II" star Angie Dickenson.

Match

$36

160 Mercer St. (212) 343-0020
bet. Prince & Houston Sts. in SoHo
If a trendy restaurant is only as hip as its line outside, then this SoHo American/Asian Fusion place (sister spot to Lucky Strike) is still "trend city." Like the crowd, the food may "look good," but is somewhat lacking in taste: "Great sushi?" "I don't think so." How can you tell with all that cigarette and cigar smoke, anyway? Still, not many places are as "good for a bottle of wine at 3 a.m."

Match Uptown

$41

33 E. 60th St. (212) 906-9177
bet. Madison & Park Aves. on the Upper East Side
Whether you find it "chic" or "Eurotrash meets Upper East Side," the Uptown version of a Downtown trendmonger has attitude to spare. The modern-American-slash-Pacific-Rim cooking is "great if you can't decide what genre of food you want," and it's as "beautifully presented" as those eating it. Late-night jazz and a buzzing bar are magnets for arrivistes and "wanna-bes."

Matthew's

$45

1030 Third Ave. (212) 838-4343
at 61st St. on the Upper East Side
This may be the most you'll pay for Morrocan food in NYC, but our voters assure us it's "imaginatively refined," in a "quiet setting" (good for romance or business) that's worth the cost. The staff can be "snooty," but this is the Upper East Side: snoot 'em right back!

Matt's Grill

$19

932 Eighth Ave. (212) 307-5109
at 55th St. in Midtown W.
So it's "loud," but what bar and grill isn't. The service is mighty friendly and they deal out "great burgers" in neighborhood environs. It's nestled nicely near the theater district, so if you spent all your money on orchestra seats, a "great value" burger here will take a little sting out of the evening's bill.

Mavalli Palace

$22

46 E. 29th St. (212) 679-5535
bet. Park & Madison Aves. in Murray Hill
One of the top Vegetarians in the city, this Murray Hill restaurant is also one of the best Indians: "Superb Southern Indian food" is brought to your table by a "helpful and sincere staff," and at low, NY Indian prices. "A find," "be prepared to sit and enjoy." Mavallous!

▉ = SUPERIOR ▇ = EXCELLENT ▅ = V. GOOD ▬ = GOOD

Maxim's
Le Bistro de Maxim

680 Madison Ave. at 61st St./Upper East Side (212) 980-6988
If shopping hasn't maxed out your credit cards, you can max 'em out at this large new offering, billed as a replica of Maxim's of Paris. Vote on it on next year's poll.

Mayrose

920 Broadway at 21st St. in the Flatiron District (212) 533-3663
This Flatiron Diner has a lovely, spare setting, and is usually filled with a "trendy designer crowd" (including more than a few celebs) who go for "great comfort food" after the movies or for "funky breakfast" or "great brunch." Portions are "generous," but the service has an "attitude."

Mazzei

 $39

1564 Second Ave. bet. 81st & 82nd/U.E. Side (212) 628-3131
Word is the "food is fabulous" at this Upper East Side sleeper. It's a "neighborhood Italian" known for freshly made specialties from the Puglia region cooked in a wood-burning oven. A welcoming staff and unintimidating atmosphere make it a "favorite local spot" worth remembering.

McGee's

240 W. 55th St. (212) 957-3536
bet. Broadway & Eighth Ave. in Midtown W.
This Irish-American pub now appears in a former firehouse just off-Broadway, having lost its fight with CNS to stay at the Ed Sullivan Theater. Good for a beer, a burger, or a chicken pot pie.

McSorley's
Old Ale House

15 E. 7th St. bet. Second & Third Aves./E. Village (212) 473-9148
For "atmosphere galore" head over to this East Village pub that's been brewing its own since the 1800s. "Too many Wall Street types," so-so pub eats, and a divey feel don't deter devotees who appreciate the "excellent beer on tap" and vintage decor at this "unique" NYC "legend." No credit cards.

Meandros Greek

 $21

118 MacDougal St. (212) 505-7627
bet. Bleecker & W. 3rd Sts. in the Washington Sq. Area
This Central Village Greek is "good" for family-style service, but "the food is not as rewarding." While some call it the "best home delivery for Greek food," others say "skip it and go to Astoria."

Mee Noodle

 $13

219 First Ave. bet. 13th & 14th/E. Village (212) 995-0333
795 Ninth Ave. at 53rd St. in Clinton (212) 765-2929
922 Second Ave. at 49th St. in Midtown E. (212) 888-0027
The "fastest restaurants in the world" have "great noodles," but voters call them little more than an "imitation Ollie's." "Hot, uncomfortable, but insane portions of well-prepared food for a pittance."

FOOD ROOM STAFF COST

Mekka
$23

14 Ave. A bet. E. Houston & 2nd/E. Village (212) 475-8500
The "good," "solid and reasonable" Southern/Cajun food at this
two-year-old attracts a "hip, diverse, beautiful-people crowd." A
little expensive for some East Villagers, and with more than a
few detractors who did not order the "best batter-dipped catfish
this side of the Mississippi."

MeKong

44 Prince St. (212) 343-8169
at Mulberry St. in SoHo
Brian Bui's new Little Italy Vietnamese, across from St. Patrick's Old
Cathedral, has an Americanized atmosphere and outdoor seating .
Fans laud the "good food" and love the view from the "tiny patio."

Meltemi
$34

905 First Ave. (212) 355-4040
at 51st St. in Midtown E.
With solid scores in every category, this Sutton Place Greek
transports voters with some of the "finest" seafood specialties
around. The "cool, calm atmosphere" and moderate prices enhance
an authentic experience that makes voters declare: "You can smell
and taste the Aegean."

Menchanko-Tei
$19

131 E. 45th St. (212) 986-6805
bet. 3rd & Lexington Aves. in Midtown E.
39 W. 55th St. (212) 247-1585
bet. 5th & 6th Aves. in Midtown W.
5 World Trade Ctr. (212) 432-4210
bet. Vesey & Church Sts. in the Financial District
"Like a scene out of Tampopo," these Chinese/Japanese restaurants
are "upscale noodle shops with large sake selections." "Great lunch
spots" for "huge bowls of yummy noodle soups," there are also
great off-rush hour bargains.

Merchants
$24

112 Seventh Ave. (212) 366-7267
bet. 16th & 17th Sts. in Chelsea
521 Columbus Ave. (212) 721-3689
bet. 85th & 86th Sts. on the Upper West Side
These sibs are "great for an after work drink," or for "wine,
sandwiches and salads," "a must on those cold winter nights, a
beautiful fire burning and the onion soup is awesome." "Nice for
brunch before a walk in Central Park?" "Decent bar fare" for a mostly
under-30 crowd and a "staff with attitude" is what you'll find here.

Meriken
$27

162 W. 21st St. at Seventh Ave. in Chelsea (212) 620-9684
Some folks are loyal to this 15-year-old Chelsea Japanese, once trendy and
still "unique." However, as the evenly mixed (good and bad) food ratings
and diminishing younger crowd attest, a "good wine list," "funky" look,
and "good" sushi don't manage to make this place a standout.

Merlot/Iridium Jazz

 $37

44 W. 63rd St. (212) 582-2121
bet. Broadway & Columbus Ave. on the Upper West Side
The operative word is "wow!" for this Lincoln Center-handy cafe
with its "funky" "Cat in the Hat" meets "Jetsons" decor. The
Regional American food is only "so-so," but a new chef promises to
upgrade the menu. It's still "more than enough for pre-opera" or a
"chic jazz hangout." Floating stairs, "tooth-shaped chairs"...this is
one "fantastic spot" (one fan wants to "be there at their auction").
Go for "appetizers" or "the scene," but "don't go while tripping."

Mesa City

1059 Third Ave. (212) 207-1919
at 62nd St. on the Upper East Side
A downscale version of Mesa Grill, this new Upper East Sider will
serve chef Bobby Flay's creative Southwestern cuisine.

Mesa Grill

 $42

162 Fifth Ave. (212) 807-7400
bet. 15th & 16th Sts. in the Flatiron District
Serving what many consider "the best" and most "innovative"
Southwestern food in the city, Bobby Flay's "vibrant" still-hot-spot
has attained the status of trendy classic. Yes, the "acoustics are
appalling" and "the tables are too close," but at least you're sitting
cheek-to-cheek with a "cool crowd," and "the food is worth the
noise." "You can't go wrong" with this "spicy winner." (Hint:
Brunch is "even better than dinner.")

Meskerem

 $21

468 W. 47th St. (212) 664-0520
bet. Ninth & Tenth Aves. in Clinton
Go to Hell...'s Kitchen for a culinary delight. This top Ethiopian
sleeper is the "best buy all around in NYC for the food, and fun
eating it." The "most authentic ethnic" is "too cheap"—the prix fixe
lunch is seven bucks.

Metisse

 $27

239 W. 105th St. (212) 666-8825
bet. Broadway & Amsterdam Ave. in the Columbia U. Area
Way up the West Side, this "cozy and intimate" Nouvelle French has a
ferocious group of local followers who don't want us telling anyone
about it. The "good, imaginative menu" changes with the seasons, and
is "much needed in the neighborhood." The "reasonable prices" also
help make this "gem" a "great Columbia hideaway."

Metro Diner

2641 Broadway (212) 866-0800
at 100th St. on the Upper West Side
The food is "just a little better than general diner fare," as is the
ambiance at this way-Upper West Sider. They do their baking on
premises, serve "cheap, adequate breakfast" and make a "great
burger." Its strength? Not much competition for blocks and blocks.

FOOD ROOM STAFF COST

Metropolitan Cafe

959 First Ave. (212) 759-5600
bet. 52nd & 53rd Sts. in Midtown E.
A "lovely garden patio" and convenient location keep this
Midtown write-in popular with business lunchers and locals. It's
a "neighborhood" favorite for reliable, "average" American fare
in a spacious setting.

Mexican Radio

 $18

250 Mulberry St. (212) 343-0140
bet. Spring & Prince Sts. in Little Italy
A unique vibe to this Little Italy newcomer (a Mexican restaurant in
Little Italy—now there's a vibe) has voters raving. "A really fine
hot Mexican" is made even better by discount drink hours and a
"fun staff." It won't be a "neighborhood secret" for long.

Mezzaluna

 $32

1295 Third Ave. (212) 535-9600
bet. 74th & 75th Sts. on the Upper East Side
Brick-oven pizza and "delicious pasta" are plusses at this "kind
of trendy" Upper East Side Italian. Complaints for the "rude,
rude, rude" staff and "there's no excuse for no credit cards." The
name means "half-moon," but to many it's just half—well, you
make the joke.

Mezzogiorno

 $36

195 Spring St. (212) 334-2112
at Sullivan St. in SoHo
"Great pizza, too packed" is the skinny on this SoHo North Italian
that is "always a treat," especially if you like having "fun with
Eurotrash." More upscale than other brick-oven joints, with "pizza
and pastry top rate," it's also much more expensive.

Michael's

 $46

24 W. 55th St. (212) 767-0555
bet. Fifth & Sixth Aves. in Midtown W.
The "lovely" ambiance and fresh flowers complement the fine art at
this spacious, "casual" West Midtowner. "Delicious" Californian
fare and a private garden room make it a "solid choice for a power
lunch" or "business dinner." Service is "sweet" and
"accommodating" but some adrenaline-addled NYers bark: It's too
"relaxing," "take it back, California."

Mickey Mantle's

 $29

42 Central Park S. (212) 688-7777
59th St. bet Fifth & Sixth Aves. in Midtown W.
"Great for kids"and tourists, this Midtown American-cum-sports bar
boasts TVs, museum-quality memorabilia and prime sidewalk seats
facing Central Park. Needless to say, the food is "less than ordinary"
but the staff is "well intentioned" and "it's a must for Yankees fans."

≣ = SUPERIOR ≣ = EXCELLENT ≣ = V. GOOD ≡ = GOOD

Mi Cocina

⬛🍴⬛ 🌹 ⬛🍷⬛ $28

57 Jane St. (212) 627-8273
at Hudson St. in the W. Village

Voters easily spot the food at this West Villager as "real Mexican," not Tex-Mex or fast food: "it goes way beyond burritos." A bit "fancier than the norm," it offers "complex flavors" though, if making comparisons with other Mexicas, the portions are somewhat smaller. De rigeur comment: "excellent margaritas."

Mike's Bar & Grill

🍴 ⬛🌹⬛ 🍷 $25

650 Tenth Ave. (212) 246-4115
bet. 45th & 46th Sts. in Clinton

Hidden away "in the middle of nowhere" on Tenth Avenue is this funky but somewhat dated "neighborhood" spot that offers "homey" if unexciting eclectic American food, "great drinks" and "more fun than a barrel of monkeys." Though it's strictly "no big deal" unless you're already in the vicinity, fans say they have "always had a good time here."

Minetta Tavern

⬛🍴⬛ 🌹 ⬛🍷⬛ $30

113 MacDougal St. (212) 475-3850
bet. Bleecker & W. 3rd Sts. in the W. Village

It's been around since the '30s, performing consistently year after year. Frequent diners call it "a good-old Italian favorite" "haunt" and "a little tucked-away gem" with "caring" service. Celebs like it too so keep your eyes peeled. It's popular with smokers, kids and for pre-theater eats.

Mingala Burmese

⬛🍴⬛ 🌹 🍷 $18

21 E. 7th St. (212) 529-3656
bet. Second & Third Aves. in the E. Village

Just like Burma, this restaurant is somewhat smaller and just outside little India, in this case in the East Village. "Good on all counts," most think it's among the "best Burmese," "reliable and consistent," with "fresh salads," and "curries and noodles" as standouts.

Mingala West

⬛🍴⬛ 🌹 ⬛🍷⬛ $22

325 Amsterdam Ave. (212) 873-0787
bet. 75th & 76th Sts. on the Upper West Side

The Upper West Side sibling to Downtown's Mingala Burmese, and, though bigger, folks say it's just as good. With "interesting and exotic food at reasonable prices," and all "delivered with verve."

Miracle Grill

⬛🍴⬛ 🌹 ⬛🍷⬛ $28

112 First Ave. (212) 254-2353
bet. 6th & 7th Sts. in the E. Village

Southwestern "food this good, in a charming garden" at "East Village prices" truly "is a miracle." So much so that MG ranks high on our lists of outside dining, first date and large party spots. Very popular weekend brunches and "good drinks" help to make it "the Mesa Grill without all the hype."

	FOOD	ROOM	STAFF	COST

Mirezi

59 Fifth Ave. (212) 242-9709
at 13th St. in the Central Village
Formerly the Markham, redone to become Mirezi, this new now-Asian restaurant borrows cuisine from the entire Orient: Korea-based, with influences from Japan, Thailand and China. 14 tiny televisions on the walls show Korean commercials and Japanimation—Mirezi means "futureland" in Korean.

Miss Saigon

1425 Third Ave. (212) 988-8828
bet. 80th & 81st Sts. on the Upper East Side
Don't worry, while the portions at this Upper East Side Vietnamese restaurant are as big as the Broadway show, the quality is much better. "Super fresh and super delicious," it's "new and crowded," a "great value."

Mitali East $20

334 E. 6th St. (212) 533-2508
bet. First & Second Aves. in the E. Village
A standout on the East Village's Curry Lane, this Indian serves "very good" food to a crowd of all ages (not just bargain-hunting youngsters). While an "exotic experience," it's a reliably good one (this "grandfather of the Indian restaurant row" has a liquor license, for example), "at a price" for this area. But, at $20 per, it's a very cheap date indeed.

Mitali West $22

296 Bleecker St. (212) 989-1367
at Seventh Ave. S. in the W. Village
While affiliated with Mitali East, we treat this one separately as voters are somewhat disappointed with this West Village Indian. Despite a "good location" ("more light and open than Mitali East") and "good food," "you can get better elsewhere" including the East Village branch.

Monkey Bar $44

Elysee Hotel, 60 E. 54th St. (212) 838-2600
bet. Madison & Park Aves. in Midtown E.
Those who "remember the old days" (it's gone from chic to shabby-chic to now ultra-chic) say this Elysee Hotel offshoot and now-attendant restaurant's "old comfortable ambiance" is such eye-candy, it would make a "great setting for a movie." One of Midtown's best after-work drink spots (especially for martinis), there's a dress code down to the shoes so the crowd can't help looking good. The Contemporary American food can't live up to the room, and folks say the staff "needs more training."

Monsoon $19

435 Amsterdam Ave. (212) 580-8686
at 81st St. on the Upper West Side
You don't get "none of that upscale French/SE Asian melange" here; just "good old Vietnamese/Thai peasant food," though many say it's "not too authentic," or at least less authentic than courthouse-area spots. "A welcome relief to the boredom in Morningside Heights."

Monte's Trattoria

97 MacDougal St. (212) 228-9194
bet. Bleecker & W. 3rd Sts. in the W. Village
Romackateers praise the authentic "Goodfellas" atmosphere and
"wonderful specialties" at this West Villager. Though service can be
"quirky," it's a "good value" for "fresh," "well-prepared" Italian fare.

Montrachet $56

239 W. Broadway (212) 219-2777
bet. Walker & White Sts. in TriBeCa
Drew Nieporent's flagship is still at the top of the heap, or Drew's
heap, at least. The "excellent" food and "very knowledgeable staff"
have helped to put it in New Yorker's Top 25 overall favorite spots.
With one of the best wine lists in town, voters find it "worth the
search" through TriBeCa, if they find it at all: Keep looking, it's one
of the "best dining experiences in NYC." Some say the ambiance
("too yuppie" means "destination spot") can't hold its own against the
food and staff: Most lump them together and come up with "bliss."

Moondance Diner

80 6th Ave. (212) 226-1191
bet. Grand & Canal Sts. in SoHo
Here's a "kitschy, fun" "punk diner" with "pretty good food" and
"fabulous grease." Regulars tout the "cool-ugly adjacent room" and
recommend the "best onion rings and apple pancakes."

Moonstruck

400 W. 23rd St. (212) 924-3709
at Ninth Ave. in Chelsea
"When all else fails," you've got this 24-hour Chelsea diner to fall
back on. "Very good breakfasts" are only part of a "large selection,"
on a huge menu. That's a-more, if not amore.

Moran's $31

146 Tenth Ave. (212) 627-3030
at 19th St. in Chelsea
Moran Bldg., 103 Washington St. (212) 732-2020
bet. Rector & Carlisle Sts. in the Financial District
Reasons to visit: "good beers and a great pick-up scene," a
"charming room," and a "great, quiet, out-of-the-way location,"
complete with water view that's swell for business lunches. Reason
not to: the "overpriced" Continental fare is "mediocre at best."

Moreno $37

65 Irving Pl. (212) 673-3939
at 18th St. in Gramercy
A "feel-good place" dispensing "decent food" and "good value and
quality," "this "serviceable Gramercy Italian" gets as much
feedback for its "romantic" atmosphere and "wonderful sidewalk
dining" as for its fairly typical Italian menu. Moreno Maltagliati is
the "consummate host," inspiring a solid neighborhood following.

FOOD ROOM STAFF COST

Morton's of Chicago

$53

90 West St. at Wall St. in the Financial District (212) 732-5665
551 Fifth Ave. at 45th St. in Midtown E. (212) 972-3315
"Boy's restaurants" indeed: Breathe in that macho mingling of sirloin sizzle and cigar smoke. This chain so good you forget it's a chain features steaks that are "the best in town except for Peter Luger"—or simply "as good as you can get." Either way, it's the ideal men's business lunch place.

Mo's Caribbean

1454 Second Ave. (212) 650-0561
at 76th St. on the Upper East Side
While some voters only see this Upper East Side Caribbean as a "noisy pickup bar," a closer look reveals "good music and atmosphere," with big crowds and a good "Monday night lobster special." And the food? "Good," with some standouts, like the "fantastic coconut shrimp."

Motown Cafe

$25

104 W. 57th St. (212) 581-8030
bet. Sixth & Seventh Aves. in Midtown W.
The Four Tops here: live Motown music every hour, a jivin' jukebox, "great interior design," and "must-try" sweet potato fries. "The best of the 57th Street theme parks" is "a great place to bring visitors or "the kids—they'll have a ball." Fries aside, the food offers few Temptations: It's "surprisingly bland" and more burger-y than soulful.

Moustache

$16

90 Bedford St. (212) 229-2220
bet. Barrow & Grove Sts. in the W. Village
No reservations mean occasional long waits at this teeny West Village Middle Eastern, but most voters keep a stiff upper lip: "The food is amazing." "The Middle Eastern 'pitza' is fabulous" made to order on a pita, of course. The staff could be more attentive; still, for many voters, Moustache is a "favorite."

Mr. Chow

$47

324 E. 57th St. (212) 751-9030
bet. First & Second Aves. in Midtown E.
Trendoids say it's "not the same since Warhol died," but, to answer their question: Yes, Mr. Chow is still open and still tasting great. This Sutton place Chinese may be "a bit pricey," and not everyone's first choice for what some call "overbearing" Asian, but the food is still "delicious."

Mueng Thai

$18

23 Pell St. (212) 406-4259
bet. Mott & Bowery in Chinatown
"For a 101 education" "bring a big party" to this "small" but "fine" "starter Thai" in Chinatown. The servers may be "unknowledgeable" and the premises nondescript, but the owner's the "friendliest" and the food's "cheap" and "delicious."

▦ = SUPERIOR ▦ = EXCELLENT ▦ = V. GOOD ▬ = GOOD

Mughlai  $24

320 Columbus Ave. (212) 724-6363
bet. 75th & 76th Sts. on the Upper West Side
Some folks just can't get used to the idea of an Indian restaurant outside of the East Village. This Upper West Sider is at least "pretty good," and some think even better than "any place on Sixth Street," though "pricey" for Indian. Hey, you pay for the neighborhood.

Mumbles

179 Third Ave. at 17th St. in Gramercy (212) 477-6066
Tasty Caesar salad and "good value" brunch keep tongues wagging about this Gramercy New American. "Generous portions" and late hours make it a popular "hangout" though service sometimes fumbles.

Museum Cafe

366 Columbus Ave. at 77th St./Upper West Side (212) 799-0150
Aside from its "good location" opposite the Museum of Natural History, there's "nothing special" about this Upper West Side American. "Satisfactory" fare and a "pleasant atmosphere" featuring an enclosed atrium make it a "nice" neighbor.

Mustang Grill  $23

1633 Second Ave. (212) 744-9194
at 85th St. on the Upper East Side
The "average" Southwestern fare is "okay," but hipsters gallop to this "trendy" Upper Eastside "hangout" for the huge tequila menu and "fair prices." A popular destination for "good fried things" at brunch, it looks "better on the inside" than it does from Second Avenue. After dark the "noise" and "poor service" make it best for imbibing.

My Most Favorite Desserts  $22

120 W. 45th St. (212) 997-5130
bet. Sixth Ave. & Broadway in Midtown W.
While this little Theater District dessert spot isn't on the Romac "Bestest Restaurant Names" list, it is an easy choice for post-theater or post-dinner desserts. They also serve pretty "good" other light fare, but Romac Reporters advise, "stick to the sweets."

Ñ  $23

33 Crosby St. (212) 219-8856
bet. Broome & Grand Sts. in SoHo
The copper top bar's the thing at this SoHo Spanish, with "great entertainment" and "excellent tapas." "Watch out for the flamenco dancers" at this "little hot spot," a Romac Top 10 for Thursday night out. "Nice and small and dark."

Nadaman Hakubai

Kitano Hotel, 66 Park Ave. (212) 885-7111
at 38th St. in Murray Hill
The expensive Kaiseki dinners are the draw here, the experience of a trip to Japan without the airplane. This is a great spot to celebrate that big business deal, in one of the private tatami rooms.

	FOOD	ROOM	STAFF	COST

Nadine's

$26

99 Bank St. (212) 924-3165
at Greenwich St. in the W. Village

"Fancy on the outside, homey and friendly on the inside," this West Village Eclectic serves one of the best brunches in town. Chandeliers, "funky music," "congenial staff" and nude paintings make it "campy and fun": large portions and low prices make it a good value. "Congenial everything."

Nanni Il Valletto

$46

133 E. 61st St. (212) 223-8720
bet. Park & Lexington Aves. on the Upper East Side

Though it's only been around for 20 years (not a mean feat in the NYC restaurant world), Nanni's has a "1950s feel," an old-style "elegance" that includes sumptuous surroundings and pampering service. "Very distinguished," the "very good" Italian food has earned a roster of "loyal diners" who always dress for dinner.

Nanni's

$49

146 E. 46th St. (212) 599-9684
bet. Third & Lexington Aves. in Midtown E.

Intimate, elegant and pricey, this East Side Italian is nearly 30 and still going strong, serving "Italian food like it is in Italy." The management recommends the Angel Nanni, but voters say any of the pasta and fish dishes are "great." It may be time for a makeover: The decor has become "a little worn."

Naples

MetLife Bldg., 200 Park Ave. (212) 972-7001
at 45th St. in Midtown E.

Restaurant Associates strikes again: This one is a Midtown redsauce Italian, which celebrates the tradition of Naples cuisine by naming its ovens after Italian volcanoes.

Negril Island Spice

$23

362 W. 23rd St. (212) 807-6411
bet. Eighth & Ninth Aves. in Chelsea

"From Chelsea to Jamaica in a second," say voters, or at least to a Jamaican bar: the "nice ambiance" that includes a cool crowd, a "relaxing fishtank at the bar," and "great calypso music on the weekends" outstrips the food, that, though "delicious," is a bit "Americanized."

Nellos

$42

696 Madison Ave. (212) 980-9099
bet. 62nd & 63rd Sts. on the Upper East Side

"Crowded and mediocre for the price," this Madison Avenue shopping stop is not without its merits. "Sidewalk people-watching" includes street performers who stop by in the summer, but locals "just can't understand its popularity with tourists."

New City Cafe

 $36

246 DeKalb Ave., Brooklyn (718) 622-5607
bet. Vanderbilt & Clermont

If you're looking for the New City you'll have to go to Brooklyn:
Most think it's "worth the trip." The New American food at this
two-year-old is "very good" and the 35-seat room means you
should call ahead. Garden dining in nice weather.

New York Noodletown

 $17

28 Bowery (212) 349-0923
at Bayard St. in Chinatown

"A unique and frenzied dining experience" can be had at this Cantonese
joint, where the standard menu is "not standard at all," and the specials
are really special. While some think it's the "best in Chinatown," be
warned: it's a "dive with communal seating." No credit cards.

Nha Trang

 $14

87 Baxter St. (212) 233-5948
at Canal St. in Chinatown

Don't come for the decor, come for the "terrific real Vietnamese in a
no-frills environment." The food here falls neatly into the top 200 so
try the "fresh seafood," but leave the credit cards home. No matter,
you "don't need much cash" at the "best value in New York."

Nicola Paone

 $50

207 E. 34th St. (212) 889-3239
bet. Second & Third Aves. in Murray Hill

While this upscale Italian has been a staple of Murray Hill for
nearly 40 years, and owner Nicola Paone has made every effort to
create an "intimate and cozy" atmosphere in a large setting, even
the mostly older crowd who dine here think it's "overpriced" and
has slipped from past glory.

Nicola's

 $41

146 E. 84th St. (212) 249-9850
bet. Third & Lexington Aves. on the Upper East Side

While folks aren't exactly bellowing Nicola's name from the tops of the
Italian Alps, this Northern Italian does have some Upper East Siders who
identify it as a "reliably good local" spot. Like its older core clientele, the
decor is "getting dowdy," but this place is "still very active."

Night Gallery

 $24

117 Seventh Ave. S. (212) 675-0350
bet. Christopher & W.10th Sts. in the W. Village

The attraction at this West Villager is repulsion: filled with macabre,
often disgusting artwork and a corny, clubby computer-graphics
screen, the "strange decor" includes obnoxious animatronic skulls and
satyrs, explained by "curators" (actors) to a mostly "tourist" crowd.
The American food is "terrible: stick with a burger in this funhouse."

FOOD ROOM STAFF COST

Niko's
$22

2161 Broadway at 76th St./Upper West Side (212) 873-7000
Okay. A Greek, a Turk, an Italian and a Middle Easterner walk into a
kitchen on the Upper West Side...and come up with one of the
"friendliest places in New York," with a "kind staff" that serves "fresh
Mediterranean food." The punch line? The "fake grape vines."

9
$14

110 St. Mark's Pl. bet. Ave. A & First/E. Village (212) 982-7129
Most recommend this East Village Tex-Mex and Eclectic/Vegetarian
for "coffee and dessert." It's a "cool, artsy cafe" (the furniture is hand
painted), "good for conversation and late dining" and "coffee served in
a French press." Though loud, it's not uncomfortably crowded (the
name hasn't managed to get them an outside line).

9 Jones Street
$33

9 Jones St. (212) 989-1220
bet. Bleecker & W. 4th Sts. in the Washington Sq. Area
This "dark" but "intimate Village hideaway" has a DJ on Sunday
evening and Jazz on Thursday. Relax and enjoy good "middling"
old-fashioned American food and sidewalk dining on a "perfect
Village street." Throw a party in their private loft.

Nine Muses Cafe
$26

569 Hudson St. at W. 11th St. in the W. Village (212) 741-0009
This "excellent and unusual Greek" is a newcomer to the West Village
food scene: "excellent" for classic dishes like the lamb and "unusual"
for the "light, open, airy atmosphere." Some call it "another quiet
find," though the way they go on about it, that may not last for long.

Nino's
$28

1354 First Ave. bet. 72nd & 73rd Sts. in Yorkville (212) 988-0002
This Yorkville Italian serves "great food" standards like Fra
Diabolo, to an appreciative neighborhood crowd. There's a cheap
prix fixe dinner, and smoking is allowed.

9th St. Market
$16

337 E. 9th St. (212) 473-0242
bet. First & Second Aves. in the E. Village
Serving "good homebaked" treats, this tiny (and we mean tiny)
storefront is "nice for coffee or brunch,"and features "Mr. Tony" at
dinner, who serves Eclectic/Southern fare and "great desserts" to a
very casual East Village crowd. The "laid- back atmosphere" makes
a "cozy place to read" during the day.

Nippon
Hya Tan Nippon
$35

119 E. 59th St. bet. Lexington & Park/Midtown E. (212) 751-7690
155 E. 52nd St. bet. Lexington & Park/Midtown E. (212) 751-7690
The lovely and sedate atmosphere is "very good" at these
very-Japanese Japanese, outshone by the professional, doting staff,
including "Nippon's three presiding beauties." Sushi and sashimi are
"consistently very good and fresh" (with vegetarian options, too).

= SUPERIOR = EXCELLENT = V. GOOD = GOOD

Nirvana  $41

30 Central Park S. (212) 486-5700
59th St. bet. Fifth & Sixth Aves. in Midtown W.

True to its name, atmosphere-wise, this upscale Indian offers a "romantic, beautiful" setting with Central Park views (especially heart-melting at sunset), augmented by live sitar music and fortune-telling ("precise" fortune-telling at that). But your taste buds won't be transported: "there's better food on Sixth Street."

Nobu  $57

105 Hudson St. at Franklin St. in TriBeCa (212) 219-0500

Multiple cries of "orgasmic!" greet the sushi and the special chef's tasting dinner at the "best Japanese in the city." The room is as "innovative" and "imaginative" as the food, raw or cooked, at this "celeb haunt"; the mood is "L.A. in TriBeCa," but "the cellular phones stop once the food arrives." "Extraordinary," "pure perfection"— you get the idea. In sum, "not all raw fish are created equal; Nobu is the proof."

Noho Star  $24

330 Lafayette St. at Bleecker St. in the E. Village (212) 925-0070

Though packing in a "lively" crowd, the good brunch and an open "sterile" space cannot shore up the mixed results of this NoHo American, which serves Asian dishes at dinner. When in doubt, stick to the burgers, though even those have "gone downhill of late." While "friendly," the staff doesn't earn big points. Check out the new outdoor seating: It's prime for Lafayette people-watching.

Noodle Pudding  $22

38 Henry St., Brooklyn (718) 625-3737
bet. Cranberry & Middagh

The name might lead you to think this was some kind of Asian restaurant lost in the translation, but this Brooklyn Heights newcomer (of two years) is actually a casual Italian, and by early reports, a good one at that. They still don't take credit cards, but you might want to call ahead and see if they still let you BYOB.

Novita  $39

102 E. 22nd St. (212) 677-2222
at Park Ave. S. in the Flatiron District

A family-run Flatiron find that's "underrated but better than many 'in' places." The "creative," "very high quality" regional Italian food, from homemade pastas to homemade gelato right down to the "excellent breadsticks," is served by a "welcoming staff" in a "delightful, low-key" atmosphere. To know it is to love it.

Nyona

194 Grand St. (212) 334-3669
at Mulberry St. in Little Italy

Malaysia comes to Little Italy via Nyona, a new restaurant which features authentic peasant dishes from Penang. Hike a couple blocks from SoHo, and tell us what you think on your questionnaire next year.

FOOD ROOM STAFF COST

Oak Room & Bar $48

The Plaza, 768 Fifth Ave. (212) 546-5330
at Central Park S. in Midtown W.
In business since 1907, this venerable old "classic" in the Plaza Hotel must be doing something right. Perhaps it's the "great ambiance" ("very dark," "very woody"), the "good" "solid American food," or the surefooted staff who make you "feel important." Whatever the virtues, it's a "great spot to talk to someone," and quite possibly the "nicest place to go for tea-time in NYC." To a certain "sedate," "older crowd," The Oak Room is one "classy joint."

Oceana $54

55 E. 54th St. (212) 759-5941
bet. Madison & Park Aves. in Midtown E.
Romac Reporters find "perfect" preparations and service at this "fancy" yet "unintimidating" East Midtown seafooder. The "elegant" atmosphere makes it "wonderful for business lunch (especially if someone else is paying)." A "top notch" favorite that serves "unreal bouillabaise," Oceana has a new upstairs oyster bar.

Odeon $35

145 W. Broadway (212) 233-0507
at Thomas St. in TriBeCa
"Night and day," this "art-deco" icon in TriBeCa is "still happening." For "great people-watching" and "reliable" American/Continental fare, it's a "classic and cool" late-night "favorite." Most voters consider it a Downtown "institution" that's "always a great place to be."

Odessa

119 Ave. A (212) 473-8916
bet. 7th & St. Mark's Pl. in the E. Village
A 24-hour East Village "mainstay," this diner dishes up "plentiful" portions of "standard" Ukrainian fare at "low prices." Locals appreciate the "improved" decor and "great" pierogi but say service can get "mean."

Official All Star Cafe $25

1540 Broadway (212) 840-8306
at 48th St. in the Theater District
Yeowch! This stadium-sized sports bar American gets blasted by our voters: The all-stars are a host of owner/sports figures (you get to see their pictures!) and sports legends (you get to see their jerseys!) while splash-cut video assaults your senses from a football-field of big screens. "A sports fan's heaven," the food is bad enough to send them there early.

Oishi Noodle $11

1117 Ave. of the Americas (212) 764-3075
at 43rd St. in Midtown W.
You'll find "good, quick Japanese-style comfort food" at these little Noodle Shops around town. Not the "best Japanese noodles in the city," the "Big Bucket of Noodles" on the menu is more the speed here.

Old Devil Moon $18

511 E. 12th St. (212) 475-4357
bet. Aves. A & B in the E. Village
While the "yardsale atmosphere" ain't La Grenouille, it perfectly
suits the "good," "down-home" American Southern cooking. "A bit
dark" at night, brunch is an East Village fave, and desserts (Key
lime and peanut-butter pies) are "stellar."

Old Homestead Steakhouse $45

56 Ninth Ave. (212) 242-9040
bet. 14th & 15th Sts. in Chelsea
A "shrine to beef" for the last 128 years (with plenty of touristy
touches in the "old-time decor"), this Meat Packing District
steak-and-lobster house wins raves for "primal red-meat
satisfaction," but the staff is quite uneven, and many diners
complain the "old world atmosphere" needs a good airing out.

Old Town Bar $19

45 E. 18th St. (212) 529-6732
bet. Broadway & Park Ave. S. in the Flatiron District
The "brewskis" are the most nutritious things at this historic
Flatiron pub (the "mountain of fries" is its prize feature"), but the
century-plus Old New York charm can be food for the soul, with a
good bar for "after work" or to "end the night."

Olive Tree Cafe

117 MacDougal St. (212) 254-3480
at Bleecker St. in the Washington Sq. Area
With above average Middle Eastern food, this Washington
Square restaurant has plenty of extras: "Slate tables and chalk to
write on them" and "great desserts" happen upstairs, and there's a
comedy club downstairs.

Ollie's Noodle Shop $16

200B W. 44th St. bet. Bdwy & 8th/Theater Dist. (212) 921-5988
2957 Broadway at 116th St. in Harlem (212) 932-3300
199 Broadway bet. 68th & 69th Sts./U.W. Side (212) 595-8181
2315 Broadway at 84th St. on the Upper West Side (212) 362-3111
This chain of Chinese supershops may be an "assembly line
success," but most voters think the best of the food is limited to the
Upper West Side, original location. As for the rest, it's "cheap,"
with "rushed service" that's actually convenient: They "get you to
the theater" in "record time." However, some think the other
locations should be renamed "Oily's."

Omen $42

113 Thompson St. (212) 925-8923
bet. Prince & Spring Sts. in SoHo
You won't find Gregory Peck giving Satan's kid a haircut at this SoHo
"special place," but you will find "very good" sashimi and other Japanese
dishes. A "good example of Japanese soul," it's a lovely, "quiet" place
with a "very good" staff, and, alas, "small, Japanese portions."

___ = FAIR   [blank] = POOR   ▓ = NOT RATED   165

FOOD · ROOM · STAFF · COST

One If By Land Two If By Sea

 $55

17 Barrow St. (212) 255-8649
bet. Seventh Ave. S. & W. 4th St. in the W. Village

Most wax poetic (and the remaining few, vulgar) of this fine vintage New York Continental, far and away the most romantic restaurant in town (and No.1 on our poll, for that matter). Even Don Juan couldn't live up to the romantic hype this place receives, so a few are disappointed, but for the most part, voters like to make extravagant claims as to the power this place has over one's partner, voting it into the Top 3 for first dates and quiet chats. "Propose here: s/he'll accept."

101

 $29

10018 4th Ave. (718) 833-1313
at 101st St. in Brooklyn

"Okay food" and "lots of big hair" set the tone at this Brooklyn Italian, though don't get us wrong: It's a "fun place to hang out," and has a "homey feeling," like you're "sitting in a brownstone dining room." "Great for a holiday dinner when you don't want to cook."

Opaline

85 Ave. A (212) 475-5050
at 5th St. in the E. Village

This French bistro was too new for our participants to vote on: Walk a couple extra blocks south and east, and vote on Opaline on next year's poll.

Opus II

 $43

242 E. 58th St. (212) 753-2200
bet. Second & Third Aves. in Midtown E.

This Bloomie's-area Steakhouse has only been around for a few years, and has been slow to find fans. The staff is still trying to find itself, the decor is "too bright for a steakhouse," and the food is only average. The "prix fixe steak dinner is a good value."

Orienta

205 E. 75th St. (212) 517-7509
bet. Second & Third Aves. on the Upper East Side

No infants, sidewalk dining, late-night menu and smoking: sounds like a Village hipster hangout. Wrong. This 40-seat charmer brings chic to the Upper Eastside with its cool crowd and innovative SE Asian fare.

O.G. (Oriental Grill)

 $25

507 E. 6th St. (212) 477-4649
bet. Aves. A & B in the E. Village

Former China Grill chef Chris Genoversa opened this little Nouvelle Asian on the very outskirts of civilization (that is, past Avenue A in the East Village), serving "well-priced," well-portioned and "tasty" food that is "fab." Gin drinkers, take note: wine and beer only.

≣ = SUPERIOR ≣ = EXCELLENT ≣ = V. GOOD ▬ = GOOD

Orleans

$27

252 Bleecker St. at Leroy St. in the W. Village (212) 929-5089
1438 Third Ave. bet. 81st & 82nd Sts./U.E. Side (212) 794-1509

Folks prefer the West Village version of this Cajun/American over the Upper East Side location, and in both cases they don't remind voters "of the Louisiana they know." Sometimes the spicy flavors of the Big Easy are not to everyone's taste, and sometimes it's the restaurant that's unreliable.

Orologio

162 Ave. A (212) 675-3100
bet. 10th & 11th Sts. in the E. Village

Folks find this little East Village Italian one of the "best in Alphabet City": A "good value in an iffy neighborhood," the dark ambiance, with tons of clocks everywhere, makes some "feel like they're in Tuscany (at night, we presume).

Oren's Daily Roast

$7

985 Lexington Ave. at 71st St./Upper East Side (212) 717-3907
31 Waverly Pl. bet. Greene St. & Wash. Sq. E. (212) 420-5958
434 Third Ave. bet. 30th & 31st Sts. in Murray Hill (212) 779-1241
1144 Lexington Ave. bet. 79th & 80th/U.E. Side (212) 472-6830
33 E. 58th St. bet. Madison & Park/Midtown E. (212) 838-3345

Chipping away at their own vein in the coffee gold mine, these dark roasted ("bitter") coffee shops don't stand out, except for their "good chocolate covered espresso beans."

Orso

$38

322 W. 46th St. bet. Eighth & Ninth/Clinton (212) 489-7212

Known as "that rave celebirty hangout with excellent food," Joe Allen's Clinton Northern Italian is "an experience." While most find "everything excellent," some say that after fifteen years it has become "a bit overrated" (or maybe they're miffed since it's still "hard to get a table"). Whatever. Go post-theater and spot the actors offstage.

Osso Buco

$27

88 University Pl. bet. 11th & 12th/Central Village (212) 645-4525

"Family-style" Italian food at "excellent prices" are what attracts bargain seekers to this "neighborhood" mainstay. Big and convivial, it's good for "business affairs," "groups of friends," or "whenever Carmine's has a large wait list," but the truth be told, "some of the food is boring."

Osteria al Doge

$35

142 W. 44th St. (212) 944-3643
bet. Broadway & Sixth Ave. in Midtown W.

"Venice does it better," but this "much-needed" Theater District Northern Italian does a respectable job, dispensing "nice decor," "good antipasto," and "reasonable" prices. It's a "bit noisy" pre-theater, so "bring a book—you'll never hear a word anyone says to you." Small wonder the "best time to go is after the theater crowd."

▬ = FAIR   [blank] = POOR   ▦ = NOT RATED   **167**

FOOD ROOM STAFF COST

Osteria del Circo $49

120 W. 55th St. bet. Sixth & Seventh/Midtown W. (212) 265-3636
The sons of Sirio (as in Le Cirque) are knockin' 'em dead at this "new
neighborhood favorite" in Midtown West, with its bright, circus-theme
atmosphere and "expensive" but interesting Italian food. To fans "Circo"
is "something remarkable"—"this family is the best"—but there are
more than a few detractors who say the brothers are "too pretentious for
their own good," and there's "too much trading on Dad's name." In any
case, it's "getting difficult to get reservations."

Otabe $42

68 E. 56th St. bet. Park & Madison/Midtown W. (212) 223-7575
There's lots to see and more than the usual choices at this Midtown
Japanese, busy at lunch (reservations, please) and more "serene" at dinner.
"The chef can be quite entertaining," the food "excellent," and you can
"eat inexpensively or indulge in kaiseki." "The decor is great," too.

Ottoman Cuisine $22

413 Amsterdam Ave. (212) 799-6363
bet. 79th & 80th Sts. on the Upper West Side
Don't expect to put your feet up at this Upper West Side
two-year-old: The name refers to the Turkish origin of the food
here. While still on their way up the learning curve, the "staff is
eager to please," and the "wonderful Turkish food," including good
vegetarian options, rises well above the level of the "fair" decor.

Oyster Bar at the Plaza $41

The Plaza, 768 Fifth Ave. (212) 546-5340
at Central Park S. in Midtown W.
"Fabola crab cakes," "terrific oysters" and a "great oyster poor boy"
in "landmark surroundings" in The Plaza Hotel more than make up
for steep tariffs, too much noise, and a setting that's "a little too
cafeteria-like for the prices." Those in the know suggest you "sit at
the counter" for the most "acceptable" service.

Palio $57

151 W. 51st St. (212) 245-4850
bet. Sixth & Seventh Aves. in Midtown W.
Aesthetics attract "mostly businesspeople" to this "high-end"
Midtowner. A "beautiful" Sanro Chia mural above the downstairs
bar covers four walls and moves voters to praise the "outstanding"
ambiance. While the Italian fare is "delicious" and service sparkles,
many criticize prices that are "too high" for portions that are "too
little." Try the $35 prix fixe lunch.

Palm $49

837 Second Ave.bet. 44th & 45th/Midtown E. (212) 687-2953
Voters "love" the wall of caricatures and "huge" slabs of "fabulous"
meat at this "macho" steakhouse that's been sizzling since 1926.
Popular for business lunch, it serves "monster lobster" prompting
voters to ask "why go to Maine?" when you can crack 'em open in
Midtown. All agree that the staff, while "knowledgeable," could at
least "try smiling."

Palm Court

$44

The Plaza, 768 Fifth Ave. at CPS in Midtown W. (212) 546-5350
Quite possibly "the nicest place to go for teatime in NYC," the
legendary "bright and airy" Tea Room Cage is also "reliable to
impress out-of-towners" with a "superb" Sunday brunch buffet and
"some of the most delicious cakes and pastries" in the city. Full of
"old-world charm" and "music" (harp or violin, depending on the
time of day), this classic bit of Manhattan is truly "special." "If you
want upscale," "this is the place."

Palm Too

$48

840 Second Ave. bet. 44th & 45th/Midtown E. (212) 697-5198
"Consistently good," with "huge portions," some think this
Midtown Steakhouse is among the city's best, at least for the
old-fashioned, meat-and-potatoes meals. However, the room needs
a revamp and staff gives off a grumpy vibe. P.S. For better service,
try "greasing 'The Palm' of the maitre d'."

Pamir

$26

1065 First Ave. (212) 644-9258
at 58th St. in Midtown E.
1437 Second Ave. (212) 734-3791
bet. 74th & 75th Sts. on the Upper East Side
It's unique and "always a treat" for what may be the "best kebabs in
NYC." This Upper East Side Afghan delights diners with "varied
tastes and textures" and an "attentive," "accommodating" staff. For
most, it's "unusual and fun" with a subdued atmosphere that
includes walls covered with traditional Afghan carpets.

Panarella's

513 Columbus Ave. (212) 799-5784
bet. 84th & 85th Sts. on the Upper West Side
Sure, there are plenty of "delicious neighborhood Italians" with
"wonderful pasta" all over town. This Upper West Sider,
however, is made special by their "Italian library" decor younger
voters find "very romantic."

Panna

93 First Ave. bet. 5th & 6th Sts. in the E. Village (212) 598-4610
330 E. 6th St. bet. First & Second Aves./E. Village (212) 475-9274
These teeny East Village Indians have some of the closest tables in
town, and the First Avenue location has perhaps the most preposterous
decor ever attempted in any kind of room, anywhere. So what? The
food is "incredible," and some call the look "funky." "CHEAP!"

Pao

$29

322 Spring St. (212) 334-5464
at Greenwich St. in SoHo
Are you ready for this? There's an affordable restaurant in SoHo.
One of the newest arrivals below Houston, this Portuguese is
starting to take hold with food of both the funky and classical
variety. Early ballots from voters say, "food and service is
POW!—in-your-face amazing."

■ = FAIR   [blank] = POOR   ☰ = NOT RATED   **169**

Paola's

FOOD	ROOM	STAFF	COST

Paola's $34

343 E. 85th St. (212) 794-1890
bet. First & Second Aves. on the Upper East Side
Voters tell us that when you go to this fine little Yorkville Northern
Italian, "you're in Paola's house." Er, not quite, for though "the
owner is always there," they've just moved two doors down 85th
Street. Don't worry, it's still "quaint and wonderful," serving
"delicious gourmet Italian, home-cooked to perfection." "A very
rare find on the Upper East Side."

Paradis Barcelona $42

Kimberly Hotel, 145 E. 50th St. (212) 754-3333
bet. Third & Lexington Aves. in Midtown E.
Flamenco dancers and sangria are not enough to attract folks to this East
Midtown Spanish. Voters call it "fake Catalan," saying it's "expensive,"
"never crowded," with "poor" food. "Where are the tapas?"

Parioli Romanissimo $80

24 E. 81st St. (212) 288-2391
bet. Fifth & Madison Aves. on the Upper East Side
The intimate, "excellent" atmosphere in this former townhouse off
Central Park (with a menu that, like the park, reflects the seasons)
overlooks a skylit garden; autumn game dishes by the fireplace;
"excellent service"; and a show-stopping cheese cart to end the
evening. What could be better? Well, the food, according to voters,
though it's still "good."

Paris Commune

411 Bleecker St. (212) 929-0509
bet. Bank & W. 11th Sts. in the W. Village
"Warm and intimate" this West Villager wins fans with
"consistent" French cuisine and a "romantic" atmosphere that's
beyond "cozy." It's great for dates or a "quiet" dinner with friends,
but beware, while the staff is "gorgeous," "service is lacking."

Park Avalon $33

225 Park Ave. S. (212) 533-2500
bet. 18th & 19th Sts. in Gramercy
A big room, a late weekend menu, live entertainment at brunch, a
Park Avenue South address, a "fine bar crowd" and a Top 10 rank
for Thursday night out all add up to a "trendy" and "terrific
atmosphere." "Surprisingly pleasant staff and better-than-average"
Mediterranean/Italian food are bonuses at a restaurant that
specializes in "beautiful people."

Park Avenue Cafe $48

100 E. 63rd St. (212) 644-1900
bet. Park & Lexington Aves. on the Upper East Side
"David Burke is the most whimsical chef around," waxes one satisfied
Park Avenue patron, "and can be quite brilliant." Plenty of Romac
voters agree: "I could hardly believe my taste buds," "exquisite food,"
and "desserts are a highlight." Downtown trendsetters beware: "The
food is as super and hip as the clientele is not."

Park Bistro

$41

414 Park Ave. S. (212) 689-1360
bet. 28th & 29th Sts. in Murray Hill
"Like being in Paris," this "small" Murray Hill Provençal bistro is judged "original," "exciting," and "never disappointing." "Jammed tables" and occasionally "brusque service" (another "little bit of Paris") do nothing to detract from the "good," "very French bistro fare."

Parma

$38

1404 Third Ave. (212) 535-3520
bet. 79th & 80th Sts. on the Upper East Side
This old-line Northern Italian on the Upper East Side still inspires solid scores and a loyal, local following, if not a lot of superlatives.

Pascalou

1308 Madison Ave. (212) 534-7522
at 93rd St. in Carnegie Hill
Formerly the Carnegie Hill Cafe, Pascalou got a name and menu change with the arrival of Pascal Bonhomme, who had been the chef at Bistro du Nord. The neighborhood needs more like this one.

Passage To India

$18

308 E. 6th St. (212) 529-5770
bet. First & Second Aves. in the E. Village
"One of the most genteel" East Village Indians, a source of "good, cheap spicy food." The atmosphere may need a little "updating," there are unusual options on the menu ("mango juice!") and, though it's not the best in town, it's possibly "the best on the block."

Pasta Eater

$17

6 E. 48th St. (212) 223-3322
bet. Fifth & Madison Aves. in Midtown E.
Yawn. For a pasta haven that proclaims to having over 15 varieties, "too bland to describe" is not a great review. How about, "average"? Better? But then again the prices are "really decent" and you can bring your own drinks. Oh, they don't take reservations, but that's okay because you might already have some.

Pasta Lovers

142 W. 49th St. (212) 819-1155
bet. 6th & 7th Aves. in Midtown W.
158 W. 58th St. (212) 582-1355
bet. Sixth & Seventh Aves. in Midtown W.
A "no-frills" atmosphere, that includes pasta-themed photographs that can be less-than-appetizing, doesn't stop voters from getting in the long cafeteria line for "heavenly, huge portions" of "good" pasta.

Pasta Presto

959 Second Ave. at 51st St. in Midtown E. (212) 754-4880
What's so special about this East Side Midtowner? "Cheap food," consisting of "standard plus" pasta, though the service could use a boost. "You'll pay a lot more for a lot less at some trendier, spendier places."

FOOD ROOM STAFF COST

Pasteur

$18

85 Baxter St. at Canal St. in Chinatown (212) 608-3656

Vietnamese soups and barbecue are "very good" at this popular, "charming and cheap" Chinatown hole-in-the-wall. By the looks of the place, we hope they utilize the discoveries made by namesake Louis.

Pastrami King

$16

124-24 Queens Blvd. (718) 263-1717
at 82nd Ave. in Queens

The deli wars don't stop at Manhattan's doors; "Queens's answer to Katz's" has, to many, the "leanest," "best pastrami," cured and smoked Romanian style and piled to the rafters in a "mouthwatering, huge" sandwich—and the corned beef's a contender for "best anywhere" as well. The new decor is "cold and barren" and they "don't know the meaning of service," so "get takeout."

Patria

$45

250 Park Ave. S. (212) 777-6211
at 20th St. in the Flatiron District

"Fire and ice" in a "unique and eclectic mix of food" via Douglas Rodriguez's "creatively different" "nouvelle" "Latino deluxe." The "loud," "thrilling atmosphere" makes for a "party every night." "Fun! Food makes you laugh, and it tastes great, too." Bottom line, while the "execution doesn't always match the" "eclectic" "ideas," there's still "nothing like it."

Patrissy's

$33

98 Kenmare St. (212) 226-2888
at Mulberry St. in Little Italy

Old fashioned pine wood and brass interior provide the "very authentic" charm at this Little Italy spot. The "great" food and service rate well here so you won't go wrong.

Patroon

158 E. 46th St. (212) 883-7373
bet. 3rd & Lexington Aves. in Midtown E.

Ken Aretsky ("21" Club, Arcadia, BUtterfield 81) joins forces with Franck Deletrain, late of the Four Seasons, to create a new French/American in a large, comfortable, conveniently located Midtown space. Tell us about it on your questionnaire next year.

Patsy's Pizza

$18

2287-91 First Ave. bet. 117th & 118th/E. Harlem (212) 534-9783
61 W. 74th St. at Columbus Ave./Upper West Side (212) 579-3000
509 Third Ave. bet. 34th & 35th/Murray Hill (212) 689-7500

For more than sixty years, the Harlem location has been firing up the "best thin crust" brick oven pizzas north of the Village. The rumor is that "Frank Sinatra has their pizza flown to him," so we're guessing they make it his way. We mortals now have two more locations, in Murray Hill and on the Upper West Side, where we can dip our bread in the "special olive oil."

▤ = SUPERIOR ▤ = EXCELLENT ▤ = V. GOOD ▬ = GOOD

Patsy's Pizza (Brooklyn)

$18

19 Old Fulton St. (718) 858-4300
bet. Front & Water/Brooklyn

This Brooklyn Heights "Peter Luger of pizza joints" serves up
brick-oven "pizza from heaven" in a "loud, informal atmosphere."
Voters are virtually unanimous in praising the "smoky delicious
pies" as "the epitome of greatness" and "worth a walk" over the
bridge. Bring cash and expect a wait.

Paul & Jimmy's

$38

123 E. 18th St. (212) 475-9540
bet. Park Ave. S. & Irving Place in Gramercy
Family-owned and-operated since 1950, this "small"
"neighborhood Italian" serves up "solid" regional specialties in a
relaxed setting. Over-30 regulars report that it's a "reasonably
priced" Gramercy option that's never crowded.

Peacock Alley

$45

Waldorf-Astoria, 301 Park Ave. (212) 872-4895
at 50th St. in Midtown E.
Provincial French cooking, with "aromas from Gascony" and
other Southwestern French locales, while voted "very good" by
Romac Reporters, doesn't hold a candle to the ambiance and
"excellent people-watching" in the Waldorf-Astoria lobby. One
of the "best choices for high tea" (guess what—jacket and tie
required) there's also an "outstanding buffet brunch," and
cost-conscious ($44) prix fixe dinner.

Pedro Paramo

$21

430 E. 14th St. (212) 475-4581
bet. Ave. A & First Ave. in the E. Village
Fed up with all those Cal-Mex megafeeds? Try this "lovely,
family-owned Mexican hangout," "so much better than any
overstuffed California burrito." This is "one of NYC's real
Mexicans," "quiet and homey" and above all, "authentic." How do
they do it? "Real Mexicans run it, that's how."

Penang

$26

240 Columbus Ave. (212) 769-3788
at 71st St. on the Upper West Side
109 Spring St. (212) 274-8883
bet. Greene & Mercer Sts. in SoHo
38-04 Prince St. (718) 321-2078
at Roosevelt Ave. in Queens
This authentic" trio pleases with its "beautiful" sarong-clad servers
and "enjoyable selection" of "exotic, spicy food." Downtown's
"sexy," "jungle-like setting" ("indoor waterfall," "bamboo rest
rooms") makes for the "best interior" ("the decor in SoHo is funkier
than the West Side"), though our reporters could of course do
without "waiting in line." A few grouse that it's "too trendy to be
good," but they're just plain wrong.

FOOD · ROOM · STAFF · COST

Periyali

$44

35 W. 20th St. bet. Fifth & Sixth/Flatiron District (212) 463-7890
This Flatiron favorite garners more kudos than an octopus has tentacles
(the grilled version here "alone is enough of a reason to go," by the way).
"Right down to the Hellenistic waiters" offering "gracious service,"
every detail is right. Price is no object when it buys the "best grilled fish
in town" and makes you feel like you're "on vacation." "Almost too
good to be Greek"? Well, don't say that in front of the waiters.

Pesce Pasta

$28

262 Bleecker St. (212) 645-2993
at Morton St. in the W. Village
1079 First Ave. (212) 645-2993
at 59th St. on the Upper East Side
What makes these Italians "neighborhood gems?" The food's "very
good," (especially—what else?—the fish and pasta) the staff is
"friendly" and the price, if not "cheap" is at least a "good value,"
since portions are "fresh and hefty."

Petaluma

$36

1356 First Ave. at 73rd St. in Yorkville (212) 772-8800
"Best for lunch," this "authentic" Northern and Southern Italian
generally pleases "all around" with its fresh grilled fish and meats
from the wood-burning oven, plus specials like osso buco and
risotto. The flower-filled outdoor dining area is a plus.

Peter Luger
Steakhouse

$46

178 Broadway, bet. Bedford & Driggs/Brooklyn (718) 387-7400
The most expensive restaurant in the five boroughs that doesn't take
credit cards, this just-over-the-bridge ("what a neighborhood")
Brooklyn restaurant serves the undisputed "best steaks in New
York," even "the best aged porterhouse in the country." Creamed
spinach, shrimp cocktail and French fries help fill out the "small
menu," voters call "glorious." This vintage NYC spot is a Romac
Top 5 favorite, despite a notoriously "intolerant" staff.

Peter's Backyard

64 W. 10th St. (212) 477-0076
bet. Fifth & Sixth Aves. in the Central Village
The Peter's Backyard of the '60s and '70s (the spot where the
script for Rear Window was born) has recently been reincarnated.
Its menu features the usual variety of meats and fish, a reflection
of its steakhouse past.

Pete's Tavern

$25

129 E. 18th St. (212) 473-7676
at Irving Pl. in Gramercy
Get "that old-time feeling" at this circa-1864 Gramercy pub where
Romac Reporters advise: Check out "O. Henry's table, but don't
bother with the food." "The bar is where the action is" and it's "noisy"
and "crowded" after-work so be prepared. Tavern-lovers know it's a
"good place to drink" in an atmosphere "rich with history."

▤ = SUPERIOR ▤ = EXCELLENT ▬ = V. GOOD ▬ = GOOD

Petrossian

 $61

182 W. 58th St. (212) 245-2214
at Seventh Ave. in Midtown W.

"Death by caviar!" Now here's a restaurant you can sink your teeth into, never mind your wallet. Break the bank because this one breaks the records for food (top 100)—"order chocolate soufflé"— and ambiance: "dangerously romantic." You have to dress for ecstasy—jackets and ties are a must. But it's worth it for a place diners call "Russia's loss."

Pho Bang

117 Mott St. bet. Canal & Hester in Chinatown (212) 966-3797
3 Pike St. at E. Broadway in Chinatown (212) 233-3947
6 Chatham Sq. at Bowery in Chinatown (212) 587-0870
102 W. 86th St. at Columbus/U.W. Side (212) 579-9696

Fans wrote in these "high quality," "cheap Vietnamese," which boast "great BBQ beef and noodles" in "tawdry" "authentic Chinatown" settings—there's also a newer, more upscale location on the Upper West Side.

Phoebe's

 $21

380 Columbus Ave. (212) 724-5145
at 78th St. on the Upper West Side

"Friendly" and "comfortable as home" this Upper West Side American prepares "plain," "tasty" basics in a convenient spot opposite the Museum of Natural History. The fireplace and "quaint country atmosphere" make it a "good date place."

Phoenix Garden

 $25

242 E. 40th St. (212) 983-6666
bet. Second & Third Aves. in Murray Hill

This "creative" (i.e. large menu) Cantonese is the "best in the Midtown East area," according to voters who "can't say enough" about how much they like the food. It's also one of the few BYOBs around.

Piadina

 $29

57 W. 10th St. (212) 460-8017
bet. Sixth Ave. & Greenwich St. in the W. Village

You get "great Italian food and service in an out-of-the-way West Village location" at this cozy little yearling. Early reports say it's "very good."

Piccolo Angolo

 $24

621 Hudson St. (212) 229-9177
at Jane St. in the W. Village

Folks say this "family-run" and home-cooked Italian is "worth the trip to the West Village" (unless you already live there), where the "family style" runs toward "cheek-pinching" and food-pushing. Stares from people in line make some voters uncomfortable while they eat, but that feeling dissipates after a "bottle of their homemade wine." Tie your shoes: the "sorbet will knock your socks off!"

▬ = FAIR   [blank] = POOR   ▦ = NOT RATED

	FOOD	ROOM	STAFF	COST

Picholine
$50

35 W. 64th St. (212) 724-8585
bet. Broadway & Central Park W. on the Upper West Side
"What the West Side needs," say voters, is this "wonderful pricey" French spot that makes a "fine plus to the area." The "excellent" food "gets more and more imaginative," and the "service is superb." Though "noisy," the room is lovely, and it's open late to accomodate the opera crowd. "Lincoln Center's greatest restaurant" also includes a good wine list and the best selection of cheeses in town: It even sports NYC's only "cheese cave" to house them.

Pierre au Tunnel
$36

250 W. 47th St. (212) 575-1220
bet. Broadway & Eighth Ave. in the Theater District
It may be dated and somewhat "old-fashioned," but an older clientele appreciates this "solid" Times Square-handy bistro for its "decent" Traditional French favorites and accommodating, gracious service. A "favorite for years in the Theater area."

Pietrasanta
$26

683 Ninth Ave. (212) 265-9471
at 47th St. in Clinton
This "Clinton gem" "never lets you down," dispensing "great" homemade bread and all-around delicious Northern Italian food at "good prices." Its convenient location "near theaters but away from the tourist traps" may be a little "too cramped," but this one's "still a favorite after many years."

Pietro's
$46

232 E. 43rd St. (212) 682-9760
bet. Second & Third Aves. in Midtown E.
Few are seated but many are satisfied at this little Murray Hill Italian Steakhouse. In business since the prohibition era (though only at this location for the past 12 years), this unassuming and "very good" spot is the very definition of "sleeper."

Pig & Whistle
$22

165 W. 47th St. (212) 302-0112
bet. Sixth & Seventh Aves. in Midtown W.
No whistle blowing here: a recent relocation to the Midtown from Rockefeller Center hasn't done much to improve the quality of the food at this Irish/American drinkery. It's "nothing to write home about."

Pig Heaven
$23

1540 Second Ave. (212) 744-4333
bet. 80th & 81st Sts. on the Upper East Side
"Pork galore..." Folks don't come running like they used to when this Upper East Side Chinese hollers "sooey" these days. The room is big and kid friendly (and "pinker than *Seventeen Magazine*"), but the suckling pig, ribs, dim sum and moo shoo are on the "oily" side: You're "better off going to Chinatown."

▤ = SUPERIOR ▤ = EXCELLENT ▤ = V. GOOD ▬ = GOOD

Pink Teacup

$18

42 Grove St. (212) 807-6755
bet. Bleecker & Bedford Sts. in the W. Village
"Where else can you get fried chicken for breakfast" if not at a
Southern place? Fried chicken aside, the breakfast at this "cute," West
Village "down-home"-y "getaway" with "down-home prices,
down-home staff" is tops. Of course, "Soul Food" tends to be "a little
greasy." But that's its charm, so wipe your mouth on your sleeve, this
is "just like Mamma used to make." Leave the credit cards on the
dresser, bring the beer and the kids not necessarily in that order.

Pintaile's Pizza

$10

1443 York Ave. (212) 717-4990
bet. 76th & 77th Sts. in Yorkville
26 E. 91st St. (212) 722-1967
at Madison Ave. in Carnegie Hill
"Trendy pizza by the slice" can be had at this Carnegie Hill brick
oven joint that's not much too look at but can be a ton of fun.
Cheeseless pizzas and "good salads" make even the finickiest voters
happy, and the kids love the "make your own pizza day."

Pisces

$28

95 Ave. A (212) 260-6660
at 6th St. in the E. Village
A "very good" and "real cheap" upscale (if tiny) "artful" Seafood
restaurant in the East Village? Yes indeed, with a legion of fans
who make it a destination despite views of needle park. "Noisy,"
and no wonder: While some restaurants have a TV in the bar, at
Pisces you can watch NYPD Blue as it happens, through the
wide-open, floor-to-ceiling windows.

Pitchoune

$37

226 Third Ave. (212) 614-8641
at 19th St. in Gramercy
This "cute" Provencal newcomer has emerged as one of the "best
Gramercy restaurants" thanks to its "sensitively seasoned food"—
what a "welcome addition to the 'hood." "Tight quarters" that make
"you feel like a sardine in a can" and "aggressive servers" who are
wont to give you the "bum's rush." Still, let's "hope they do well."

Pizzeria Uno

432 Columbus Ave. (212) 595-4700
at 81st St. on the Upper West Side
220 E. 86th St. (212) 472-5656
bet. 2nd & 3rd Aves. in Carnegie Hill
89 South St. (212) 791-7999
at Pier 17 at the South St. Seaport
391 Sixth Ave. (212) 242-5230
bet. 8th St. & Waverly Pl. in the Washington Sq. Area
55 Third Ave. (212) 995-9668
bet. 10th & 11th Sts. in the E. Village
Poll participants know the pizza is "reliable" and "boring" at this
East Village outpost but they really go for the Caesar salad. Open
late, it can get "overcrowded" and "noisy" but it's kid-friendly and
"better than most" chains.

FOOD　ROOM　STAFF　COST

P.J. Clarke's $25

915 Third Ave. at 55th St. in Midtown E. (212) 759-1650
This Old New York Saloon is "among the best for cheeseburgers and fries in NYC," and is likely to continue to outlive its patrons. "The streaky mirrors and buckled bar need some restoring," and the "social club" (i.e. "dark") atmosphere reminds some of Lost Weekend. P.S. Credit cards are accepted, typewriters are not.

Plan Eat Thailand $15

184 Bedford Ave., at N. 7th St. in Brooklyn (718) 599-5758
It was probably some kind of a cease and desist order that prompted this "excellent" Williamsburg Thai to change its name from "Planet Thailand": From the "excellent" food scores, "nice atmosphere," and "all good" comments, there is no mistaking this "best Thai food" spot with another similarly named joint. "Good enough to make the trek": Plan to Eat here.

Planet Hollywood $24

140 W. 57th St. (212) 333-7827
bet. Sixth & Seventh Aves. in Midtown W.
"Cool props" are the mainstay of the "very good" decor at this tourist super mecca. Tops for celebrity spotting and out-of-towners, it's child-friendly and the food's just perfect for their little unsophisticated palates. If "you're better off just burning your money," why is this one of the most popular places on the poll?

Po $34

31 Cornelia St. (212) 645-2189
bet. Bleecker & W. 4th Sts. in the Washington Sq. Area
"Say hello to Mario"— Mario Batali, that is—whose "perfectly modern Italian" food wows the Village. "Warm," "accommodating service" and a "creative" and "delicious" menu that "takes full advantage of the region's freshest bounty" are the reasons you must "reserve well in advance." And prices are "great to boot"—"Po won't make you po'." The only off-note concerns the ever-present "tight seating."

The Polo $62

Westbury Hotel, 840 Madison Ave. (212) 439-4835
bet. 69th & 70th Sts. on the Upper East Side
P is for power at The Polo. As in power breakfast, lunch and dinner. So, if you need to cut a deal in a ritzy part of town, do it here—this hotel restaurant has been the home for wheeling and dealing for years. For dinner try the "succulent" "attractively presented" seafood and on Sunday go for the oceanic brunch. Bring your favorite gold-colored plastic.

Pongsri Thai $20

244 W. 48th St. bet. 8th Ave. & Bdwy/Theater Dist. (212) 582-3392
106 Bayard St. at Baxter St. in Chinatown (212) 349-3132
Not just "great jury duty dining," this little Chinatown spot may be the "best Thai this side of the Pacific." It goes further than that: The "coconut milk and lemongrass soup is out of this world," with "the most perfect spices anywhere!" "Great, delicious, simple."

Popover Cafe

551 Amsterdam bet. 86th & 87th Sts./U.W. Side (212) 595-8555
A brunch and breakfast mecca, this Upper West Side American draws flocks for "outstanding" signature popovers and "creative" comfort food. It's the "epitome of a neighborhood restaurant" and a great place to "gab with friends" and "teddy bears."

Portico $28

1431 Second Ave. bet. 74th & 75th/U.E. Side (212) 794-1032
Hand-made pastas, breads and desserts may or may not be enough to recommend this new Upper East Side Italian with high hopes. The light traffic makes it "good for weekends" so check it out and let us know if you agree with the few voters who say "good menu with a wide price range."

Post House $53

Lowell Hotel, 28 E. 63rd St. (212) 935-2888
bet. Park & Madison Aves. on the Upper East Side
Part of the Smith & Wollensky crowd, this "nice, manly" steakhouse has an atmosphere that's a bit more elegant than its competitors'. "Don't order light"— not when there's "good steak," "good wine," and "good cigars" adding up to "a great choice" when you're in the mood for such things. The "chopped salad" and "Cajun rib steak" come in for extra mention. "It's not Peter Luger," but then again, it doesn't try to be.

Pot Belly Stove

94 Christopher St. (Bleecker & Hudson/W. Vill.) (212) 242-8036
It sure is "cozy" at this 24-hour West Village American. Choose from a "huge menu" of "hearty" standards and expect "plentiful portions." The "nice back garden" is a plus but be prepared for "seat-you-and-forget-you" service.

Pravda $39

281 Lafayette bet. Prince & Houston Sts. in SoHo (212) 226-4696
This super "trendy" SoHo Russian speakeasy is all caviar (6 kinds), vodka (75 kinds), and "scene, scene, scene." It's a top-celebrity spot, so before you go, decide whether you want to satisfy your stomach or your curiosity. There's a DJ for your entertainment if the famous faces aren't enough, and the menu runs late, late, late through the week. There are three prerequisites to gaining access to the "amazing martini": You need saintly patience for the service, deep pockets, and to be able to "get past the door Czars." Reservations essential—even for drinks only.

Primavera $43

1578 First Ave. at 82nd St. in Yorkville (212) 861-8608
Though it still ranks respectably, there's a sense that this "solid traditional Itailian" may be "slipping a bit." A quiet, nonglitzy exception to the Upper East Side Italian rule, it offers a warm, comfortable atmosphere—well, as comfortable as you can be in the requisite jacket and tie, that is—and "consistently good," if consistently unadventurous, cuisine.

▬ = FAIR   [blank] = POOR   ≣ = NOT RATED

Primola

🍴 🌹 🍷 $41

1226 Second Ave. (212) 758-1775
bet. 64th & 65th Sts. on the Upper East Side
Here's a quiet little Upper East Side Italian with an "amazing chef" and a "sleepy room." The price reflects the quality of the food so brace yourself.

Prince St. Bar/Rest.

🍴 🌹 🍷 $22

125 Prince St. at Wooster in SoHo (212) 228-8130
While it may seem to have trendy trappings—SoHo loft location, Continental/Indonesian food—it's better described as "an old neighborhood standby": The bar is "great," but the food is "nothing memorable."

Provence

🍴 🌹 🍷 $42

38 MacDougal St. bet. Prince & Houston/SoHo (212) 475-7500
For a "taste of France in NY," head down to SoHo where "civilized" Provence dispenses "incredible food with a neighborhood feel." The helpful staff and "authentic" "French country atmosphere" of this "very laid-back restaurant" will transport your cares away. "Great wines" and a "heavenly" garden open year-round are other earthly delights.

Quantum Leap

88 W. 3rd St. (212) 677-8050
bet. Thompson & Sullivan Sts. in the Washington Sq. Area
This macrobiotic Vegetarian has the usual core group of fans, surprised to find so much flavor with so little meat. Who'd have though that "veggies and fish (with no booze)" could be "habit forming?" Or, that you'd get "a lot for your money?" All that, and a "wonderful staff" to boot.

Quatorze Bis

🍴 🌹 🍷 $44

323 E. 79th St. (212) 535-1414
bet. First & Second Aves. in Yorkville
The move from Quatorze Street hasn't put a damper on the ratings for this Yorkville French. Consistent, "very good" food ratings makes voters say "we miss you on 14th St., please come back."

Queen

84 Court St., Brooklyn (718) 596-5955
bet. Livingston & Schermerhorn
Second-generation chefs serve up "consistent" favorites at this "old-fashioned" Brooklyn Italian. "Low prices" and "high quality" make many loyalists exclaim: "If I could eat there everyday, I would."

Quisisana

🍴 🌹 🍷 $44

1319 Third Ave. (212) 879-5000
bet. 75th & 76th Sts. on the Upper East Side
Upper East Side Italian seafood has never been better. The "very welcoming and caring owners" show these qualities by supplying a restaurant with a "homey feel," "nice decor" and "very good food." Voters say "you'll find no bigger place in terms of food."

Rachel's

 $25

608 Ninth Ave. (212) 957-9050
bet. 43rd & 44th Sts. in Clinton

It's "small," and it's hard to "avoid elbow contact with the
next table" but the "good" American food at a "great value"
has won a following with the pre-show crowd in the Clinton.
The post-show crowd rolls back in for the homemade "the
best" desserts. Brunch Wed/Sat/Sun.

Rain

 $31

100 W. 82nd St. (212) 501-0776
at Columbus Ave. on the Upper West Side

A year-and-a-half-old and already a favorite, this urbane
Pan-Asian attracts "celebrities" and trend-followers who savor its
"romantic" Downtown atmosphere and culinary "innovations."
With a bar and full-service lounge, it's a comfortable Upper West
Side "hangout." Though the "trendy" Thai, Vietnamese, and
Malaysian fare is "interesting," it's not as impressive as the
style-saturated decor.

Rainbow Room

 $58

G.E. Bldg., 30 Rockefeller Plaza, 65th Fl. (212) 632-5000
bet. 49th & 50th Sts./5th & Sixth Aves. in Midtown W.

For swanky "art-deco" ambiance (ranked second in our survey)
and "breathtaking" "top-of-the-world views," "it doesn't get
much better" than this "special-occasion" Midtowner. It's
"worth every penny" for jazzy big bands and retro "glamour"
that make it swell for romancing and for older out-of-towners.
The Continental menu looks to improve under Waldy Malouf
(ex-Hudson River Club) and service soars, but nothing can
match the "1940s-movie-set" atmosphere. "A unique NY
experience," "everyone must do it once."

Rao's

 $47

455 E. 114th St. (212) 722-6709
at Pleasant Ave. in E. Harlem

Recently reopened after a little, er, fire trouble, this East Harlem
Italian makes you feel like you're "one of the familia." They don't
take reservations, but "what's a reservation?" ask voters, when "the
table is yours for the night." "No rush," with "excellent" food and
"friendly atmosphere." "Worth the wait," they say, "especially if
you know the right people." What are they hinting at?

Raoul's

 $43

180 Prince St. (212) 966-3518
bet. Sullivan & Thompson Sts. in SoHo

Most agree that this "very lively" SoHo French bistro had "slipped"
when it lost its chef a few years ago: However, it's "back up again, and
service has improved" too, making it one of the most charming spot in
the city." Fans say to start with the artichokes and order the house
specialty, steak au poivre. In all, it "makes you feel warm and fuzzy."

	FOOD	ROOM	STAFF	COST

Raphael

$52

33 W. 54th St. (212) 582-8993
bet. Fifth & Sixth Aves. in Midtown W.

With a garden and fireplace in a West Midtown location, this French is smooth for both biz and l'amore. And if you can combine the two, all the better. Wear a jacket and go before a show. With vegetarian selections and no smoking, it keeps up with American attitudes while maintaining classic French tastes .

Ratner's

$20

138 Delancey St. (212) 677-5588
at Norfolk St. on the Lower East Side

They have food on the Lower East Side? How about good "typical kosher dairy fair" in a "no-nonsense atmosphere." "The egg barley" is "a blast from the past" at a "Noo Yawk restaurant your out-of-town relatives will remember and talk about." "The vegetable cutlet makes it worth the trip" despite, or maybe because of "rude" service. "Ask the waitress to talk about her grandchildren." This is "a NYC tradition for fans of noise, stress and traditional deli" cuisine, one of those joints that's probably always looked like "it's seen better days."

Redeye Grill

890 Seventh Ave. at 56th St. in Midtown W. (212) 541-9000

The space is large, and so are the portions at this new American/Continental, where you can choose from large selections of fish, salads, pastas and meats, and a trend-of-the-moment raw bar.

Red Tulip

$29

439 E. 75th St. at York Ave. in Yorkville (212) 734-4893

"Hearty Hungarian food in a somewhat tacky but cozy setting" is one way to describe this Yorkville restaurant. "Good peasant food with wandering violinists" who " encourage clapping and dancing," is another. Check out the "Transylvanian decor," ah, that is, "old-fashioned atmosphere." A fireplace is always nice too.

Regional Thai Taste

$21

207 Seventh Ave. at 22nd St. in Chelsea (212) 807-9872

You won't usually find "authentic" food in such a stylish space but the fare is "surprisingly tasty" at this Chelsea Thai. Expect innovative presentations and a staff that is "entertaining" but "slow."

Remi

$48

145 W. 53rd St. (212) 581-4242
bet. Sixth & Seventh Aves. in Midtown W.

Ahh, Venice. Well, not exactly, (it's in Midtown, not on Canal St.) but pretty close according to voters, who call the atmosphere at this Midtown Northern Italian just "beautiful" and "great," with "delicious food, too," A "nice place for dinner," they single it out as one of the city's top picks for business lunch, with "fair prices" at lunch to boot. A big dinner tab keeps out the riffraff.

= SUPERIOR   = EXCELLENT   = V. GOOD   = GOOD

Rene Pujol $41

321 W. 51st St. (212) 246-3023
bet. Eighth & Ninth Aves. in Clinton
A Clinton perennial, owner Rene Pujol has a loyal (mostly older) crowd
of fans, though passing the baton to his son and daughter-in-law may
appeal to younger diners. The atmosphere tries to create "countryside of
France in Manhattan," and you "can't beat the value" of their "excellent
prix fixe." "Soft-shell crab in season is a must."

Republic $19

37 Union Sq. W. bet. 16th & 17th Sts. (212) 627-7172
"Welcome to the People's Republic of Noodles." "Funky
pan-Asian" noodles are the specialty of Indochine's newer sib, a
"futuristic" "community lunchroom" (you eat at long tables with
strangers) with "designer, school-cafeteria tables," "too-cool"
servers, and "loads of good food" for "not much money," including
"tasty" and "addicting" pad Thai for the "Union Square beau
monde." Even fans say it's got "all the warmth of a bus station," but
that's probably why it's so "hip."

Revolution

611 Ninth Ave. bet. 43rd & 44th Sts. in Clinton (212) 489-8451
The DJ's records turn at 33 1/3 rpm, and that's not the only
revolution going on at this Theater District Eclectic. The "great bar
scene" and "top value," "great" food has crowds of pre- and
post-theater goers giving this place a spin.

Rice 'n' Beans $18

744 Ninth Ave. (212) 265-4444
at 50th St. in Clinton
"Perfect for lunch," this Clinton Brazilian is little more than a
"cabbie food stop." The "tiny," "cafeteria-like room" houses a
"surly staff," but still they rave: A "favorite find this year," it's
"great Brazilian at giveaway prices."

Right Bank $27

822 Madison Ave. (212) 737-2811
bet. 68th & 69th Sts. on the Upper East Side
You don't get free checking, but there's still plenty of interest in this
"informal and lively" Upper East Side Continental, approaching forty
and going strong. Cheap for the area, some think it's a bit "dicey," but
tell it to the crowd. P.S. "Go late if you want to talk"—and be heard.

Riodizio $32

417 Lafayette St. (212) 529-1313
bet. E. 4th St. & Astor Pl. in the E. Village
You may find you "can't face meat for a few days" after an all-you
can-eat Brazilian feast at this noisy,
great-for-(nonvegetarian)-groups "cholesterol heaven." You'll need
to "bring a stun gun to stop the servers from passing you by," but
the charm of limitless quantities overrides any concerns over
"uneven" quality. "Eat everything, then go for a long, long walk."

FOOD	ROOM	STAFF	COST

Rio Mar

$27

7 Ninth Ave. (212) 242-1623
at W. 12th St. in the W. Village

"Tucked away in the Meat District" in the "Wild West" Village is
this cheap, "authentic" Spaniard with its atmospheric bar,
all-"Spanish juke box," and "partylike" late-night atmosphere.
Those in the know suggest you try the "great paella" and "the best
octopus salad" (plus "grilled sardines on summer weekends"). No
entertainment, unless you count who you meet in the street.

River Cafe

$59

1 Water St., Brooklyn (718) 522-5200
at Cadman Plaza W.

Teeming with tourists and romantics, this upscale Brooklyn Heights
cafe gives voters a reason to leave Manhattan, if only to gaze right
back at the "magical" skyline. The "great" American/Continental fare
and ultra-attentive service are top notch and almost a perfect match for
the "stunning view." It's an "expensive" favorite, but most voters
vow: It's "worth it" for "the best" waterside dining in NYC.

Riverrun Cafe

176 Franklin St. (212) 966-3894
bet. Hudson & Greenwich Sts. in TriBeCa

This is a "great saloon" with "good" Eclectic/American "food," but
the bartenders, many microbrews on tap, and especially the Top 10
jukebox are the real attractions here. This "good after-work drink"
spot is an "upscale mom and pop place with no pretentions,"
making it "a TriBeCa find."

Rocco

$25

181 Thompson St. (212) 677-0590
bet. Bleecker & Houston Sts. in the Washington Sq. Area

There's a nice "Mom-and-Pop place" with "food just like
Grandma's" in SoHo, and it doesn't cost an arm and a leg. The
"fresh cannelloni" will fill you up and it's not high traffic so you
can count on decent service. The neighborhood is prime for
people-watching, so sit outside. It offers high chairs, and that
usually means kids are welcome.

Roettele A.G.

$29

126 E. 7th St. bet. Ave. A & First Ave./E. Village (212) 674-4140

Grab your lederhosen and head down to this East Villager for
"unusual" Alpine fare in a "cozy," "Swiss" atmosphere. Though the
eats can be "inconsistent," diners say danke to "friendly" service
and an outdoor garden that's "better than Prozac."

Rolf's

$29

281 Third Ave. at 22nd St. in Gramercy (212) 477-4750

If you can't get to Germany for the holidays we hear that Rolf's is
"decorated for Christmas all year long" (and Gramercy is quite a bit
closer). Grab a "nice booth" some great "sauerbraten and
dumplings," a mug of the "best beer on tap," and all there is to
worry about is the "brusque service."

Rosa Mexicano

$36

1063 First Ave. (212) 753-7407
bet. 57th & 58th Sts. in Midtown E.

Is it the "best Mexican in NYC?" Appetizers, particularly the "best guacamole, made at your table to taste" though some say "it's all excellent." "Hard to get a reservation," though worth it they say for the "pomegranate margaritas that make the room spin." This ain't "Mexican food, it's Mexican cuisine."

Rose Cafe

$30

24 Fifth Ave. (212) 260-4118
at 9th St. in the Central Village

With the "best mini-muffins on Sunday," this "comfortable local eatery" gets mixed reviews on everything but its "great location." The glass-enclosed front is "good for watching the world go by," and the simpler items on the Eclectic/American Bistro menu are the best.

Rosemarie's

$39

145 Duane St. (212) 285-2610
bet. Church St. & W. Broadway in TriBeCa

You won't find any former cast members of the Dick Van Dyke Show here, but you will find "nice ambiance" and "consistently great," Northern Italian food in a cozy room that, though understated, "can get loud." Attentive service helps make it TriBeCa's "undiscovered gem."

Rose of India

$15

308 E. 6th St. (212) 533-5011
bet. First & Second Aves. in the E. Village

For first-timers and out-of-towners, the birthday ritual with disco ball and flashing lights is worth the trip to this East Village Indian. "Decent food," solid service, and a "wacky" but "cheerful" atmosphere make it a good value for open-minded twenty-somethings, though there's "better available on 6th Street." BYO.

Royal Canadian Pancake House

$16

180 Third Ave. at 17th St.in Gramercy (212) 777-9288
2286 Broadway bet. 82nd & 83rd Sts./U.W. Side (212) 873-6052
1004 Second Ave. at 55th St. in Midtown E. (212) 980-4131

The portions are legendary at these popular pancake and Canadian fooderies, so big that you must either "doggy bag most of your order, or leave it tidy for City Harvest." Though some think "bigger is not better," they're still ranked No. 1 for the best breakfast in town, with a top 10 brunch and big weekend crowds. Good for kids, and "a good place to take fat relatives."

Royal Siam

$21

240 Eighth Ave. (212) 741-1732
bet. 22nd & 23rd Sts. in Chelsea

"The best little Thai in the neighborhood, if not the city" say folks of this "little-known Thai Gem" in Chelsea. Pad thai and dumplings are standouts, of course, though some spice hounds say they are "a bit timid on the spices, to accommodate American palates."

	FOOD	ROOM	STAFF	COST

Rubyfruit

531 Hudson St. (212) 929-3343
bet. Charles & W. 10th Sts. in the W. Village

It's a hotspot for "lesbian lovelies," but "straight friends are welcome too," at this West Village write-in. A "great staff" and "very intimate" atmosphere complement the "wonderful" Continental cuisine. The one complaint: "if only it weren't so cramped."

Rumpelmayer's $25

St. Moritz Hotel, 50 Central Park S. (212) 446-5525
at Sixth Ave. in Midtown W.

This American/Continental at Central Park South may be "running on reputation" since a "poorly conceived makeover" but it's still a "great happy kid place" with the "best hot chocolate" and "hot fudge sundaes"—"Stick to the desserts and you'll be happy." Breakfast is offered as is afternoon tea and there's a buffet brunch on the weekend. We repeat: They love kids and vice versa.

Rungsit Thai $15

161 E. 23rd St. (212) 260-0704
bet. Third & Lexington Aves. in Gramercy

While this Gramercy Park-area Thai does have its fans, the majority describe it as "only run-of-the-mill Thai in a greasy-spoon setting." While the staff is more busy than helpful and the room is not much to look at, and if the food falls short of superb, it's "superbly fast."

Rush 'n Express $10

306 E. 86th St. bet. First & Second/U.E. Side (212) 517-4949
303 Park Ave. S. (212) 982-8383 at 23rd St. in Gramercy

"Fast and good Russian food" is their motto, and everyone agrees at least with the first part. They're "great for starving artists," that is, they're "cheap and fast." The portions are "swell," though only the soups draw raves. "Borscht to go, enough said."

Russian Samovar $37

256 W. 52nd St. (212) 757-0168
bet. Broadway & Eighth Ave. in the Theater District

An "amazing choice of flavored vodkas" and live classical singing help make this Midtown Russian "good," though flagging service detracts from attempts to make it a romantic spot.

Ruth's Chris Steakhouse $46

148 W. 51st St. (212) 245-9600
bet. Sixth & Seventh Aves. in Midtown W.

"The filets and steaks are close to perfect" and the portions come hefty at this Top 5 Midtown Steakhouse. Diners also appreciate the "nice atmosphere" that's "not a man's club like most other steakhouses," and makes for fun after-work gatherings and productive biz lunches. While the chops are "primo" some groan that the veggies and side dishes could use a boost. Service is as reliable as it should be, and there are cigar dinners monthly.

Sahara East $17

184 First Ave. (212) 353-9000
bet. 11th & 12th Sts. in the E. Village

This East Village Moroccan/Middle Eastern is "surprisingly good and inexpensive." The "good" comes from the "pleasant food" (including "best falafel") and "friendly staff," while the surprise is in contrast (especially the rear garden) to the dishevelled block on First. It's so authentic, you can say "waiter, there's Sahara in my soup..."

Sakura

615 Hudson St. (212) 645-2128
bet. Jane & W. 12th Sts. in the W. Village

Voters call the West Village version of these Japanese a "great neighborhood sushi bar," with "fabulous special sushi rolls." With "good," "cozy" atmosphere, and a "nice" staff. The Upper West Sider has more competition, but is still reliable, especially for bargain lunch boxes.

Salaam Bombay $31

317 Greenwich St. (212) 226-9400
bet. Duane & Reade Sts. in TriBeCa

This is no false salaam: Voters find this TriBeCan to be the "most refined, delicious, and varied Indian food in New York City." Of course they have a lunch buffet that turns out to be way above the average, and though "out of the way" it has "great service and a nice room." "Try the fish, any style."

Sal Anthony's $33

55 Irving Pl. (212) 982-9030
bet. 17th & 18th Sts. in Gramercy

"Good Italian fare and ambiance," at this 30-year-old Gramercy standby, and the "outside's (even) nicer." "Homey and comfortable," this is a "neighborhood spot" that's "refreshing if you're tired of trendy." Some see it as "reliable" and unchanging, though others, perhaps fixed on an ideal of the place from years ago, insist that the quality is "slipping."

Sal Anthony's
Caffe Adeline $18

119 E. 17th St. (212) 674-6677
bet. Park Ave. S. & Irving Pl. in Gramercy

The new cafe/takeout version of the venerated Sal Anthony's, folks are enthusiastic about this Gramercy yearling for it's cafe-style, "excellent food" and "very cheap prices." "Tucked away," it's "nice to sit out front at lunch."

Sal Anthony's S.P.Q.R. $32

133 Mulberry St. (212) 925-3120
bet. Grand & Hester Sts. in Little Italy

For parties and large groups don't miss this Little Italy restaurant with "desserts to die for" and a two course, $8.50 prix fixe lunch that's "a steal." The "huge, airy room" could be the reason the service is a little "slow," but it's a great spot for a "retirement party," so settle in for the evening.

	FOOD	ROOM	STAFF	COST

Sala Thai

$27

1718 Second Ave. (212) 410-5557
bet. 89th & 90th Sts. in Carnegie Hill
What's a Thai this good doing so far North and East? Serving "very good," "authentic Thai," that is "cheap" and therefore "worth it." The decor may be "typical," and service sometimes "slow," but for "simple and clean Thai" they've got the goods.

Saloon

1920 Broadway (212) 874-1500
at 64th St. on the Upper West Side
A "huge menu" and "convenient" location make this "unexceptional" American a "comfortable," reliable, inexpensive choice for pre-and post-theater dining. With sidewalk seating and "abundant portions," it can get "touristy and "loud" at peak hours.

Sammy's Noodle Shop

$15

453-461 Sixth Ave. (212) 924-6688
at W. 11th St. in the W. Village
There's "never a dull moment" at this West Village Chinese yearling: A "lightning fast staff" (that's "bad" during overcrowding), serves "great cold sesame noodles" to a demanding crowd in a "neon setting." "The freshest Chinese" to some is just an "Ollie's clone" to others: An accountant waxes "same assets, same liabilities."

Sammy's Roumanian

$36

157 Chrystie St. (212) 673-0330
at Delancey St. on the Lower East Side
"You'll need angioplasty after supper" at this Lower East Side Romanian Jewish restaurant, but judging from the "big spenders" who frequent the joint, you can get the procedure performed at your table. Features: fifths of vodka served in solid iceblocks; "flank steaks the size of Milwaukee (save room for an egg cream); and a band that plays "lower-middle-class bar mitzvah party" versions of '70s Top 40 classics. What is to some "wonderful and ridiculous" is to others "rude staff, dive atmosphere, annoying entertainment."

San Domenico

$57

240 Central Park S. (212) 265-5959
bet. Seventh Ave. & Broadway in Midtown W.
"Elegant," thy name is San Domenico, a "wonderfully romantic" Italian housed in a "beautiful room" on Central Park South. "Star studs visit" for the "smashing food" and "excellent prix fixe" (at $29.95, the pre-theater menu's a "great bargain"). San Domenico exudes "style" and "class," and it "deserves more recognition."

San Giusto

$42

935 Second Ave. (212) 319-0900
bet. 49th & 50th Sts. in Midtown E.
Don't you just love those family-run places where you actually see the family doing the running. And they even chat with you. Go here for Northern Italian fare and Midtown hominess.

Santa Fe

 $31

72 W. 69th St. (212) 724-0822
bet. Columbus Ave. & Central Park W. on the Upper West Side
Here on the Upper West Side, a "peaceful," "genteel" townhouse setting and a transition from standard Tex-Mex to "satisfying," "always reliable" upscale Southwestern rate fewer kudos than "great frozen margaritas."

Sanzin

180 Spring St. at Thompson St. in SoHo (212) 965-0710
Chuck a big career at Le Bernardin, Bouley and Pitchoune, and open a tiny restaurant in SoHo? That's what Johannes Sanzin did, and, having received big press, this new spot is already a tough dinner res. Open until 4 a.m. weekends.

Sapporo East

 $18

245 E. 10th St. at First Ave. in the E. Village (212) 260-1330
This East Village Japanese is the best of the chain, partly for the low price but mostly for the "good" quality of food, given the slightly grungy setting. The sushi here is "inexpensive," and, like its Midtown cohort, it has "very good noodles and gyoza" and "authentic Ramen." The crowd, mostly in their '20s, is a trip in itself.

Sarabeth's Kitchen

 $27

Whitney Museum, 945 Madison Ave. (212) 570-3670
at 75th St. on the Upper East Side
423 Amsterdam Ave. (212) 496-6280
bet. 80th & 81st Sts. on the Upper West Side
Hotel Wales, 1295 Madison Ave. (212) 410-7335
bet. 92nd & 93rd Sts. in Carnegie Hill
The "awesome" tops-in-the-city brunch is "perfect" if you're out "with mum, especially if she pays" and you feel like you're sitting in her kitchen "eating her homemade cooking." Breakfast and desserts are also major draws at this NYC minichain that seniors and out-of-towners dig too. The rap on the place is that it's "too expensive" and weekend crowds jam it, but at least they don't take reservations, so locals and hotel guests have equal shots at the tables. Bring the kids and the grandparents.

Saranac

 $28

1350 Madison Ave. bet. 94th & 95th/Carnegie Hill (212) 289-9600
A little out-of-the-way escape in Carnegie Hill with "pleasant American food" can be a welcome experience. It's "a little pricey for so far uptown," and the food isn't as uptown as the tab suggests, but the "comfortable" atmosphere may even things out.

Sardi's

 $38

234 W. 44th St. (212) 221-8440
bet. Broadway & Eighth Ave. in the Theater District
You may find "delicious gossip" at this Continental Theater District "tourist trap"-cum-"institution," but you won't find anything delicious on the menu. Despite "robotic service," the "fun" caricatures, "great maitre 'd" and star-spotting keep this "legend" alive.

___ = FAIR   [blank] = POOR   ▦ = NOT RATED

	FOOD	ROOM	STAFF	COST

Sasso

 $34

1315 Second Ave. (212) 472-6688
bet. 69th & 70th Sts. on the Upper East Side
The fact that the menu changes weekly or that the noodle dishes are homemade doesn't seem to keep this from being "just another Upper East Side Italian."

Savann

 $31

414 Amsterdam Ave. bet. 79th & 80th/U.W. Side (212) 580-0202
181 E. 78th St. bet. 3rd & Lex./Upper East Side (212) 396-9300
"Who needs another restaurant in the Upper East/West Sides?" "We do," when the food is this "delicious" and the atmosphere this "cozy." The "wonderfully well-crafted" Contemporary French food draws raves, the service is very "particular," and the moderate prices make this a "best deal for dinner." Only the "close" tables and the "wine list need work."

Savannah Club

 $26

2420 Broadway (212) 496-1066
at 89th St. on the Upper West Side
"Mature and mellow" Upper West Side regulars aren't "thrilled" or "disappointed" by the Southern fare at this "neighborhood" eatery. It can be "noisy" and smoky after dark when the "cool" but "casual" scene ("not the menu") "has 'em lining up to get in."

Savore

 $35

200 Spring St. (212) 431-1212
at Sullivan St. in SoHo
Northern Italy is well known for its "out-of-this-world risotto" which gives it something in common with this "classy" Soho trattoria that also has "great salads and specials," and a "knowledgeable and attentive staff." Stop in for a great "noncrowded, romantic dining experience." Okay so we'd like the pasta "a little al dente per favore!" But nobody's perfect.

Savoy

 $42

70 Prince St. (212) 219-8570
at Crosby St. in SoHo
Dining around a fireplace will do it almost every time for those in search of the "charming" and "intimate." Both floors at this SoHo Mediterranean blaze the hearth, and it will even use one to cook its "inventive," "creative" cuisine. Order a bottle from the "excellent wine list," and hang out in the lounge before dinner. From "soup to nuts, it's a fantastic place." Kind of like your New York apartment, "too small, too expensive, worth every penny."

Sawadee Thai

 $21

225 Columbus Ave. (212) 787-3002
bet. 70th & 71st Sts. on the Upper West Side
Here's an Upper West Side Thai that might be a good choice for a "cheap biz lunch that includes soup and salad." It's got a "solid menu" though "some dishes taste like Chinese."

Sazerac House
 $25

533 Hudson St. (212) 989-0313
bet. Charles & 10th Sts. in the W. Village

Though the Cajun/American cuisine can be "uneven," voters say it's "getting better all the time" at this family-owned Greenwich Villager. Housed in a circa-1826 landmark building, it's a "neighborhood favorite" for "comfortable atmosphere," hospitable service and moderate prices—especially at lunch.

Screening Room

54 Varick St. (212) 334-2100
1 block S. of Canal in TriBeCa

This new TriBeCan American cafe gives "dinner and a movie" a more concrete meaning: 30 bucks gets you both. The small adjoining moviehouse shows independent films, with a schedule that includes midnight shows on the weekends.

Sea Grill
 $49

Rockefeller Center, 19 W. 49th St. (212) 332-7610
bet. Fifth & Sixth Aves. in Midtown W.

"For the view" often means "for the tourists" in this town, but then again the ice rink at Rockefeller Center is one of the biggest tourist attractions in the US. Luckily, the Sea Grill delivers "excellence" in all categories, a Romac top 100 for delicious seafood and the top 40 for room and staff. And while many "take their out-of-town guests," the location and quality (and high price tag) makes it a "great business lunch" destination. "Try the crab cakes."

Second Avenue Deli
 $18

156 Second Ave. at 10th St. in the E. Village (212) 677-0606

"Irresistible chopped liver," "great pastrami," "chicken in a pot" to "live for" served by a "surly staff?"—must be the "the finest Jewish deli in NYC, hands down." Think about it for a sec, "you don't go for the 'polite' staff" ("authentic," not "arrogant") and the scene becomes "most interesting to watch, a comedy." "The matzoh ball soup is a miracle cure-all."

Seeda Thai
 $23

309 W. 50th St. (212) 586-4040
bet. Eighth & Ninth Aves. in Clinton

Mentioning that this is a Thai restaurant would be redundant if it didn't also serve Vietnamese. Clinton sports a hot little cache of tasty hideaways: This one is "average." Try the "excellent peanut chicken" (that's chicken satay to you and me). There are prix fixe and pre-theater dinners that won't break you, but the "slow" service might not get you to the church or show on time.

Sel et Poivre
 $34

853 Lexington Ave. bet. 64th & 65th/U.E. Side (212) 517-5780

Popular with a salt-and-pepper (i.e. older) crowd, this "unpretentious" East Side bistro offers French basics at "reasonable prices." Some claim it survives on "location," but well-seasoned regulars return for the "flavorful" fare and "helpful" service.

FOOD   ROOM   STAFF   COST

Sequoia

$30

69 Fulton St. (212) 732-9090
at Pier 17 at the South St. Seaport
"Overpriced for mediocre food, but... it's the Seaport" writes one concise voter, summing up this Downtown American seafooder. Long on ambiance and view and short on food, it's as big as its mighty namesake, with a surprisingly low price tag and "not too touristy."

Serendipity 3

$22

225 E. 60th St. bet. Second & Third/Midtown E. (212) 838-3531
"Oh, those frozen hot chocolates." Frozen hot chocolates? Dessert is an art form at this Eclectic/American in East Midtown, so "skip the food" but please "don't go without the kids" (if you don't have any, borrow some). A "tourist's delight" isn't complete without tiffany lamps, a gigantic clock and a boutique to make it "too cute" and "a New York treat." But did we mention those "amazing," "gotta have..." "addictive" frozen hot chocolates? Well, "there's nothing more to say..." except breakfast and brunch. Oxymorons and alliteration at the same restaurant.

Seryna

$49

11 E. 32nd St. at Fifth Ave. in Murray Hill (212) 980-9393
The top sleeper in the book also happens to be "very quiet." Murray Hill isn't too chaotic after work, and this upscale Japanese is quietly winning raves. "Everything here is perfection" from the "attentive service" to the "juicy steak" and "delicious appetizers." And they'll cook that steak right in front of you. Wake up and give it a try on one of those nights when you feel like splurging.

Sette Mezzo

$39

969 Lexington Ave. bet. 70th & 71st/U.E. Side (212) 472-0400
You may not be treated well until you've been a couple of times, then again, the "rude reception for first timers" might deter you from another visit to this plain but good Upper East Side Italian. The grilled red snapper is a specialty and the food is enjoyable enough that "you don't mind the cash-only policy."

Sette MoMA

$33

MoMA, 11 W. 53rd bet. Fifth & Sixth/Midtown W. (212) 708-9710
"Decent" "food and service in a divine space" sums up this Contemporary Italian, overlooking the sculpture garden (Moore! Matisse! Miro!) in the Museum of Modern Art. Summer concerts make it "beautiful and romantic," but the food is "like a school lunch cafeteria." Here's an idea: go for a concert, but sneak in a Snickers (that would be with white wine).

7A

109 Ave. A at 7th St. in the E. Village (212) 673-6583
"It's a dive" but 24-hour convenience and "excellent people-watching" keep this East Villager popular with a diverse, "interesting" crowd. Locals rely on it for "satisfying" American/Eclectic eats and sidewalk seating opposite entertaining Tompkins Square Park.

Sevilla $28

62 Charles St. at W. 4th St. in the W. Village (212) 929-3189
You don't just eat this food, you dive into it. The "enormous portions" are "definitely worth the money," which you dole out in "very reasonable" sums by the way, at this West Village Spanish. The decor and ambiance are as "authentic" as the food and service but it's the paella, arroz con pollo, garlic bread and sangria that pull in the most praise. It's "loud," "squished" and "a bit rushed."

Sfuzzi $34

58 W. 65th St. (212) 873-3700
bet. Columbus Ave. & Central Park W. on the Upper West Side
2 World Financial Center, 225 Liberty St. (212) 385-8080
at S. End Ave. in the Financial District
It gets "hectic" around here. The "great drinks," especially that frozen sfuzzi, and "nice wine list" draw the after-work crowds. Brunches, Saturday nights, and lunch hours are also hopping. Regulars like the "good eats at happy hour" but "so-so" is about as exciting as it comes for the dinner comments on the "standard" Italian fare. You might find "long waits" and service can get "snobby."

Shaan $38

57 W. 48th St. bet. Fifth & Sixth/Midtown W. (212) 977-8400
The Theater District offers some of the "best Indian food in New York," in a "beautiful place," with solid service, a "creative" menu, validated parking, a fairly priced prix fixe lunch, and live entertainment on the weekends. The high dinner tag makes some voters call it "touristy."

Shabu Shabu 70 $27

314 E. 70th St. bet. First & Second Aves./U.E. Side (212) 861-5635
With sushi and other Japanese dishes available, the real draw at these clean, well-lit places is the Japanese barbecue, that you cook yourself on your tabletop. It's "fun to cook the lean meats," and the "selection of vegetarian plates is awesome." "The special for two is a deal."

Shabu Tatsu $28

1414 York Ave. at 75th St. in Yorkville (212) 472-3322
216 E. 10th St. bet. 1st & 2nd Aves./E. Village (212) 477-2972
483 Columbus Ave. bet. 83rd & 84th/U.W. Side (212) 874-5633
"Stay on that long line"—"you won't regret it" once you get a taste of the "delicious," "low-fat healthy" shabu-shabu and other Japanese specialties that you cook yourself on an "authentic grill built into the table." It's "lots of work," but "lots of fun," and the "exotic yet relaxed setting" is "filled with Japanese people," so you know you've "come to the right place."

Shaliga Thai $28

834 Second Ave. (212) 573-5526
bet. 44th & 45th Sts. in Midtown E.
Well, the "quiet calm surroundings" may "allow you to enjoy the conversation" but the food at this Murray Hill Thai is another issue. Nothing here cuts it above fair so don't go out of your way.

FOOD ROOM STAFF COST

Shark Bar

307 Amsterdam bet. 74th & 75th Sts./U.W. Side (212) 874-8500
The bar may be "too tight," but everything else is "smooth" at this
Upper West Side Soul Fooder with a "cool vibe." With a brunch
that some say is one of the "best" in NYC, and vittles "like Mom
used to make," it can be "pricey" but "holds its own."

Shinbashi

 $38

280 Park Ave. (212) 661-3915
at 48th St. in Midtown E.
Before you even think of going to this Murray Hill Japanese, check
your bank account. The "awesome, fresh sushi/sashimi" is "quite
expensive," then again you're paying for "one of New York's best"
and a top sleeper at that. You get personal service in a relaxing,
uncrowded space, but you'll pay for it.

Shinbashi-An

 $36

141 E. 48th St. (212) 752-0505
bet. Third & Lexington Aves. in Midtown E.
The "sukiyaki" and "fresh sushi and sashimi" at this Murray Hill
Japanese "will raise you from the dead." Once you've risen, the
service will make you feel at home. Add another holiday to your
life and "try the New Year's Banquet in February" whether you're
Japanese or not. Other than that it's quiet, quiet, quiet.

Shun Lee
Shun Lee Cafe

 $36

43 W. 65th St. (212) 595-8895
bet. Columbus Ave. & Central Park W. on the Upper West Side
Not just fancy alternatives to the corner Chinese, these restaurants
have their place in the NYC fine dining pantheon. "Haute Chinese,
very well done," "expensive but fabulous food" is the concensus.

Shun Lee Palace

 $39

155 E. 55th St. (212) 371-8844
bet. Third & Lexington Aves. in Midtown E.
"The best gourmet Chinese in the city?" You bet, say Rorhac
voters, who rank Shun Lee Palace right at the top. "Exquisite"
"excellent" "well prepared and presented" food served by a
competent staff in a "nice new setting" makes for a "perfect place
for a business lunch."

Siam Inn

 $21

854 Eighth Ave. (212) 757-4006
bet. 51st & 52nd Sts. in the Theater District
916 Eighth Ave. (212) 489-5237
bet. 54th & 55th Sts. in Midtown W.
"Great for takeout" and pre-theater, these "uncrowded" Siamese
twins serve consistent, "delicious" dishes in "cozy" quarters. With
"authentic" fare, moderate prices and accommodating service,
they're convenient for the Midtown lunch crowd.

Sidewalk Cafe

94 Ave. A (212) 473-7373
at 6th St. in the E. Village
Live music with no cover, a late menu that serves 24-7, great breakfasts and of course sidewalk people-watching make this East Village eatery a favorite dive for "nighttime eating, drinking and hanging." All in all, it's "very busy, popular and" above all, "inexpensive."

Sign of the Dove $54

1110 Third Ave. at 65th St. on the Upper East Side (212) 861-8080
In her 30s and still as "beautiful" as ever, this "elegant," "classy," and "timeless" Contemporary American is "one of NY's best, still," with "fabulous food," "gracious service," and drop-dead "heavenly" decor —"truly a classic." "The food's almost as good as the place is romantic," and that's saying a lot. Cranks suggest they should change the name to "Dollar Sign of the Dove," but its many fans liken it more to an "orgasmic experience."

Silk Road Palace $15

447-B Amsterdam Ave. (212) 580-6294
bet. 81st & 82nd Sts. on the Upper West Side
"A cut above the run-of-the-mill Chinese," as the lines outside this Upper West Side Szechwan attest. (Though some may be lining up for the "free wine while you wait.") Opt for takout or delivery—you won't be missing out on atmosphere.

Silver Palace

50 Bowery (212) 964-1204
at Canal St. in Chinatown
We didn't survey every Chinatown Chinese, but voters insisted we not leave this dim sum destination out of the book. With "long lines on weekends" it's "still the best for Chinese style banquets."

Silver Swan

41 E. 20th St. (212) 254-3611
bet. Broadway & Park Ave. S. in the Flatiron District
Normally, traditional German/American places get a nod and a shrug from most diners. A top selection for beer on tap, and "hearty," "authentic German fare" ("moist sauerbraten" is hard to find) and good desserts (including "crisp strudel") make this Flatiron place one of the "few good Germans still around."

Sloppy Louie's $28

92 South St. (212) 509-9694
at the South St. Seaport
Good bouillabaisse is hard to find, but if you look for a "charming old" landmark building located at the South Street Seaport you'll find a "touristy" American seafooder. It's been around since 1930, serving "good," "reasonably priced seafood." The inside of the space may not live up to the outside and the service doesn't swim. So dive into "fresh and tasty grilled fish," or don't.

FOOD ROOM STAFF COST

Smith & Wollensky

$50

797 Third Ave. (212) 753-1530
at 49th St. in Midtown E.

Tops in such manly categories as Business Meal and Cigar Spot, S&W joins that legion of "granddaddy steakhouses" that includes Sparks and Peter Luger, to which it is frequently compared—and not unfavorably, we might add. "Killer portions" of "good meat," plus an enviable Scotch selection conspire to make this a "rewarding splurge." "Not for vegetarians," no, but it's a "NY institution."

Smith & Wollensky Grill

$37

201 E. 49th St. at Third Ave. in Midtown E. (212) 753-0444

Men, men, men, men, "mooo." That's mostly what you'll find at this Midtown beef bash. It's "testosterone city" "full of stuffy stogie smokers," but "for great steak, deal with it." Okay. So let's talk about those "amazing" steaks. Or how about those "great steaks." Even those "big beautiful burgers" that just might be the most expensive in town. The professional service will also help you out with the creamed spinach on the side, "great chocolate cake" for dessert, and a scotch, beer, vintage, or cider.

S.O.B.

$33

200 Varick St. at W. Houston St. in SoHo (212) 243-4940

If you want to "eat and party at the same time," go down to SoHo and "get your groove back, where the multicultural music is world class." The music and fun are the real deal at this popular club where bands from across the globe hit the New York music scene. Unfortunately the Brazilian food is "quite mediocre and should only be sought out after dancing" has "brought on starvation."

Sofia Fabulous Pizza

$29

1022 Madison Ave. bet. 78th & 79th Sts./U.E. Side (212) 734-2676

A "beautiful" Euro-crowd of all ages packs this "trendy" Upper East Sider for "designer pizza" at designer prices. The "loud music" can be "too loud," but the outdoor patio and elegant upstairs provide options for a "quiet" refuge.

Soho Kitchen & Bar

$26

103 Greene St. bet. Prince & Spring Sts. in SoHo (212) 925-1866

Yeah they have a kitchen, but everyone one goes for the bar. This SoHo Continental has the No. 1 wine list and "more beers than have probably ever been assembled under one roof." Order a 'flight' of wine, or one of the 35 drafts and sit back and pretend you're flying in one of the airplanes hanging from the ceiling. They do have "surprisingly good pizza" but it comes with "huge portions of attitude from the staff." Go after work for some of the "best wine on the planet" in a "trendy" but "fun" atmosphere that's "great for groups."

SoHo Steak

90 Thompson St. bet. Prince & Spring Sts./SoHo (212) 226-0602

"Put this in your book"—a "European-style" Steakhouse bistro that is "noisy and cramped," but it's "pretty cheap," and especially "fun for SoHo."

Solera

$44

216 E. 53rd St. bet. Second & Third/Midtown E. (212) 644-1166
No matter what your favorite Spanish place might be, the upscale "elegance" here in Midtown is hard to beat. It offers an "unbelievable tapas selection"—voters walk away from this one chiming, "every course was fabulous," "sophisticated" and "super fresh." The "quaint, airy atmosphere," "pretty garden" and top-notch service add up to a "warm and friendly" experience and the reasons why it lands on several of our tops lists.

Sonia Rose

$45

132 Lexington Ave. (212) 545-1777
bet. 28th & 29th Sts. in Murray Hill
"A true hidden gem" in a quiet Murray Hill neighborhood is this "charmingly romantic" French restaurant, whose "exquisite" food, "wonderful" service, and "attention to detail" will make you feel "removed from hectic NYC." "Like dining in someone's fine home"; "thank goodness the masses are still unaware of it." "A real find."

Sotto Cinque

$15

417 Third Ave. bet. 29th & 30th/Gramercy (212) 685-2037
1644 Second Ave. bet. 85th & 86th Sts./U.E. Side (212) 472-5563
Whether you consider these "good food at awesome prices" or just "food that's worth under $5" (the name Sotto Cinque means "under five," and refers to some of the menu prices) probably depends on your age and the condition of your pocketbook. Fans like the "decent," "filling pastas" (did we mention "cheap") and "nice courtyard in back for summer dining," but if you have six bucks "you're better off spending more and going elsewhere."

Souen

$21

28 E. 13th St. bet. Univ. Pl. & Fifth/Cen. Village (212) 627-7150
210 Sixth Ave. at Prince St. in SoHo (212) 807-7421
"An absolute must for vegetarians," these austere, "relaxing" Japanese/Macrobiotics allow voters to "meditate and eat at the same time." They offer a "great variety" of "healthy" options, but some say the "organic" cuisine "needs flavor" and the stark, "Zen" atmosphere is "depressing." Most prefer the less-cramped SoHo original to its Central Village sibling and encounter "no-nonsense" service at both locations.

Soul Fixins'

$14

371 W. 34th St. (212) 736-1345
at Ninth Ave. in Chelsea
Before a Knicks game, how about some "serious ribs" or candied yams at this "delightful" and "funky" Soul Food shack near The Garden. Both the food and service are "dependable" and the prix fixe lunch is a steal.

Soup Kitchen

359-A W. 55th St. bet. Bdwy & 8th/Midtown W. (212) 757-7730
This takeout only spot (made famous on *Seinfeld*) serves a hearty, eclectic soup menu—plus bread and fruit, if you follow the owner's unwritten rules of behavior. If you didn't catch that *Seinfeld* episode, watch the folks ahead of you, and you'll be fine.

FOOD ROOM STAFF COST

Spain

113 W. 13th St. (212) 929-9580
bet. Sixth & Seventh Aves. S. in the W. Village
This West Villager has "great sangria," and "for less than $30 two
people can eat like kings." One of our voters' very favorite Spanish
spots, with "great paella," where "you'll be amazed at the
authenticity of the food and atmosphere."

Sparks Steakhouse $54

210 E. 46th St. bet. Second & Third/Midtown E. (212) 687-4855
With "fantastic," massive steaks and an "incredible wine list," this
Midtown East institution impresses Romac Reporters who call it
one of the "best" steakhouses in NYC. The "pleasantly boisterous"
"male" atmosphere and professional service make it perfect for a
power lunch or business dinner. If you "look up 'steakhouse' in the
dictionary, you'll find a picture of Sparks."

Spartina $34

355 Greenwich St. at Harrison St. in TriBeCa (212) 274-9310
A TriBeCa view of the Hudson from a Mediterranean restaurant
may not be the thing to transport you to the Riveria, but it's better
than staring out at a dusty airshaft. Reporters say they like the
"tasty" fare from the "imaginative menu" and while it's "relaxing at
lunch" it can be loud and "pricey."

Spring St. Natural $22

62 Spring St. at Lafayette in SoHo (212) 966-0290
In the Top 10 for vegetarian plates, the scores will show you what
most voters think of "multi-ethnic organic vegetarian, with seafood
and poultry," even a pretty good one. "Great" though
"unimaginative" is the general consensus. Though "tucked away in
SoHo," "the clientele has less attitude than the waitstaff" (gee!).

Spy $37

101 Greene St. bet. Spring & Prince Sts. in SoHo (212) 343-9000
Fortunately the name changed from Kaptain Banana to something a
little less phallic, or whatever. But word about this hip Nouvelle
spot in Soho is that people-watching is the deal, so you're liable to
spy someone cool or famous or at least someone who's trying to be.

Stage Deli $21

834 Seventh Ave. bet. 53rd & 54th/Midtown W. (212) 245-7850
Is that a turkey sandwich or an entire Butterball? If you don't try one
of the "sandwiches big enough for two or more meals" order one of
the "mammoth portions" of something else from the mammoth menu
(they'd put mammoth on rye if they could). This West Midtown spot
is "another old NY tradition" in a long line of famous diners. Like the
others, the service sucks, its a "tourist trap" and a dump. But if you
want "a great Danish" or "the best cheesecake in the universe" before
a show, stop in and see what a real NY deli has to offer.

Stanhope  $49

Stanhope Hotel, 995 Fifth Ave. at 81st/U.E. Side (212) 288-5800
Don't let out-of-towners monopolize this Upper East Side
Continental. It's one of those places that gives NYC a good name:
The only attitude you'll get will probably be from the cab driver
who drops you off. It won't be from a friendly and efficient staff
that makes you feel an expensive meal is worth a night out again
and again. The "three-course prix fixe is a good buy" and the
ambiance is never a downer. Try it for a weekend brunch before
visiting the Met or the Guggenheim.

Starbucks  $9

(many, many locations)
This No. 1 Coffeehouse on our survey provokes hundreds of
"justifiable rage" comments: "You must be joking," "I don't find
McDonald's on your list, why include" the "Microsoft of
coffeehouses? Don't feed the sharks." The decaf comments are
more like: "great at what they do," "Starbucks has great coffee,"
and "chains make me gag, got to have the frappuccino."

Steak Frites  $33

9 E. 16th St. bet. Fifth Ave. & Union Sq. W. (212) 463-7101
The Top 10 steak, burgers and "relaxed atmosphere" pull in the traffic
at this French steakhouse in Union Square, but the "expensive" tab
and the "incompetent but beautiful staff" that just can't get it together
don't win fans. The "sidewalk cafe in good weather is very French"
and is ideal for brunch. Try the black Angus steak sandwich, mussels
appetizer or the monkfish with lobster mashed potatoes.

Stella Del Mare  $39

346 Lexington Ave. bet. 39th & 40th/Murray Hill (212) 687-4425
"Pomposity" and "high prices" must be keeping the traffic light,
because the food is deemed fine at this dressed-up Midtown East
Northern Italian. The bottom line seems to be, "if you're limited to
the Grand Central area, then it's okay."

Stick To Your Ribs  $15

5-16 51st Ave., Queens (718) 937-3030
at Vernon Blvd.
While the Upper West Side location was claimed by fire, the
original Queens version is still going strong. Once the best in the
five boroughs, more Southern options in Manhattan have made the
drive across the bridge to "cholesterol city" seem more onerous of
late. Plus, it closes at 9 p.m., disappointing the after-midnight
grease hounds who are so ready to travel.

Stingray  $25

428 Amsterdam Ave. (212) 501-7515
bet. 80th & 81st Sts. on the Upper West Side
This is the kind of place where you wait at a table to get a seat at the bar:
It's the "best part," and clearly the focus of this Upper West Side
Seafood, uh, restaurant. However, some take exception to the new wave
mixology here. "When you order a martini, they use vodka. Heathens!"

FOOD ROOM STAFF COST

Stingy Lulu's

$16

129 St. Mark's Pl. (212) 674-3545
bet. Ave. A & First Ave. in the E. Village
The food is "not so hot" but the milkshakes are "awesome" and
you're liable to see the freak of the week at this "funkiest East
Village hang," "Denny's on Acid." The American fare is "cheap,"
the drag queens provide the entertainment and best of all it's open
till 5am on weekdays, 6am on weekends. "Try the herbal burger,"
the onion rings or one of those early-morn breakfasts. As for
service, "be pierced and be patient."

Sukothai West

$27

411 W. 42nd St. bet. 9th & 10th Aves./Clinton (212) 947-1930
East meets West (Clinton, that is) at this "delicious, reasonably
priced Thai." It is "dependable," and has "one of the most beautiful
rooms to dine in in all New York. Is it possible for ceiling height to
enhance the flavor of lemon grass?"

Sullivan's Restaurant and Broadcast Lounge

$39

1697 Broadway bet. 53rd & 54th/Theater Dist. (212) 541-1697
SO HEEEEEEERRRE'S a new Chinese/American place on
Broadway in the historical Ed Sullivan theater building with
(naturally) "live and lively" entertainment and "mammoth,
marvelous desserts." Who knows, maybe Ed Sullivan'll drop by.

Sunny East

$32

21 W. 39th St. (212) 764-3232
bet. Fifth & Sixth Aves. in the Garment District
It's in the Garment District, so don't let the name fool you. If
you're dragging those relatives around Times Square, this Chinese
is close enough to hit when the stomach grumbles. Voters say
"good food and service" and you can eat dim sum in a comfortable
smokeless section. Check out the "great fish tank."

Supper Club

$36

240 W. 47th St. (212) 921-1940
bet. Broadway & Eighth Ave. in the Theater District
"Supper is not the draw here." Instead, what this Theater District
American offers is "splendidly esoteric entertainment" in a
"beautiful room" that's "perfect for romance." Swing bands, rock
bands and jazz/blues greats show up here and make for a rip-roaring
good time. The food is only "so- so" and the staff is average but if
you don't have a good time here, then you might want to find a
place that serves prozac appetizers.

Sushiden

$38

19 E. 49th St. bet. Fifth & Madison/Midtown E. (212) 758-2700
This place has everything you want in a sushi bar. The Midtown
atmosphere is "just like having sushi in Tokyo among Japanese
businessmen." Participants say "piece by piece" it's among "the
best in NY," which is why it makes the Top 20 by way of fresh
seafood (spicy tuna is a fave). They also have a "nice private room"
but might be a little "too eager to turn over tables."

≡ = SUPERIOR ≡ = EXCELLENT ≡ = V. GOOD ▬ = GOOD

Sushihatsu

$47

1143 First Ave. (212) 371-0238
bet. 62nd & 63rd Sts. on the Upper East Side
With "excellent sushi" that's so authentic, this Sutton Place-area Japanese restaurant is best attended "with a Japanese speaker in your party." "The sushi bar's the place to be," for some of the freshest fish around, though its Far-East location keeps it going at a laid-back pace.

Sushisay

$47

38 E. 51st St. (212) 755-1780
bet. Park & Madison Aves. in Midtown E.
"Sushi so tender it melts in your mouth" comes at "Tokyo prices" to be sure, but this "fresh fish paradise" offers some of the "best sushi in town." "Reliable staff" and comfortable Midtown quarters (hard by the BMW showroom, natch) are an added plus, and did we mention "excellent sushi"? The two magic words: "expense account."

Sushizen

$47

57 W. 46th St. (212) 302-0707
bet. Fifth & Sixth Aves. in Midtown W.
"Very expensive," yes, but those in the know say Sushizen's got the "best sushi" and the "most unusual hand rolls in town." The soothing setting is enhanced by an attractive outdoor garden, and the menu that changes seasonally.

Sutton Watering Hole

$24

209 E. 56th St. (212) 355-6868
bet. Second & Third Aves. in Midtown E.
The drinking reference is more than appropriate for this restaurant. "Happy hour hell" accompanied by the animal sounds coming through the bathroom speakers make "you feel like you're in the jungle." The American food rating has difficulty rising to a level of mediocrity. Fortunately the prix fixe dinner and the jazz brunch are affordable with a capital 'A'.

Sweet 'n' Tart Cafe

$19

76 Mott St. (212) 334-8088
at Canal St. in Chinatown
Despite its unlikely name, folks call this one-year-old Chinatown hole-in-the-wall a "great new, real Chinese." That goes for the food, including the "finest dumplings." As for the extras, people love the health shakes and various sweets from the Orient.

Sweet Ophelia's

430 Broome St. (212) 343-8000
at Crosby St. in SoHo
"Swing loooww..." country cuisine from the south in SoHo. Say that ten times fast with a mouth full o' "bitter greens." Suck back some "interesting tonics and health drinks" on the patio and squeeze the sweet buns at the full-service bakery, then let us know how it went because frankly my dear, we do give a damn, and voters were scarce on this one.

FOOD · ROOM · STAFF · COST

Sweet Potato

$12

1466 Second Ave. bet. 76th & 77th/U.E. Side (212) 535-8423
Just when you thought the healthy stuff was always going to be the most expensive, along comes this Upper East Sider that's not only cheap, but it tastes good. It's known for "great fruit smoothies and sandwiches." There's little in the way of decor, and "the service is in slow motion," but both your heart and wallet will walk out of here feeling full.

Sylvia's

$24

328 Lenox Ave. bet. 126th &127th Sts. in Harlem (212) 996-0660
For "the ultimate in comfort food, if you don't mind arteriosclerosis," head up to Harlem, where you'll find what fans deem "the best Soul Food outside Georgia." Sylvia's still gets many votes for "best ribs" and "great chicken wings," but with its growth from cult favorite to tourist mecca, some wonder if it's fallen prey to "the emperor's new clothes" syndrome. Still, the "great gospel brunch" is no illusion, and despite claims of "overrated"-ness, "Sylvia's still has soul."

Syrah

1400 Second Ave. at 73rd St./Upper East Side (212) 327-1780
This new Upper East Side American/French bistro gets its name from the Syrah grape, which is found in many fine French wines. Let us know what you think about this spot on your questionnaire next year.

Szechuan Hunan Cottage

$19

1433 Second Ave. bet. 74th & 75th Sts./U.E. Side (212) 535-1471
1588 York Ave. bet. 83rd & 84th Sts. in Yorkville (212) 535-5223
"Very good food and congenial staff" make this Yorkville Chinese very popular for "great" takeout or dine-in. The "sesame noodles are still the best around," and the chef's specials, while somewhat Americanized, are fine. Of course, the free wine with dinner doesn't hurt, either.

Table d'Hote

$43

44 E. 92nd St. bet. Madison & Park/Carnegie Hill (212) 348-8125
It's "very small" and "very intimate" but "the food, oh the food." This real sleeper on the Upper East Side just down the street from the 92nd St. Y is like being in a "rustic" "romantic" corner of Vermont for "amazing" Contemporary American fare. The "neighborhood goodie"/"charming little hideaway" appeal of this one is never lost and is worth going to no matter where in the city you dwell. The early-bird dinner until 6:30pm cuts the price tag in half.

Takahachi

$23

85 Ave. A bet. 6th & 7th Sts. in the E. Village (212) 505-6524
Who says you have to go to a fancy Midtown place for "amazing" sushi. And at these low prices, it's worth the hike from the subway to deep into the heart of the East Village for "great," "fresh" seafood and "great homemade soy sauce." There's always a "cool crowd," competent service and regulars advise "get there for the early-bird menu." No reservations=always a wait.

≣ = SUPERIOR ≣ = EXCELLENT ≣ = V. GOOD ≡ = GOOD

Takesushi

 $29

71 Vanderbilt Ave. (212) 867-5120
bet. 45th & 46th Sts. in Midtown E.
With a price tag that's higher than most Japanese, this Grand
Central-area Sushi restaurant is also much larger than most. While
not the highest rated, you can't argue with 20 years of success, that
includes a $50 pre-theater menu for two.

Tammany Hall

 $32

393 Third Ave. (212) 696-2001
at 28th St. in Murray Hill
Voters go to this Murray Hill American for "great early-bird
specials" and "classy, low-key" ambiance with banquette seating.
Prices are "reasonable," but some say the "initial signs of promise
are fizzling" and the staff and menu can be "spotty."

Tang Pavilion

 $30

65 W. 55th St. (212) 956-6888
bet. Fifth & Sixth Aves. in Midtown W.
"You must order only from the Shanghai menu..." say voters (who
seem to be reading too many fortune cookies). Everyone agrees,
calling the food at this West Midtowner at least "good," and usually
well above average. "A godsend for Midtown," the lunch menu is
full of good bargains.

Tang Tang

 $20

243 Third Ave. (212) 477-0460
at 20th St. in Gramercy
1328 Third Ave. (212) 249-2102
at 76th St. on the Upper East Side
These Chinese sibs are doing their best to feel like they're in
Chinatown: The room and staff ratings are simply poor. The food
does a little better, owing to a few die-hard fans who appreciate the
"duck soup," "cold noodles," and "best sesame beef."

Tanti Baci

 $22

163 W. 10th St. (212) 647-9651
bet. Seventh Ave. S. & Waverly Pl. in the W. Village
Self-described as "strictly Italian," some find this West Village
basement "simple and charming" (BYOB is ultra-charming in these
parts) and call it "a Village experience," though most agree it's
closer to "a hole in the ground" with "cheap eats."

Taormina

 $37

147 Mulberry St. (212) 219-1007
bet. Grand & Hester Sts. in Little Italy
Everything's homemade at this Little Italy Southern Italian, to the
delight of most voters who call it "the best Italian on Mulberry
Street." The food places well into the Top 100 overall, and the
"very good" staff nearly makes it into the Romac Top 50. However,
"now that they don't have to impress Gotti," grumbles one
conspiracy theorist, "the quality slips."

	FOOD	ROOM	STAFF	COST

Tapas Lounge

$28

1078 First Ave. (212) 421-8282
at 59th St. in Midtown E.

"An interesting venue" on the Upper East Side that includes wrought-iron fixtures, candlelight and even flamenco night culminates in better-than-average Spanish food and "authentic," "very good" tapas.

Tapika

$41

950 Eighth Ave. (212) 397-3737
at 56th St. in Midtown W.

Like a "cross between Arizona 206 and Patria," this "inventive Southwestern" in a soaring Midtown space offers "flavorful" food, "incredibly wonderful" service" and a "delightful atmosphere" that strikes our reporters as a "nice theme." Rising-star-chef David Walzog puts out "really fresh" and "most interesting" Contemporary American food with "American West" flair. Though locals thought they'd "miss the Symphony Cafe," now they're in "love" with Tapika.

Taqueria de Mexico

$15

93 Greenwich Ave. (212) 255-5212
bet. W. 11th & W. 12th Sts. in the W. Village

"Small prices" go with the "small portions" at this West Village taco stand, okay "for a quick snack or takeout."

Tartine

$22

253 W. 11th St. (212) 229-2611
at W. 4th St. in the W. Village

While high marks in the "closest tables" and "weekend crowding" categories makes it hard to just drop by this West Village French (with Mediterannean influences), the "very good" food places well into Romac Reporters' top fifty faves. "Charming, cheap and crowded," this "tiny" BYOB is "a great deal—if you can get in."

Tatany

$27

380 Third Ave. (212) 686-1871
bet. 27th & 28th Sts. in Gramercy

The "best sushi in the 'hood" is yours for the asking at this "sedate," "refreshingly beautiful" Gramercy storefront, with its "fresh and affordable sushi" and other well-prepared, "very traditional" Japanese specialties. The accommodating staff will help you forget the "long waits on weekends."

Tatany 52

$31

250 E. 52nd St. (212) 593-0203
bet. Second & Third Aves. in Midtown E.

In some ways, this East Side Japanese is a typical Midtowner: busy at lunch, it's mellow in the evening making it a "great date place." However, it goes beyond that, with "very good," "consistent" and "fresh" sushi and a very late-night menu until 3:30 a.m.

Tatou

$42

151 E. 50th St. (212) 753-1144
bet. Third & Lexington Aves. in Midtown E.
Say what you will about the "scary" crowd, this "too trendy"
Midtowner offers constant "entertainment" in a "theatrical setting."
At dinner time there's a "fun" cabaret or live jazz but later it "turns
into a nightclub" rumored to be an "older pick-up" zone. The
French/American fare is "overpriced" and nothing special but "who
goes here to eat?" Upstairs try Le Cigar for stogies and single malts.

Tavern on Jane

$25

31 Eighth Ave. at Jane St. in the W. Village (212) 675-2526
While there wasn't a desperate need for another American Tavern
in the West Village, there's always room for another "cozy" (it
doesn't get much cozier than two fireplaces) room, and this yearling
fills the bill. The food "isn't so great for the price," at least so far.

Tavern on the Green

$47

Central Park & W. 67th St./Upper West Side (212) 873-3200
"Hollywood comes to Central Park." This is a feast for the eyes, not the
appetite. Come for the classic, NYC atmosphere, the music, the dancing,
not the food. New Yorkers call it "overhyped and overpriced" and a
"tacky tourist trap," but it's Number 1 for out-of-towners: "The patio is
enchanting on summer evenings and fairy-tale-–esque on winter nights;
a NY gem." Fun for big family brunches, but avoid it weekends and
"don't go on any holiday." If you want to live a black-and-white movie
dream for an evening, this is your place.

Tea and Sympathy

$19

108 Greenwich Ave. bet. 12th & 13th/W. Village (212) 807-8329
Its many fans "can't live without treacle pudding," "jam rolli
pollis," "real scones," and other "English comfort food" served up
by "waitresses who call you 'luv'" at this "tiny," "charming
restaurant" that specializes in a "fabulous afternoon tea." For those
"homesick for England," "this is the place to go." Too bad it's
"almost impossible to get in."

Tea Den

$18

940 Eighth Ave. at 56th St. in Midtown W. (212) 265-8880
This Midtown West Cantonese/Szechuan may have the "super fast
delivery" part down cold (or actually, hot), but for the most part
voters find the food (including daily eat-in dim sum) only "fair."

Telephone Bar

$21

149 Second Ave. at 10th St. in the E. Village (212) 529-5000
"Blimey, it's a limey bar!" with "food only the British could love." But
the meal might taste better after tapping into the beer which ranks in the
top 20. Try "classics" like the "excellent fish and chips" or the "great,
authentic shepherds pie." But, beware, the "noise level makes it hard to
talk." Laugh it up during Wednesday "comedy spots," or try Monday
poetry readings and Sunday jazz. If the pot calls the kettle it will probably
be in one of the charming red phone booths at the entrance.

▬ = FAIR   [blank] = POOR   ▦ = NOT RATED

| | FOOD | ROOM | STAFF | COST |

Temple Bar $28

332 Lafayette St. (Bleecker & Houston/E. Village) (212) 925-4242
The martinis here have achieved mythic status (No. 1), as have the
bartenders who serve them (top 20) and the "romantic," "quiet
enough to talk," "wood-paneled speakeasy" room they are served in
(top 100). Other than the "delicious nibbles" the "overpriced" food
is not the pull. Voters call this the "perfect spot to experience
THE MARTINI," when you're "in the mood for decadence." This
East Village bar is an after-work fave, but they don't take
reservations, so claim your space early.

Tennessee Mountain $25

143 Spring St. at Wooster St. in SoHo (212) 431-3993
"The best ribs south of Harlem"? Some may have a bone to pick
with that claim, but our voters go hog wild for the
"fall-off-the-bone" tenderness of this barbeque. It's SoHo goes
down home, complete with a farmhouse setting, a family-friendly
atmosphere, and all-you-can-eat specials, perfect for all those who
"can't get enough."

Teresa's

70-34 Austin St., at 71st in Queens (718) 520-2910
80 Montague St., at Hicks in Brooklyn (718) 797-3996
103 First Ave. bet. 6th & 7th Sts. in the E. Village (212) 228-0604
Some say this East Villager (with outposts in Brooklyn and Queens) is
"best at breakfast" but others appreciate the "hearty," "wholesome"
Eastern European eats anytime. "Friendly" service and sidewalk seats
make it a staple for a "filling," "inexpensive" meal.

Terrace $53

Butler Hall, 400 W. 119th St. (212) 666-9490
bet. Amsterdam Ave. & Morningside Dr. in Harlem
"The food matches the glorious view" at this "very special"
French dining room, worth the schlepp up to Morningside
Heights for the "perfect food" and "excellent service." There's
"no problem getting a table," despite the fact that this is
"absolutely NY's premier romantic spot" in the star-struck eyes
of many of our reviewers. "Go when the harpist plays," or when
you can enjoy the moonlight on the outdoor terrace.

Thai House Cafe $18

151 Hudson St. at Hubert in TriBeCa (212) 334-1085
This cash-only TriBeCa Thai has scads of Pad Thai fans who have
"never been disappointed." Maybe that's because they offer your
choice of meats for each Thai cooking style, and if, somehow, and
"if it's not on the menu, ask the owner and he will prepare."

13 Barrow $32

13 Barrow St. bet. 7th Ave. S. & W. 4th St./W. Vill. (212) 727-1300
"Delicious," inventive cuisine and a comfortable setting makes
voters "want to stay all night" at this West Village Eclectic. Luckily
the "creative" cuisine is available until 4 a.m., though, inevitably for
this neighborhood, it can get "noisy" and "crowded."

Thomas Scott's　　　　🍴 🌹 🍸　$34

72-74 Bedford St. (212) 427-4011
at Commerce St. in the W. Village
Folks "love the look of this little gem" in the West Village, though they
disagree somewhat on the food and feel of the place. What is "gay
romantic" to some is "stuffy and weird" to others, though everyone
seems to enjoy the great Sunday brunch and "very good desserts."

Three of Cups　　　　🍴 🌹 🍸　$21

83 First Ave. at 5th St. in the E. Village (212) 388-0059
While an East Villiage Italian named for a Tarot card might seem
too spooky for some, our voters find plenty to recommend here.
"Good brick-oven pizza, but much more" including "cool couches"
and "candlelight" that make it a "great hangout where every kind of
person can be themselves." Increasingly crowded, some preferred it
"before it was 'discovered.'"

Tibetan Kitchen　　　　🍴 🌹 🍸　$18

444 Third Ave. at 31st St. in Murray Hill (212) 679-6286
You won't find enlightenment at this Murray Hill Tibetan, but there's
no guarantee you'll find it in Tibet, either. With little to compare it
with, voters are disappointed with the "rather ordinary" food here,
have come to "expect a wait" for it and call the atmosphere "dull"
(except the "rowdy" basement, down a precarious spiral staircase).

Time Cafe/Fez　　　　🍴 🌹 🍸　$26

87 7th Ave. S., at Barrow St. in the W. Village
380 Lafayette St. at Great Jones in the E. Village (212) 533-7000
A "very lively, huge brasserie," this NoHo New American three-
parter has something for everyone funky. The big, pretty Time
Cafe, the Fez cocktail lounge (with limited menu) next door, and
the performance space downstairs attract the "Village Cool," the
"very hip" and especially the "18-24-year-olds (none overweight!)."
You can "never go wrong with the cafe outside."

Tio Pepe　　　　🍴 🌹 🍸　$23

168 W. 4th St. (212) 242-9338
bet. Sixth Ave. & Seventh Ave. S. in the W. Village
A longtime Villager, Uncle Pepe started out Spanish but changed
over the years to meet the Tex-Mex trend. That means "good
margaritas," and the "best piña coladas in NYC," and still includes
"great paella," though some say the kitchen has lost its focus. The
all-you-can-eat Sunday brunch buffet, in the "great garden in back,"
is a good value and attracts the smoker crowd.

Tito Puente's　　　　🍴 🌹 🍸　$32

64 City Island Ave., at Horton St. Bronx (718) 885-3200
"Popular with the young and beautiful" who don't mind the trek to City
Island for the seafood-intensive Puerto Rican/Cuban specialties served at
this year-old restaurant owned by the great Latin jazz percussionist. The
rollicking atmosphere features live music Thursday and Friday nights,
and the restaurant prides itself on its Happy Birthday fetes. The aurally
challenged say "go for the salsa, as in the music only."

FOOD ROOM STAFF COST

Tivoli

515 Third Ave. (212) 532-3300
bet. 34th & 35th Sts. in Murray Hill
One of the few 24-hour Italian restaurants on our poll, this East
Midtown spot has many fans, who also like it during regular hours.
It's more a "deli with home cooking," or a "great neighborhood
coffee shop" than a formal restaurant, but it's "reliable," and that's
the way voters like it.

Toast
$30

428 Lafayette St. (212) 674-4066
bet. E. 4th St. & Astor Pl. in the E. Village
From the name, you might think they had a pretty limited menu
here. However, this East Village Continental has plenty of "great
food," in a "fun atmosphere" with a "doting staff," and they don't
even serve breakfast. Eclectic touches like Thai Salmon and "Pot of
Chocolate" dessert make this place special.

Tomoe
$27

172 Thompson St. (212) 777-9346
bet. Bleecker & Houston Sts. in the Washington Sq. Area
The sushi's "soooo good" that you don't mind the hour's wait and
"shabby surroundings" that go with the territory at this
bargain-priced Thompson Street specialist. Tomoe has the "best and
largest sushi in the city" (the other Japanese fare "lacks"), so long
as you are prepared to join the "long lines" outside.

Tompkins 131
$29

131 Ave. A (212) 777-5642
bet. St. Mark's Pl. & 9th St. in the E. Village
The East Village being the competitive market that it is, this
American eatery might not "really fit pricewise." Try the twice per
month liquor tastings: a novelty. We hear the food is "upscale," but
you tell us. They serve until late, so make a last minute decision.

Tom's Restaurant

2880 Broadway (212) 864-6137
at 112th St. in Harlem
This is the Columbia U.-area Diner of *Seinfeld* fame (and
Suzanne Vega), they have "reasonable prices" and "quick
service," if only average food. But, "how many other diners have
TWO separate pop culture references?"

Tony di Napoli

1606 Second Ave. (212) 861-8686
bet. 83rd & 84th Sts. on the Upper East Side
This Upper East Side Italian may be a "poor man's Carmine's" to
some, but eyes still "bulge" when the "enormous, family-sized"
portions arrive. It's "cheap" and "great for a group," but don't
expect better than "average" cuisine.

Toraya

$25

17 E. 71st St. (212) 861-1700
bet. Fifth & Madison Aves. on the Upper East Side
This Japanese Tea Room is located in High Tea Central—East 71st
Street, just off the park. A coffee/tea shop, not a ceremonial
teahouse, the room is pretty, and the staff "excellent." A little
latitude leaves room for "the most exotic dessert in the city."

Torre de Pisa

$42

19 W. 44th St. (212) 398-4400
bet. Fifth & Sixth Aves. in Midtown W.
The "fascinating creative decor" (like a fractured leaning tower)
rates better than the Tuscan menu, but the food's "consistently"
"good" enough to warrant a visit to this "great space" in a
convenient Midtown location. The "quick service" comes in handy
if you're running late for curtain time.

Torremelinos

$41

230 E. 51st St. (212) 755-1862
bet. Second & Third Aves. in Midtown E.
Despite prix fixe specials, a live guitarist, and tasty fare, this
Spaniard is relatively unknown and uncrowded. Solid scores and a
Midtown location make it a likely lunch stop though many
surveyors find it "overpriced."

Tortilla Flats

$20

767 Washington St. (212) 243-1053
at W. 12th St. in the W. Village
Good Tex-Mex wouldn't be complete without "velvet Elvis
paintings and '70s music," and a "raucous bar scene" in a "funky
West Village" setting. This is a "fun place to go with a group of
people," it's "great for birthday parties" and it hosts "the best bingo
night in NYC," Monday and Tuesday. It's kid-friendly so bring the
whole family and the ear plugs too.

Totonno Pizzeria Napolitano

$16

1524 Neptune Ave., Brooklyn (718) 372-8606
bet. W. 15th & W. 16th Sts.
The pizza here is so good some wonder, "is this what pizza is
supposed to taste like?" Yes indeed. "Light as a feather dough, fresh
tomatoes, pure white mozzarella," make "simply the best pizza you
can find." They took grandpa's recipe from about 70 years back and
don't plan on changing a thing. It's way out in Coney Island so for
most it's a trip, but worth it for "landmark pizza." No slices—only
whole pies. No credit cards or reservations.

Tout Va Bien

$33

311 W. 51st St. (212) 265-0190
bet. Eighth & Ninth Aves. in Clinton
Everything is good—at least the ratings are—at this 50-year-old
Clinton French. "A cozy, unpretentious bistro," though sometimes
"unreliable," is one of the "last of the old Theater District haunts."

FOOD ROOM STAFF COST

Townhouse

$38

206 E. 58th St. (212) 826-6241
bet. Second & Third Aves. in Midtown E.
This East Midtown New American draws a mixed, mostly older crowd for bargain prix fixe lunches: later on, you generally "go for the view" or the great "after-work cocktails," where the atmosphere prevails over the kitchen, and the scene turns mainly male.

Tramps

$26

45 W. 21st St. (212) 633-9570
bet. Fifth & Sixth Aves. in the Flatiron District
This joint has live music (best on the poll) and the New Orleans Cajun menu can burn, baby burn. The food's only fair to middling, and the "funky roadhouse atmosphere" (right in the heart of Chelsea) isn't to everyone's liking. Still, you can "do your eating, drinking and dancing in the same joint."

Trattoria Alba

$27

233 E. 34th St. (212) 689-3200
bet. Second & Third Aves. in Murray Hill
"Good, reliable Italian food at good prices" can be had at this Murray Hill spot, hard by the movie theaters. While not outstanding, they have a cozy, "nice atmosphere," and the staff gets consistently good marks. No credit cards.

Trattoria dell'Arte

$42

900 Seventh Ave. (212) 245-9800
bet. 56th & 57th Sts. in Midtown W.
It's a good idea to call ahead to this "very good," Regional Italian that's "the best place for after Carnegie Hall," especially for groups. The "fun, bustling atmosphere" and "great Italian brunch" at a "bargain deal" help propel this spot into the Top 40 Romac Favorites. Some parts are more cramped than others, and the whole scene is presided over by what appear to be full-sized casts of the Statue of Liberty's nose, ear and other, er, parts.

Trattoria Spaghetto

$21

232 Bleecker St. (212) 255-6752
at Carmine St. in the W. Village
It's "always crowded" for "solid red-sauce Italian" here in the center of the Village. But "huge portions" that are "dirt cheap" do tend to attract an audience. The "close seating and hurried dining" make the ambiance "very New York," so it may be "too noisy." No credit cards.

Tre Pomodori

$24

210 E. 34th St. (212) 545-7266
bet. Second & Third Aves. in Murray Hill
This casual, two-year-old Murray Hill place pulls down consistent (if average) ratings for its presentation of the simpler side of Italian cooking. "Cheap, decent eats" in a family-run spot equals "a fine neighborhood restaurant."

= SUPERIOR = EXCELLENT = V. GOOD = GOOD

Triangolo

345 E. 83rd St. (212) 472-4488
bet. First & Second Aves. on the Upper East Side
There's a "great menu, with lots of choices" at this Upper East Side
Northern Italian. "Excellent home made food" is complemented by
a relaxed atmosphere, but the "inexpensive" price tag and BYOB
policy put their 45 seats in high demand.

TriBeCa Grill

 $45

375 Greenwich St. (212) 941-3910
at Franklin St. in TriBeCa
This celebrity-seekers' haunt is more famous for megawatt owner
Robert DeNiro than for its Drew Nieporent-orchestrated food,
justifiably or not. The majority cite "great American bistro/grill"
fare but admit the "power-lunch scene" and "great
people-watching" are major draws. A vocal minority say it's all
Raging Bull: "overpriced, overhyped, overloud."

Trionfo

 $48

224 W. 51st St. (212) 262-6660
bet. Broadway & Eighth Ave. in the Theater District
Here's another pre-theater Northern Italian that offers a good buy
before curtain call. The steaks, chops and homemade pasta and breads
are "delicious" say participants and the "gracious service" makes you
want to go back every time a new show hits town. It's "a shame its not
more popular because it should be," and probably will be if they keep
this up. In case you haven't guessed, it's in the Theater District.

Triple Eight Palace

78 E. Broadway (212) 941-8886
at Division & Market Sts. in Chinatown
Though it is "somewhat expensive," voters single out this
Chinatown/Hong Kong dim sum restaurant as well above average.
"Lots of variety" puts diners in "dim sum heaven," and once you get
through the "terrible weekend lines," a "nice atmosphere" awaits.

Triplets Roumanian

 $37

11-17 Grand St. (212) 925-9303
at Sixth Ave. in SoHo
"Home of the singing waiters," this "Jewish Soul Food" joint (actually,
it's a Roumanian steakhouse) is "more known as a fun place" than a
serious restaurant. "Busloads of European tourists" find the atmosphere
can be like "getting stuck at a bad wedding" in "cholesterol city." Still,
it's a "great show and the triplets are always there."

Trois Canards

 $37

184 Eighth Ave. (212) 929-4320
bet. 19th & 20th Sts. in Chelsea
Duck into this casual Chelsea bistro for "unaffected" French fare
and a winning weekend brunch. Convenient for a pre-Joyce meal, it
features polished-wood fixtures, standard service and an
"interesting" motif. Even the butter is "duck-shaped."

▬ = FAIR   [blank] = POOR   ▤ = NOT RATED   **211**

| | FOOD | ROOM | STAFF | COST |

Trois Jean

$43

154 E. 79th St. (212) 988-4858
bet. Third & Lexington Aves. on the Upper East Side
Most find the French cuisine at this Upper East Sider "very fine,"
but it's the "above-average" staff and "cozy," "elegant bistro
setting" (including 18 wines by the glass) that make this a
comfortable local favorite. In sum, "a superlative neighborhood
French" that includes daily high tea.

Tropica

$42

MetLife Bldg., 200 Park Ave. (212) 867-6767
at 45th St. in Midtown E.
This "tropical paradise" makes a "good escape from the city" with its
well-rated "creative" "Caribbean food" (jerk chicken and "seafood" a
specialty) and upbeat, Caribbean "great house" atmosphere. Although
some call it "expensive," there's a $29 three-course, prix fixe dinner
that takes the sting out of this "taste of Florida."

Tse Yang

$47

Banca DiRoma, 34 E. 51st St. (212) 688-5447
bet. Park & Madison Aves. in Midtown E.
With sophisticated service and an elegant room, this sleek Midtowner
satisfies many voters seeking an "upscale Chinese" experience. For
others, it's "lovely" but "pretentious," and "too expensive" for Peking
and Shanghai specialties that "need more imagination."

T.S. Ma

$24

5 Penn Plaza, 33rd St. (212) 971-0050
at Eighth Ave. in the Garment District
This Garment District Chinese serves MSG (that is, Madison
Square Garden) crowds in an "upscale" (for Chinese, and especially
for an area mostly populated with Red Lobsters and Blarney
Stones) atmosphere. Though pricey, it's better than you might
think, and worth a trip once every four years when you're getting
your license renewed across the street.

Tsunami

$27

70 W. 3rd St. (212) 475-7770
bet. Thompson St. & La Guardia Pl. in the Washington Sq. Area
Jaded voters are far from overwhelmed by the "gimmicky setup" at
this Greenwich Village Japanese. NYC's only water-canal sushi bar, it
offers acceptable sushi and service but the big attraction crashes hard.
Most consider the "mundane moat" a "disappointment."

Turkish Cuisine

$22

631 Ninth Ave. (212) 397-9650
bet. 44th & 45th Sts. in Clinton
Folks call this Clinton "hole-in-the-wall" a "tasty Turk," and like the
"incredible atmosphere" of tapestries and belly dancers. Specializing in
lamb and other "authentic" Turkish treats, this is a straight-up,
down-and-dirty ethnic joint that's an exotic pre-theater option. BYOB.

Turkish Kitchen

$30

386 Third Ave. (212) 679-1810
bet. 27th & 28th Sts. in Gramercy
While pricier than other ethnics, this "neat, casual" Gramercy Turk serves "food in a class of its own." Though the decor "has seen better times," a two-story setting is "good for large groups." "Skip the entrees and make a meal of the appetizers."

Tutta Pasta

26 Carmine St. (212) 463-9653
bet. Bedford & Bleecker Sts. in the W. Village
504 LaGuardia (212) 420-0652
bet. Bleecker & Houston Sts. in the Washington Sq. Area
These West Village "good, casual Italian bistros" offer "fresh, fat-free cooking," that's "inexpensive" for lunch or dinner, or a late (till 2am) snack. "Excellent for family and friends to meet and chat," voters recommend the "amazing raviolis" and advise you "don't be shy: Go off the menu!"

12 Chairs

56 McDougal St. at W. Houston St. in SoHo (212) 254-8640
Russian-born owner Naila Beniamin would cook her food in a melting pot (her brand new restaurant features dishes with Middle Eastern, American and Russian flavors) if there were room. This teeny spot is worth a look.

20 Mott St.

$22

20 Mott St. at Bowery in Chinatown (212) 964-0380
It's "a cavern" but it does "great dim sum." The "authentic Chinese" at this Chinatown spot is "reasonably priced" and "freshly made." It's "very crowded," so "be prepared to wait in line." Don't expect great service, do expect wine and beer. Children and credit cards are welcome here.

"21" Club

$54

21 W. 52nd St. bet. Fifth & Sixth/Midtown W. (212) 582-7200
1929: The stock market crashes, and the "21" Club opens. While the effects of the former soon dissipated, the latter has been denting New Yorker's pocketbooks ever since. And, though suffering "downs" in the past, it's definitely on an "up": A famously welcoming and knowledgeable staff serves up "very good" American dishes, and you can literally "soak in the atmosphere" in one of the city's premiere cigar spots. A businessmen's favorite, "21" club serves a $24 burger that's among the best in town ("that's a lot for a burger").

Twigs

196 Eighth Ave. at 20th St. in Chelsea (212) 633-6735
"Gay-friendly" and "cozy" for brunch or dinner, this "trendy" "neighborhood Italian" is always "crowded" with locals. Write-in voters praise the "great staff," "creative" fare and tasty tiramisu. They're pro-buff here, with the only "gym night" in town, Mondays: 1/2 off the second dinner when you show any gym card.

FOOD | ROOM | STAFF | COST

Twins ░ $25

1712 Second Ave. (212) 987-1111
bet. 88th & 89th on the Upper East Side
The "cute concept" at this Upper East Side Continental (co-owned
by the one-and-only Tom Berenger) is that your servers are
identically dressed identical twins. That amounts to a "silly
gimmick" to most, who find the atmosphere "SoHo wannabe" and
the food just "lousy." However, twins like it since they get
two-for-one drink specials. Each?

Two Boots $13

74 Bleecker St. (212) 777-1033
bet. Broadway & Lafayette St. in the E. Village
75 Greenwich Ave. (212) 633-9096
bet. W. 11th St. & 7th Ave. S. in the W. Village
514 2nd St. (718) 499-3253
bet. 7th & 8th Aves. in Brooklyn
37 Ave. A (212) 505-2276
bet. 2nd & 3rd Sts. in the E. Village
Buongiorno mon cher? Want some spice in your life? How 'bout
Cajun/Italian? This place lands raves for the "most interesting pizza
concoctions," and great reviews as a "family restaurant for the new
millennia" which "supplies crayons for kids." But since it's "the best
place to go with screaming" tots, it can also be "noisy and unpleasant." If
you're feeling adventurous, try the "crawfish garlic calzones."

Two Tom's $22

255 Third Ave. (718) 875-8689
at Union St. in Brooklyn
"Order what they suggest and you won't go wrong" at this
"ultimate neighborhood" Italian spot in Brooklyn. The waiters
"make you feel like an old friend."

222 $48

222 W. 79th St. (212) 799-0400
bet. Broadway and Amsterdam on the Upper West Side
Frank Valenza, known for astonishing food and even more
astonishing prices, has downscaled a bit with this still-pricey but not
stuffy townhouse Continental on the Upper West Side. Those few
who know it say that "when word gets out about the food," this
could be "Number 1 in the city." In the meantime, enjoy the lovely
antique-filled setting and luxury ingredients like lobster, foie gras,
black truffles, and white chocolate mousse, or "order off the prix
fixe menu" for a mere $36. All this, "and you can smoke" too.

Typhoon Brewery $33

22 E. 54th St. (212) 754-9006
bet. Fifth & Madison in Midtown E.
That's "Thai-phoon," and though the attraction here is the
on-premises microbrews, the Thai food get marks from "ordinary"
to "very good." Relatively (for an ethnic) high prices seem to target
"tourists and expense-accounters," since locals know there are
"scores of inexpensive Thais around town."

Ugly Joe's

46 Third Ave. at 10th St. in the E. Village (212) 677-0501
This East Village Pizza and Pasta yearling is a "great date spot" for romantics on a budget. The "fab decor" gets more consistent marks then the thin crust pizza and pasta dishes. But, a "not great, not bad" food rating doesn't diminish voter affection for the place.

Uncle George's Tavern

33-19 Broadway, at 34th St. in Queens (718) 626-0593
"One of the best taverns in Astoria" is open 24 hours, and though occasionally uneven, serves "cheap, tasty Greek peasant food" specializing in fish and lamb dishes. Cash only. "Great Greek/great prices."

Uncle Nick's $25

747 Ninth Ave. bet. 50th & 51st Sts. in Clinton (212) 245-7992
"Flaming Cheese Ball" does not refer to comedian Rip Taylor, but to this Clinton Greek's specialty of the house. "Good fish dishes" (including "great grilled octopus") are the focus of the menu, though quality has become uneven of late. Staff has always been uneven, it seems.

Uncle Vanya $18

315 W. 54th St. bet. Eighth & Ninth/Clinton (212) 262-0542
"This place could do for Russian food what Mitali did for Indian food," i.e., make it almost mainstream. Fans find Uncle Vanya "delightful": "cozy" and "homey," with a "very loving staff" and a moderately priced menu of "Russian favorites." Tourists go to the Russian Tea Room; the Russians go to this "bit of old Russia transplanted to NY."

Union Square Cafe $46

21 E. 16th St. bet. Union Sq. W. & Fifth Ave. (212) 243-4020
With food and staff scores that place in the Top 20 overall, Danny Meyer's American (with "rustic Italian flair") distinguishes itself as New Yorkers' favorite restaurant, inspiring page after page of overwhelmingly positive comments in our poll. With "friendly, funny" and the most knowledgeable service in town, the "first class service and great atmosphere are only the icing on the cake. The food is tops here." "Never disappointing," for all that excellence voters find it "surprisingly reasonable." About no other restaurant do New Yorkers advise you to "believe the hype."

U.N. Delegates Dining Room

United Nations, 4th Floor, First Ave. & 46th St. (212) 963-7626
Security is tight and it's only open for lunch, but "if you're lucky the staff will mistake you for a delegate and give you the royal treatment" at this UN International. All citizens can expect a "gourmet" buffet selection prepared by "high-quality chefs" with different offerings every month. The East River view and helpful, costumed staff make this an "excellent" choice.

FOOD ROOM STAFF COST

Universal Grill

$26

44 Bedford St. (212) 989-5621
bet. Leroy & Carmine Sts. in the W. Village
"Wild and woolly," this unrepentantly "wacky," "very gay"
"flamboyantly on cue" bar-and-grill flaunts a "very silly staff"
(i.e. "dancing around and singing to the Mary Tyler Moore Show
theme song") and "festive atmosphere," making it "great for
brunch," "a must for birthdays," and a "fun place" whenever you
want to "leave in a good mood."

Uskudar

$24

1405 Second Ave. (212) 988-2641
bet. 73rd & 74th Sts. on the Upper East Side
This Upper East Side Turkish is "always reliable" for "very good"
food and a crowd that doesn't mind the drab decor. A "nice
selection of dishes" is served by a "friendly" staff.

Va Bene

$36

1589 Second Ave. (212) 517-4448
bet. 82nd & 83rd Sts. on the Upper East Side
There's "very good" Italian food at this smallish Yorkville
restaurant, "and it's Kosher, too." Comfy and sedate, it's "great for
a date," and (for voters who don't require Kosher) the food
"surpasses expectations," if "heavy on the dairy."

V & T Pizzeria

1024 Amsterdam Ave. bet. 110th & 111th/Harlem (212) 663-1708
This Columbia University/Harlem hangout is "a must for the
students" and anyone else who wants "great pizza," in "many
varieties" complemented by the "best salad." Garlic pizza with
onions is a breath-enhancing favorite.

Vatan

409 Third Ave. at 29th St. in Murray Hill (212) 689-5666
This Indian vegetarian (owner Jita Mehta comes from Jhupdi of
Queens) specializes in the cuisine of Gujarat, in western India.
Here, you eat shoe- and sock-less on cushions in booths, and the
fixed menu features more than a dozen dishes. This new spot
looks like fun.

Vegetarian Paradise

33 Mott St. (212) 260-7130
at Pell St. in Chinatown
144 W. 4th St. (212) 260-7130
bet. MacDougal St. & Sixth Ave. in the W. Village
With one of voters' favorite vegetarian menus, these West
Village/Chinatown spots serve "imaginative concoctions" of "ersatz fish
and meat" dishes that are at least "intriguing," and at best "fabulous." The
"flawless" meals are "good enough to convert meat eaters."

▪ = SUPERIOR ▪ = EXCELLENT ▪ = V. GOOD ▪ = GOOD

Veniero's

$13

342 E. 11th St. (212) 674-7070
bet. First & Second Aves. in the E. Village
Romac Reporters' No. 1 pick for dessert in the city, and No. 2 overall for espresso and cappuccino, it's no wonder that this dessert-only Italian is packed with patrons who brave the cramped conditions, indifferent staff and East Village attitude for "undoubtedly the best cheesecake" anywhere (takeout is even more trying). So what. "If you don't already believe that chocolate is better than sex, they'll convert you."

Verbena Restaurant

$47

54 Irving Pl. (212) 260-5454
bet. 17th & 18th Sts. in Gramercy
"Be sure to speak softly while you're supping, won't you?," for the "peaceful ambiance" is perfect for "oh-so-genteel" dining in the "lovely" herb-and-flower-filled garden. As for chef/owner Diane Forley's seasonal American food, it can be "stunningly good," and the service is "very fine" indeed. There's a "great private room for a small party," and a warming hearth when the weather turns chilly. All in all, "a pleasant respite from the noise and the funk" of the city—and "don't miss the Verbena Cocktail."

Veselka

$13

144 Second Ave. at 9th St. in the E. Village (212) 288-9682
"Memorably rude service" doesn't keep the "broke and hungry" hordes away from this 24-hr East Village "old favorite." For "generous portions" of "typical Eastern European diner" fare at "reasonable prices," "get a window seat" and enjoy the local "cast of characters."

Viand Coffee Shop

$13

673 Madison Ave. (212) 751-6622
bet. 61st & 62nd Sts. on the Upper East Side
1011 Madison Ave. (212) 249-8250
bet. 78th & 79th Sts. on the Upper East Side
300 E. 86th St. (212) 879-9425
at Second Ave. on the Upper East Side
Some think of these Greek/Americans as simply "typical corner coffee shops," that you "have to be hungry—and in front of" to enter. But, they're working on their image, and there's "nothing quicker and better at 4am" than a "great fresh turkey sandwich."

Viceroy

$27

160 Eighth Ave. (212) 633-8484
at 18th St. in Chelsea
A "strong gay presence" pegs this Chelsea two-year-old, with it's long, antique mahogany bar and 1am weekend menu. An "excellent post-yaya snack joint, especially when you are too much in the stratosphere to care price" or "when will they ever get the service together" staff. The "excellent coffee" outshines the New American menu.

FOOD ROOM STAFF COST

Victor's Cafe 52

$40

236 W. 52nd St. (212) 586-7714
bet. Broadway & Eighth Ave. in the Theater District
While not exactly like "pre-Castro Havana," this upscale-for-Cuban restaurant in the Theater District is "authentic and festive," and likes to stay up late on weekends, with live piano music. The "large portions" are deemed at the very least "reliable," and folks say the appetizers are quite good.

Viet Nam

11-13 Doyers St. (212) 693-0725
bet. Bowery & Pell Sts. in Chinatown
It's "hard to spend money" at this Chinatown Vietnamese, famous for its "delicious, real" food (particularly "great summer rolls" and lemongrass chicken) at cheap prices. "Divey," its the kind of joint where "drinks come in the can."

View

Marriott Marquis Hotel, 1535 Broadway (212) 704-8900
bet. 45th & 46th Sts. in the Theater District
What tourist area would be complete without a giant, rotating cocktail lounge overlooking it? Times Square is no exception, and while the crowd-pleasing atmosphere and view are "first class," the Continental and Eclectic menu leaves something to be desired. Maybe that's why the name of this place isn't "Food."

Villa Berulia

$29

107 E. 34th St. (212) 689-1970
bet. Park & Lexington Aves. in Murray Hill
"Routine menu and specials" of "1950s classics in big portions" makes for "pleasant but not exceptional" food at this Murray Hill Northern Italian. The professional staff has been around long enough to earn high marks, however, despite reasonable prices, it's not an area standout.

Village Atelier

$37

436 Hudson St. (212) 989-1363
at Morton St. in the W. Village
Okay, it's cliched, but this small, rustic French "jewel" really deserves the mantle of "romantic hideaway." Housed in a beamed-ceilinged 1847 townhouse, it features the requisite roses and candlelight, along with a fine assortment of freshwater fish specialties. "Very comforting food and atmosphere" make for a "great escape."

Village Grill

$24

518 LaGuardia Pl. (212) 228-1001
at Bleecker St. in the Washington Sq. Area
Located in a c. 1900 building in the Central Village, this Franco/American Bistro is touted as "surprisingly good." Take a seat on the patio and enjoy "simple but well-prepared food" that's "very reasonably priced," or sit inside and watch them cook in the "nice open kitchen": maybe you'll learn something.

Villa Mosconi $28

69 MacDougal St. (212) 673-0390
bet. Bleecker & W. Houston Sts. in the Washington Sq. Area
Want to know "what the Village used to be like?" Try this "old
fashioned Italian at old fashioned prices" off Washington Square.
"Truly professional," "go for the homemade pasta," "always
satisfying in Village style.

Vince & Eddie's $36

70 W. 68th St. bet. Columbus & CPW/U.W. Side (212) 721-0068
Romackers rate the Regional American fare "good and gutsy" at
this Upper Westsider near Lincoln Center.The New England
"country"atmosphere is "comfortable" and the service "friendly,"
but it can be "crowded" and "noisy" pre-performance. The
"satisfying" brunch is a less-hectic option.

Vincent's $26

119 Mott St. (212) 226-8133
at Hester St. in Little Italy
Infamous site of mobster Joey Gallo's last meal on earth, this vintage
Italian seafood specialist also boasts "late hours" and "hot red sauce"
to, er "die for." If clams, calamari, and atmsophere that will make you
"think Little Italy" are what you crave, then Vincent's is the one.

Vinegar Factory $21

431 E. 91st St. (212) 987-0885
bet. First & York Aves. in Yorkville
Open all meals (and yes, they have a beer and wine permit), this
"elegant" Yorkville salad bar has one of the city's best weekend
brunches. A "good idea" to many, but "too expensive" and
specializing in "snobbery" to others, this gourmet shop gallery has
good prepared foods to go.

Virgil's Real BBQ $25

152 W. 44th St. (212) 921-9494
bet. Broadway & Sixth Ave. in Midtown W.
"Good and messy" "urban bar-b-que" and a "great selection of
beer" are what keep these midtown "big," "comfortable" but
"noisy" "pig-out spots" absolutely packed. "The biscuits!" "The
brisket!" "The mashed potatoes with gravy!" "YUM!" The "big,"
"tasty" portions of "hearty fare" are enough to "make Norm weep
with joy," and, man, it sure is "fun."

Vivolo $38

222 E. 58th St. bet. 2nd & 3rd Aves. in Midtown E. (212) 308-0112
138 E. 74th St. bet. Lexington & Park/U.E. Side (212) 717-4700
140 E. 74th St. bet. Lex. & Park/Upper East Side (212) 737-3533
The original Vivolo has been an Upper East Side Classic Italian standby
for 20 years: folks appreciate "quality above inventiveness" here. Anche
Vivolo, though only 6 years younger, hasn't found as loyal a local
following down by Bloomingdale's, and the new Cucina Vivolo is at the
bottom of a downward trend. Voters say, make a reservation for the
original, eat upstairs, and try the "very good" prix fixe bargains.

FOOD ROOM STAFF COST

Vong

$48

Lipstick Bldg., 200 E. 54th St. (212) 486-9592
bet. Second & Third Aves. in Midtown E.
Chef/owner Jean-Georges Vongerichten does a French interpretation
of Thai cuisine, with "spectacular" results. "Innovative and inspired,"
the "most incredible flavor combinations" place Vong in the Romac
Top 100 for food, and a pro staff does the same for service. But it's the
"elegant setting," that's "like being in a genie's bottle," that makes the
experience "surreal," and locks this Midtowner solidly in the Top 20
New York favorites.

Voulez-Vous

$36

1462 First Ave. (212) 249-1776
at 76th St. in Yorkville
Do you want to know that the twentysomethings rate the food about a
point higher than do the boomers? It is "a little cramped," but voters
appreciate the "charming host" and competent service at this Yorkville
"neighborhood French," and the fact that it can be a little "wacky" at times.

Wally's and Joseph's

$46

249 W. 49th St. (212) 582-0460
bet. Broadway & Eighth Ave. in the Theater District
This is one of the few Theater District spots known for celebrity
spotting and for "very good" Italian seafood. If you want the "best
veal chop anywhere," like extensive wine lists or just "love to look
at Al Pacino," make a reservation.

Water Club

$50

FDR. Dr. at 30th St. (via 23rd St.) (212) 683-3333
at the East River in Murray Hill
"Romantic," "first-class views" of the city and a "fabulous brunch"
keep this Murray Hill Regional American popular with tourists,
celebrants and NYers who want to "escape NYC without leaving."
Most surveyors say it's "well worth the money" for a "spectacular
setting" where the staff and chef are "trying harder these days."

Water's Edge

$46

44th Dr. & East River, Queens (718) 482-0033
bet. Vernon Blvd. & 44th Dr.
"The best view in [er, that is, 'of'] the city" can be found at this
Continental/American in Queens that rivals even the River Cafe, in
many voters' minds. Your special occasion begins with a
"wonderful ferry ride," and winds up in the Top 10 for room and
ambiance, but "don't forget to wear a jacket and tie." A piano bar
and excellent wine list add to the appeal for out-of-town guests, and
though the cuisine is "very good," the real draw is the "great view."

Westside Brewing Co.

$20

340 Amsterdam Ave. (212) 721-2161
at 76th St. on the Upper West Side
"Really bad food with pretty good beer." If you're here and you're
out of your twenties, it's time to get on with your life.

Westside Cottage  $16

788 Ninth Ave. bet. 52nd & 53rd Sts. in Clinton (212) 957-8008
689 Ninth Ave. bet. 47th & 48th Sts. in Clinton (212) 245-0800
When you think of Cottage-style Szechuan-Hunan Chinese, you
probably picture one of these Westsiders, serving
ever-so-Americanized Chinese food (complete with free, cheap
white wine) "without a lot of hoopla." Cheap, fast and good.

West 63rd St. Steakhouse  $48

44 W. 63rd St. bet. Bdwy & Ninth/Upper West Side (212) 246-6363
"Great simple salads and huge steaks" are the hallmarks of this
Lincoln Center area steakhouse, offering rare proof that sometimes
simple can be special. Though the area is still emerging as a culinary
center, voters find this two-year-old "gracious and generous" when
waiting for a table, or arriving late for a snack (before 12 midnight).
And remember: these days, "steakhouse" = "cigar club."

What's Cookin'  $19

18 E. 41st St. bet. Fifth & Madison/Murray Hill (212) 725-6096
"Kosher food with taste" is what's cookin' at this Mediterranean
spot. Portions are "small but delicious" and finding "good, healthy"
glatt kosher fare with zip to it is tough, even in this town.

Wilkinson's Seafood  $47

1573 York Ave. (212) 535-5454
bet. 83rd & 84th Sts. in Yorkville
Fans "keep coming back" for the "wonderful seafood" served at this
well-rated, "very elegant" dining room on the Upper East Side, with
its handsome mahogany paneling, etched glass, and brass and flowers
abundant. Though even boosters liken the prices to "highway robbery
without a gun," quality this "superb" never comes cheap. It's one of
the city's best when you're in the mood for fish.

Willy's Bar & Grill  $24

1538 Second Ave. at 80th St./U.E. Side (212) 734-1978
"Sit outside" at this casual American in the bustling East '80s where
dining alfresco rules supreme. The food can be "bland" but so can a
lot of American chow: Who cares anyway when the waitstaff is
slipping you complementary vino. Takeout or eat in, it's open until
2 a.m. on weekends for the bar crowd.

Windows on the World  $53

107th fl., One World Trade Center (212) 524-7011
West St., bet. Vesey & Liberty in the Financial District
After a multi-million dollar renovation, this Cadillac of New York
eateries has reopened, and it comes fully loaded: There's music every
night ($10 per table), a late night menu (2 a.m. weekends), valet
parking, rooms for private parties, and, of course, the most
"spectacular" view in town, from the 106th & 107th floor of One
World Trade Center (the room is tiered so that each table has a view).
The "World View" cuisine has something, including shabu shabu,
sushi, and a raw bar, to offer everyone. So the "food could be better?"
You probably didn't try the "excellent filet mignon." Dress up.

FOOD ROOM STAFF COST

Wo Hop

17 Mott St. (212) 267-2536
at Canal St. in Chinatown
This Chinatown oldtimer (almost 60 years old) is simply "a classic." "Good food, with very bad service," it's open all hours." "A New York tradition that packs them in."

Wolf's Rest. & Deli

57th St. & Sixth Ave. in Midtown W. (212) 586-1110
Some love it, some hate it, but this standby deli (still holding fast in the midst of the 57th Street theme park restaurants) is nothing if not a "real New York experience." "Homey" and "homely" at the same time, they have "great waitresses" who do not lack for personality.

Wong Kee

$15

113 Mott St. (212) 966-1160
bet. Canal & Hester in Little Italy
It gives new meaning to the phrase "hole in the wall," but what a "great" hole. "Great Chinese," at a "great value" comes with "no atmosphere," at this Chinatown spot, but no one cares. "The food flies at you" while the waiters ignore you, but once "the best duck in New York (only $5)," heaping plates of veggies, or pan fried noodles hit the table, everything else is moot. Bring a six pack, but not the credit cards. No reserving.

Woo Chon

$31

41-19 Kissena Blvd. (718) 463-0803
at Main St. in Queens
8-10 W. 36th St. (212) 695-0676
bet. Fifth & Sixth Aves. in the Garment Dist.
A "mostly Asian" clientele speaks well to the quality of these big Korean restaurants, one in the Garment District and the other in Queens. Open all the time, and serving "lots of little appetizers" in "clean" surroundings, the staff gets a grumpy rating, perhaps due to those onerous hours. Overall, a "good experience."

Word Of Mouth

$22

1012 Lexington Ave. (212) 570-9807
bet. 72nd & 73rd Sts. on the Upper E. Side
This "very Upper East" hidden gem has been great for lunch since 1990, serving food that is always very fresh and good. There are plans to start serving dinner—spread the word.

World Cafe

$26

201 Columbus Ave. (212) 799-8090
bet. 69th & 70th Sts. on the Upper W. Side
This "standard" Upper West Side International is "good in a pinch" for pre-theater (only $15), before Lincoln Center, or the movies. It's "adequate all the way around" for service and ambiance and the "large portions" keep it above the run-of-the-mill competition.

= SUPERIOR = EXCELLENT = V. GOOD = GOOD

World Yacht Cruises $53

Pier 81, W. 41st St. (212) 630-8100
at the Hudson River in the Convention Center Area
Every window has a water view at this restaurant, since it's on a big boat
that sets sail every night at 7 p.m. (the "fair" French food is also served at
lunch). "A great experience" that you "must do at least once in a
lifetime," it's like a mini-cruise without Kathie Lee, complete with
lounge band. "Gives 'cruising' a whole new meaning in this town."

Wu Liang Ye $28

36 W. 48th St. (212) 398-2308
bet. Fifth & Sixth Aves. in Midtown W.
While this Rockefeller Center Chinese draws a few unqualified
raves, a big buildup in the press has led to a few disappointed
voters. If anything, it's "authentic": Staff, cooks, even the decor all
come straight from the Wu Liang Ye company of China.

Xunta $19

174 First Ave. (212) 614-0620
bet. 10th & 11th Sts. in the E. Village
This one-year-old Spanish specializes in a "fun," "good" tapas bar
with a "varied selection," possibly to make up for their wine-and
beer-only permit. The "great sangria" and strolling mariachi players
might help you get through the cramped quarters, made worse by
the "uncomfortable" barrel-based tables.

Yaffa Cafe $17

97 St. Mark's Pl. (212) 674-9302
bet. Ave. A & First Ave. in the E. Village
The "cute patio" and "great late-night snacks" (it's open 24-7) come
in for lots of praise at this "very East Village" semi-vegetarian.
"Great salads," "omelets better than Mom's," and "delicious"
desserts like "three-berry pie" conspire with a "loud," "fun
atmosphere" and "very reasonable" prices to make this a
"comfortable" fave. Better hurry though, because while Yaffa's a
"cool hangout for the body-piercing set," "when the pearls and
poodles show up, its time is over."

Yama $31

122 E. 17th St. (212) 475-0969
bet. Park Ave. S. & Third Ave. in Gramercy
This little Gramercy Japanese is a Top 40 Romac Favorite: Folks
put up with a "fair" staff in ordinary surroundings to get "monster
sized sushi at a midget price." Sure, there's always a wait, for
dinner and the "great lunch specials," but from what we've seen,
there's usually a direct correlation between the length of the line
and the freshness of the food.

Yamaguchi $26

35 W. 45th St. bet. Fifth & Sixth/Midtown W. (212) 840-8185
Steady as she goes for this reasonably priced, middle-of-the-pack-rated
Japanese. It's in the running as "best place for Japanese lunch in
Midtown," because "the lunch box makes it worthwhile."

FOOD ROOM STAFF COST

Yankee Clipper

$33

170 John St. (212) 344-5959
bet. South & Front Sts. at the South St. Seaport
You may not feel like the luckiest man alive at this Seaport American Seafooder, but given the location, they have "surprisingly good food": "The New England clam chowder is ambrosia." Overall, it's "fun for the experience."

Yellowfingers

$27

200 E. 60th St. (212) 751-8615
bet. Second & Third Aves. on the Upper East Side
The food's "not so hot" but that doesn't stop hordes of weary shoppers from refueling at this East Side American. Voters praise the "charming, comfy" atmosphere and "convenient" location close to Bloomie's.

Ye Waverly Inn

$28

16 Bank St. at Waverly Pl. in the W. Village (212) 929-4377
Meat loaf, "mashed-potato heaven" and the "best chicken pot pie" means ye better expect the "hearty" but it's best ye "don't expect anything gourmet." It's American food. Love it or leave it. The garden and "stunning" early-American atmosphere vault this West Villager onto our romantic list. "Sit by the fireplace on a frigid winter night." Separate rooms for smokers and non-smokers.

Yorkville Brewery

1359 First Ave. at 73rd St. in Yorkville (212) 517-brew
This upscale Yorkville Tavern does old Germantown proud by providing "great homemade beer" and other good microbrews on tap. While the food may only be "typical burger fare," the quality is "above average" and the setting is surprisingly "clean and bright."

Yuka

$22

1557 Second Ave. (212) 772-9675
bet. 80th & 81st Sts. on the Upper East Side
"Good all-you-can-eat sushi" (at $18 per person) makes for an "extraordinary buy" in an otherwise-pretty-standard neighborhood Japanese place. The rest of the food is "inexpensive" and "unimpressive."

Yura

$21

1645 Third Ave. at 92nd St. in Carnegie Hill (212) 860-8060
This little Carnegie BYOB is open for all meals, though the French/American menu is "limited." A good choice for a reasonable lunch or dinner with the kids, this place has good burgers and "the best" angel food cake.

Zarela

$36

953 Second Ave. bet. 50th & 51st/Midtown E. (212) 644-6740
"Haute" and "sexy Mex" that's "far removed from the typical Tex-Mex joint" and "displays the true vastness of Mexican fare." Add "killer" margaritas ("they should be outlawed") and a homey, festive room that's "great for a celebration"— but not for a private conversation ("the most crowded tables in New York")—and you have "a NY treasure."

Zen Palate
$23

2170 Broadway bet. 76th & 77th Sts./U.W. Side (212) 501-7768
34 Union Sq. East at 16th St. in Union Square (212) 614-9291
663 Ninth Ave. at 46th St. in Clinton (212) 582-1669

Proving "you can make anything out of a yam" is this trio of
"spiritually transporting," "inventive Asian veggie" specialists, with
their "elegant simplicity" and "idiosyncratic"-to-"pretty weird"
food. Most love the "staggering" selection of "gourmet vegetarian
with sexy vibes," but a few "carnivores" say you'd better "bring a
microscope" to see the portions.

Zephyr Grill
$36

Beekman Tower Hotel, 1 Mitchell Pl. (212) 223-4200
1st Ave. & 49th St. in the UN Area

Located right across from the UN, this all-meals "East Side sleeper"
is a good ambassador of American/Continental food to visitors from
other lands. Located in the Beekman Tower Hotel, it has a pretty,
art-deco look and is on the inexpensive side for hotel dining.

Zeppole at the TriBaKery
$18

186 Franklin St. (Greenwich & Hudson/TriBeCa) (212) 431-1114

Lunch seems to be the main attraction at this soulful Italian situated
between The TriBeCa Grill and Nobu. "Great lunch spot," "there
should be more of these" in Tribeca, say voters. The chow grabs
good reviews, but the service gets nixed. Then again who knows,
DeNiro might even stop by.

Zinno
$34

126 W. 13th St. (212) 924-5182
bet. Sixth & Seventh Aves. in the W. Village

"A whole new Jazz experience," the "cozy and elegant" ambiance is
king at this West Village Northern Italian. Opinions vary on the
food: Some think it's "expensive" for what you get, while others
factor in the live music that they think is "the best jazz around."

Zip City
$24

3 W. 18th St. (212) 366-6333
bet. Fifth & Sixth Aves. in the Flatiron District

This "pioneering" Flatiron brewpub is "convenient" after work when
suits zip over for "real microbrewing" in a "spacious," "noisy"
atmosphere. Some say the service is the "slowest" and the menu could
definitely "use some expansion," the "interesting brews" are the big
draw. It can be "fun to watch the brewmaster," too.

Zoë
$38

90 Prince St. (212) 966-6722
bet. Mercer St. & Broadway in SoHo

A "long" all-American wine list and "zesty" "innovative" fare
prepared in an open-view kitchen make this spacious New
American a favorite for many voters. It can be "acoustically
challenged" and overpopulated with "Upper East Side transplants"
at dinner, but it's "SoHo all the way" at brunch and the
"personable" staff always delivers.

FOOD ROOM STAFF COST

Zona del Chianti

$33

1043 Second Ave. (212) 980-8686
at 55th St. in Midtown E.
Your next stop: the Chianti Zone? First looks at this yearling say it's all over the map, and not necessarily in Tuscany, where the menu's shooting for. But, for substantial portions of rotisserie roasts and fresh fish items, some call it "a real find in an otherwise high-priced area."

Zucca

$36

227 Tenth Ave. (212) 741-1970
bet. 23rd & 24th Sts. in Chelsea
Chef/owner Eric Stapleman "has done a great transformation of the old Chelsea Central" into a "comfortable and pleasant" Mediterannean bistro that specializes in organic ingredients. The room is "spare but attractive," and the "food is fabulous" according to most, who relish "healthy eating."

Zucchero

$23

1464 Second Ave. (212) 517-2541
bet. 76th & 77th Sts. on the Upper East Side
Short on looks but long on value (especially for its Upper East Side location), this neighborhood Italian has "good food" and an "extremely accommodating staff," who help to make dining here very "pleasant." Good eats and "a great buy."

Zula Cafe

1260 Amsterdam Ave. (212) 663-1670
at 122nd St. in Harlem
This Harlem Ethiopian is among voters' favorites, serving "great,"authentic West African" dishes in a small, though "reliably nice," "never crowded" setting. A "great value," it has "great cappuccino, too."

Zuni

$28

598 Ninth Ave. (212) 765-7626
at 43rd St. in Clinton
Some call it Southwest Cuisine, some call it "Tex-Mex." No matter, this "well-kept Ninth Avenue secret" serves some of the best food "for the money." The service can be "slow"— hey mosey on over here pardner—but you can always expect "too much food."

Zutto

$30

77 Hudson St. (212) 233-3287
bet. Harrison & Jay Sts. in TriBeCa
Mostly neighborhood types call this TriBeCa Japanese "incredible," at least for sushi and other special rolls. The "tranquil" setting is sometimes enlivened by the "wacky sushi chefs," who mostly mug for the kids: Folks say it's especially "child-friendly."

INDEX

CUISINE TYPES

NEIGHBORHOODS

FEATURES

CUISINE TYPES

GERMAN

GREEK

HOT DOGS

HUNGARIAN

INDIAN

INDONESIAN

INTERNATIONAL

IRISH

ISRAELI

ITALIAN

NEIGHBORHOODS

FINANCIAL DISTRICT

FLATIRON DISTRICT

GARMENT DISTRICT

GRAMERCY

MIDTOWN WEST

UPPER WEST SIDE

WASHINGTON SQ. AREA

WEST VILLAGE

YORKVILLE

OUTSIDE MANHATTAN

FEATURES

BYOB

CHILD-FRIENDLY

CREDIT CARDS (AMEX ONLY)

CREDIT CARDS (NO)

DELIVERY

DIM SUM

ENTERTAINMENT

KOSHER

LATE MENU
(2 entries means weekdays, weekends)

OUTDOOR DINING

PRE-THEATER MENU

PRIX FIXE DINNER

PRIX FIXE DINNER

RESERVATIONS NOT TAKEN

SMOKING (CIGARETTES)

SMOKING (CIGARS/PIPES)

TAKEOUT

VALET PARKING

WHEELCHAIR ACCESS